INTRODUCTION TO ANCIENT HISTORY

INTRODUCTION TO
Ancient History

HERMANN BENGTSON

Translated from the Sixth Edition by
R. I. Frank *and* Frank D. Gilliard

University of California Press
BERKELEY, LOS ANGELES, AND LONDON 1970

University of California Press
Berkeley and Los Angeles, California
Cambridge University Press
London, England
Copyright © 1970, by
The Regents of the University of California
Library of Congress Catalog Card Number: 78-118685
Standard Book Number 0-520-01723-4
Printed in the United States of America

Translated from *Einführung in die Alte Geschichte* (Munich: C. H. Beck'sche
Verlagsbuchhandlung, 6th ed. 1969)

Translators' Preface

For two decades Professor Hermann Bengtson's *Einführung in die alte Geschichte* (Munich 1949; ed. 6, Munich 1969) has been the standard introduction for German university students of ancient history. No comparable manual has been available in English.

Our translation is made especially for students who have not yet acquired facility in German. It departs from Professor Bengtson's text mainly in that the general bibliographical appendix has been reorganized to conform with the plan of the *Cambridge Ancient History* and also has been revised with the English-reading student in mind. Further, the system of abbreviations has been changed throughout to follow the usage of the *Oxford Classical Dictionary* and *L'année philologique*. The most common abbreviations used in ancient studies, as well as those used in this book, have been listed in the appendix.

We would like to thank Mr. Ernst-Peter Wieckenberg of the C. H. Beck Verlag for making available Professor Bengtson's manuscript of the sixth edition, and to acknowledge the invaluable help of Mr. Herbert J. Erlanger of New York.

R. I. FRANK

FRANK D. GILLIARD

September 1969
Laguna Beach, California

Contents

I

The Scope of
Ancient History

"Ancient history is never anything other than and never should be anything other than a part of one, universal history; and both ancient and modern historians ought never to forget that." These words of Eduard Meyer properly stand at the beginning of the study of ancient history, in spite of the fact that it has built for itself a special niche in the frame of universal history. Only reasons of expediency have been decisive for this fact. First, human incapacity to examine thoroughly and critically in the course of a single lifetime the immense field of human history. Second, the exceptional nature of ancient source material. Of course, the boundary between ancient and modern history is only conventional; that is, it has been formed by tacit agreement among those concerned with investigating it. Ultimately the tasks of historians of Antiquity are none other than those of historians of the Middle Ages and of Modern Times; to use historical analysis and to rethink the past in historical terms must in the same way inspire all students of history, regardless of the province of universal history with which they are concerned.

Thus ancient history is not to be considered detached from other historical development. A thousand threads stretch from Antiquity to the Middle Ages, and from there to the present. Only he who is at home in medieval and modern history will have a regard for historical continuity and for evaluating past events based on those of the present. Of course, the feelings, thoughts, and aspirations of ancient as opposed to modern men frequently were based on other assumptions. Ancient man grew up in an intellectual environment different from ours, an environment accessible only to one who can visualize that long-lost world in its intellectual, economic, and political aspects. The "visualization," the immersion of one's self in another time so that it awakens to life, remains the essential task of historical research, which is itself a perpetual struggle to formulate the truest picture possible of the past.

Nevertheless, the study of history (like that of all the humanities) is bound up with implicit assumptions which underlie every kind of research, as well as every kind of cognition. As a part of the intellectual life of a people, as well as of the entire civilized world, the study of the humanities is indissolubly connected with the intellectual content, with the political, religious, and economic trends of its respective time, from which the ideas of the observant student are developed. Historical understanding is further bound up with the intellectual breadth and the intellectual maturity of the inquirer. The over-all view of the historical canvas is derived from a philosophy of life that is subjected to changes by external and internal experiences. An "objective science," therefore, does not exist in the humanities; and it cannot exist—least of all in the perception and explanation of historical events. This insight into the dependence of intellectual cognition obligates the historian to reconsider constantly the assumptions of his own research, so that he may reach a better-founded knowledge of historical relationships.

In the final analysis, therefore, each view of an historical event assumes a standard derived from the knowledge and judgment of other historical events, singly or in sum. What is the case, then, for justifying historical analogy? It was used with great success by B. G. Niebuhr in his *Römische Geschichte*, although modern research is cautious about it. That each epoch—and especially Antiquity—be explained only on its own terms is a basic historical demand. An historical problem, however, can often be clarified, even if not solved, by reference to a similar situation in another time or connection. Thus analogy, often misused, is not historical evidence, but a means of illustrating historical events.

What is meant by "ancient history" or the "history of Antiquity"? Geographically, the answer is clear: it is the history of the Mediterranean Sea and of the contiguous territories which have been connected to it by historically effective political and cultural relations. The underlying unity of this area is produced not by the national characteristics of its inhabitants, but by an intensive cultural exchange, in which the Mediterranean itself played the role of the great mediator. Characteristic of the area is its enormous east-west elongation, from the Straits of Gibraltar (the "Pillars of Hercules") to the banks of the Indus. The Mediterranean, the great travel axis of the ancient world, couples its northern borderlands to the north coast of Africa, including Egypt. This cultural sphere also is comprised of the Near Eastern regions of the Hellespont (Dardanelles) and of the Syro-Phoenician coast to beyond the Persian desert—in other words, all Asia Minor, Syria, Mesopotamia, and the Iranian areas.

In the more than three-thousand-year stretch of ancient history, this enormous territory never grew together into a single, living organism. Even so, its underlying unity frequently was expressed politically in the concept of universal empire. Alexander and Caesar strove to realize it; and in the words imputed to Trajan on his Parthian campaign—"If I were young, I would advance even to India" (Cass. Dio 68.29)—the vitality of the notion of one empire embracing all the ancient civilized world shows itself.

The idea of the unity of the ancient world was at least partly realized, not on the political, but on the cultural plane. Hellenism, fostered by Alexander's victorious campaign, decisively promoted the unification of the ancient world; and Hellenism was the spiritual forerunner of Christianity, which at the close of Antiquity embraced a community extending from Iceland to India.

The spiritual unity of the ancient world laid the foundations of Western civilization, which means the contents of life in the modern world. Modern man is indebted to the ancient world, especially the Greeks, for the conception and form of Western science; and he is indebted to the Roman Empire for the creation of Roman law. The idea of a European civilization first became reality in Greece: one can think of the creations of representational art, of the appearance of tragedy and historiography, or of the beginnings of Western philosophy in Ionia. It was reserved for the imperialistic power of Rome to amalgamate a great part of modern Europe under its rule and so to lay the foundation of the political configuration of the West, in whose historical development the very idea of Rome represents an important political and cultural factor.

The chronological delimitation of Antiquity is a problem debated often and with diverse interpretations. There is no difference of opinion that the history of Antiquity reaches back to the earliest civilization in the Near East and Egypt. The special task of historical inquiry is to determine ever more exactly the lower bound-

ary, the "heavy line" between history and prehistory, whose field
is the investigation of preliterate societies. This delimitation actually
has come about in recent decades through the successful alliance
of Near Eastern with Egyptian archaeology. For the early history
of Greece and Italy we are also on surer ground than even half a
century ago, although many questions, especially concerning early
Italian history, are still strongly contested. Greek history at least
can be traced in broad outlines to the start of the second millennium
before Christ.

The point at issue is the demarcation between Antiquity and the
Middle Ages. In the face of this much-treated controversy, it should
be stressed that historical research does require periodization. Temporal divisions are an indispensable principle of order; in a way
of speaking they are a coordination system in which historical development allows itself to be displayed and classified. The common
earlier divisions which ended Antiquity with the Council of Nicaea
(A.D. 325), with the invasion of the Goths into the West (c. A.D.
375), or even with the deposition of the last West Roman emperor,
Romulus Augustulus, by the German *magister militum* Odoacer
(A.D. 476), are hardly satisfactory. All three dates fasten on an
important event of secular or ecclesiastical history and brand it
as the turning point from Antiquity to the Middle Ages. Whoever
accepts this view fails to see that the term "Middle Ages" means, in
all aspects, a new beginning. The Middle Ages mean the end of
ancient civilization, the end of the ancient state, and the end of
ancient thought. From the ruins of the ancient world there rise
with the Middle Ages new groupings of political powers, a new
way of thought, a new world outlook, and a new economic system.
Such a revolution cannot have taken place in a single year or even a
few years. Therefore, research has switched to elastically demar-
cating the boundaries between Antiquity and the Middle Ages. By
this method the end of the sixth and the beginning of the seventh
century after Christ has been reached. In that period events took
place which were decisive for the development of the medieval
world: the conquest of Italy by the Lombards (the capture of Pavia,
A.D. 572) and the invasion of the Arabs into the Western world.
The Arab storm, which broke over the East two years after Mohammed's death (d. A.D. 632), is a phenomenal event in world
history: the appearance of the Arabs is the last great reaction of
East against West; it is the response to the advance of Western,

Hellenistic culture into the wide spaces of the East. In the confrontation with the Arabs on the battlefields, a new Europe was born at the end of the seventh and beginning of the eighth century. Their invasion began a new era; and the grandson of that Charles Martel who vanquished them at Tours and Poitiers (A.D. 732), Charlemagne, founded a new empire in the West, which together with the papacy and Byzantium decided the political history of the Middle Ages.

BIBLIOGRAPHY

THE CONCEPTION OF THE UNIVERSAL HISTORY OF ANTIQUITY: Whoever holds it impossible to comprehend the world and especially the men of the ancient East on epistemological, anthropological, or other bases (so H. Berve, "Zur Kulturgeschichte des Alten Orients," *AKG* 25 [1934], 216 ff.), will not accept the idea of Antiquity within universal history which underlies this work. Definite obstacles do stand in the way of penetrating the mind of men of the ancient East, but they are hardly greater than the difficulties which, for example, exist for Europeans who want to understand the mentality of modern East Asians. The problem is set forth by B. Landsberger, "Die Eigenbegrifflichkeit der babylonischen Welt," *Islamica* 2 (1926), 355 ff., and by W. Wolf, *Individuum und Gemeinschaft in der ägyptischen Kultur (Leipziger Ägyptolog. Studien* 1, 1935), with which cf. A. Scharff, *DLZ* (1935), 985 ff. Especially recommended is W. Andrae, *Alte Feststrassen im Nahen Osten (Sendschr. d. Deutsch. Orientges.* 10, Leipzig 1941); it attempts to approach the thought of the ancient East through the meaning of ancient Oriental architecture. In any case, the adherent to the universal history of Antiquity who includes the ancient East in the sphere of his observations may refer to Herodotus, who described the great conflict between Greeks and barbarians, and thereby showed his appreciation for the strange national characteristics of Egyptians, Babylonians, Persians, Lydians, and Scythians. Opposed to H. Berve are the arguments of W. F. Albright, "How Well Can We Know the Near East?" *JAOS* 56 (1936), 121 ff., and the remarks of W. Otto, *DLZ* (1937), 1119 ff., 1161 ff.; *HZ* 161 (1940), 311. Recently J. Vogt has championed the idea of universal history: cf. the lecture "Geschichte des Altertums und Universalgeschichte," *Orbis* (1960), 362 ff.; and *Wege zum historischen Universum (Urban-Bücher* 51, Stuttgart 1961). Also see the lecture by H. Bengtson on B. G. Niebuhr, cited below, p. 21.

THE EPISTEMOLOGICAL BASIS OF HISTORICAL SCIENCE cannot be discussed here, but see Ed. Spranger, *Vom Sinn der Voraussetzungslosigkeit in den Geisteswissenschaften* (*SPAW* 1929, Abh. 2). The general reader will find much worthwhile in Wilh. Bauer, *Einführung in das Studium der Geschichte* (ed. 2, Tübingen 1928), in Moriz Ritter, *Die Entwicklung der Geschichtswissenschaft, an den führenden Werken betrachtet* (Munich and Berlin 1919), but above all in J. G. Droysen, *Historik, Vorlesungen über Enzyklopädie und Methodologie der Geschichte* (ed. R. Hübner, ed. 2, Munich and Berlin 1943). Also, "Geschichte," in the *Fischer-Lexicon* (ed. W. Besson, Frankfurt a. M. 1961) gives numerous new points of view; ancient history is there discussed by F. G. Maier. Very instructive especially for those interested in ancient history is M. P. Nilsson's discussion of K. J. Beloch, *Griechische Geschichte* I (ed. 2) in *GGA* (1914), 513 ff., in which Nilsson has excellently illuminated the boundaries of historical knowledge in regard to early Greek history. Also worthwhile is W. Pereman, "La critique historique appliquée aux sources de l'antiquité gréco-romaine," *LEC* 19 (1951), 3 ff., in which historical heuristic is discussed.

THE CHRONOLOGICAL DELIMITATION OF ANTIQUITY FROM THE MIDDLE AGES: A. v. Gutschmid, *Kleine Schriften* V (1894), 393 ff.; W. Otto, *Kulturgesch. d. Altertums* (Munich 1925), 4; E. Kornemann, *Die röm. Kaiserzeit* (in *Gercke-Norden* III.2; ed. 3, 1933), 57; K. F. Stroheker, *Saeculum* 1 (1950), 433–465; and, from the standpoint of medieval historians, H. Pirenne, *Mohammed and Charlemagne* (tr. Bernard Miall, New York 1939). Pirenne sees the establishment of Charlemagne's empire as the decisive event which marks the beginning of the Middle Ages; for another view cf. H. Aubin, *HZ* 172 (1951), 245 ff. In opposition to this, E. Manni, *Introduzione allo studio della storia greca e romana* (ed. 2, Palermo 1958), 19 ff., returns to A.D. 476 as the end of Antiquity. Completely different is F. Vittinghoff, *Geschichte in Wissenschaft und Unterricht* 8 (1958), 457 ff., who does not recognize the Middle Ages as a separate historical period.—For recent attempts at historical periodization see K. J. Neumann, "Perioden der röm. Kaiserzeit," *HZ* 117 (1917), 377 ff. and G. Ostrogorsky, "Die Perioden der byzantinischen Geschichte," *HZ* 163 (1941), 229 ff.—It is customary to call the time of transition from ancient to medieval "Late Antiquity." Although this term comes from the field of art history (A. Riegel), historians generally have long used the conception of "Late Antiquity" to refer to the time approximately from Constantine the Great (or Diocletian) to Justinian (or Heraclius I).

II

The History of
the Study of Antiquity
from the Renaissance
to the Present

The science of ancient history is a child or, better said, a stepchild of humanism. Enthusiasm for rediscovering the evidence of classical antiquity engaged the attention of the whole world of cultivated people in the age of Lorenzo Valla (1407–1457) and Desiderius Erasmus (1465–1536). The ancient authors were valued as quite unattainable exemplars, and Cicero's saying (*De Or.* 2.9.36), that history was the witness of the ages, the light of truth, the life of memory, the master of life, and the interpreter of antiquity, was the guiding principle of humanism. For these men classical antiquity was the great, unattainable model, and at the same time the best counselor in affairs of the present. In the age of humanism each newly discovered ancient author was felt to be not only an addition to knowledge, but a real enrichment of life itself. Thus the works of the humanists, the historical writings of Petrarch, Boccaccio, or Pier Candido Decembrio, as well as the patriotic passion for the ancient Germans of Jacob Wimpfeling of Schlettstadt and Beatus Rhenanus, are evidence of an uncritical attitude toward the products of ancient literature. Convinced that Antiquity was also politically the master of his own time, Cola di Rienzo (1313–1354) collected the visible signs of a great Roman past, the inscriptions. Enthusiastic about the ideal of republican government and full of admiration for the political conditions of Antiquity generally, Cola di Rienzo saw in the preoccupation with ancient works a valuable means to his own utopian political goals; he wanted to establish, in

7

league with the exiled papacy in Avignon, a Roman Republic as
a bulwark against the lust for domination of the powerful city
nobility of Rome. His political effect was ephemeral, but his collection of inscriptions had lasting influence on his contemporaries,
and introduced the first flowering of epigraphical research. Rienzo's
most famous successor was the learned merchant Ciriaco of Ancona
(died c. 1455), who, while traveling in the Levant, was the first
to collect Greek inscriptions. In his insatiable appetite for travel
and thirst for knowledge, he appears to us as an early precursor of
the gifted Mecklenburger, Heinrich Schliemann, the excavator of
Troy and Mycenae.

Political interests also led Niccolò Machiavelli to occupy himself with problems of Roman history. He was deeply moved by
the reasons for the decline of the Roman Empire, and was convinced that he lived in an age of decadence. So the aim of his *Discorsi
sopra la prima deca di Tito Livio* (which appeared in 1531, after his
death) is to ascertain, as Friedrich Meinecke said, the "causes of the
rise and fall of nations and to detect ways and means to their re-
generation."

Like Machiavelli, the French thinker Montesquieu tried to establish general historical rules by his work with Roman history. The
example here also is the decline of Rome. Montesquieu's essay, *Con-
sidérations sur les causes de la grandeur des Romains et de leur déca-
dence* (1734), is not an historical investigation, but a renewed
attempt, following Polybius and Machiavelli, to put observation of
the past in service to the present. It is the politician, the philos-
opher of civilization—not the historical inquirer—which guides
Montesquieu's argument.[1] It is with this work that the Prussian
king Frederick II argued (c. 1746) in his commentaries.

The first great historical attempt in which an unusual descriptive
power was combined with profound historical judgment deals again
with the decline of the Roman Empire. This is the *History of the
Decline and Fall of the Roman Empire* by Edward Gibbon (1737–
1797), who received decisive stimuli from the English "poetry of
ruins" of the mid-18th century. The transitory nature of all earthly
affairs, portrayed in a grandiose historical process, was Gibbon's
theme: "It was on the fifteenth of October in the gloom of evening,
as I sat musing on the Capitol, while the barefooted fryars were

---

[1] W. Rehm, *Der Untergang Roms im abendländischen Denken* (1930), 97.

chanting their litanies in the temple of Jupiter, that I conceived the first thought of my history." Gibbon's work comprises the period from the death of Marcus Aurelius (A.D. 180) to the capture of Constantinople by the Turks (A.D. 1453). With the insight of genius the Briton set forth the reign of the bizarre, degenerate Commodus (A.D. 180–192) as the prologue to the massive tragedy which the sinking empire, great even yet in its irrevocable decline, places before the eyes of posterity. Strongly influenced by the Enlightenment, Gibbon like Voltaire also reproached Christianity for having played a decisively destructive role in the gigantic process of disintegration. The cultural and historical penetration of the more-than-thousand-year epoch was Gibbon's essential achievement; as far as the basic material is concerned, the six-volume work is based on the diligence of the Frenchman Lenain de Tillemont (1637–1698), especially his *Histoire des Empereurs*, which goes from the battle of Actium (31 B.C.) to the Emperor Anastasius (d. A.D. 518). Gibbon's close connection with French culture is especially meaningful for understanding his artistic achievement: the decisive years of his intellectual development, from 16 to 21, were spent at Lake Geneva.

In Germany, however, the study of Antiquity received its decisive impulse not from Gibbon, but from Winckelmann (1717–1768) and Herder (1744–1803). It was not concern with Roman history, rather it was the relation of the late 18th century to Greece, to its art and its literary creations, which led to a new encounter with the classical world. To be sure, the nature of the Greeks was, by the enthusiastic artists and poets of that time, more divined and "felt" than understood as an historical phenomenon; yet this encounter gave German literature and art imperishable works, evidence of the marriage of Greek classicism with the German spirit.[2] This closeness to the Greeks, which is as manifest in Winckelmann's *Geschichte der Kunst im Altertum* as it is in Goethe's *Iphigenie*, Schiller's *Götter Griechenlands*, and Hölderlin's *Hyperion*, produced an enthusiasm for the Hellenic world to which the 19th century owes its great historical and philological works on the ancient Greeks—works which prepared the way for a truly historical knowledge of Antiquity. Chiefly, however, it was not enthusiasm

[2] Rehm, *Griechentum und Goethezeit: Geschichte eines Glaubens* (*Das Erbe der Alten* II.26, 1936). See also E. Grumach, *Goethe und die Antike* (2 vols., Berlin 1949).

for the Greeks, but the experience of the Napoleonic era which introduced a new epoch of historical science.

In Antiquity, especially in ancient Rome, concern with the writing of history was a domain of practical statesmen, among them Q. Fabius Pictor, the Achaean politician Polybius, and the consul Cassius Dio from the Severan period. Modern historiography likewise has exercised an especial attraction for statesmen. After Machiavelli and Montesquieu, Barthold Georg Niebuhr (1776–1831) was the third statesman who applied himself to historical observation. Niebuhr's attitude to history was completely different from that of Machiavelli and Montesquieu, who had seen their own times mirrored in the fate of the declining Roman Empire. For Niebuhr, the son of the traveler in the Orient Carsten Niebuhr (about whom he wrote a remarkable biography), the practical talent of politician was the primary impulse to the realization of something new—even revolutionary—in the past. With B. G. Niebuhr, in whom the practical statesman wrestled throughout life with the contemplative scholar, there appears a man who combined the capability for a uniquely constructive formulation of the past with a thoroughly critical talent. An active scepticism, which he derived from his own practical activity, is his unique trait. To be sure, even before Niebuhr the authority of Livy as a source for early Roman history had been questioned; Niebuhr, however, did not stop with negative criticism. With his *Römische Geschichte*, which first appeared in 1811 and was repeatedly revised, this man from Schleswig-Holstein, who served with distinction in the Danish and Prussian civil services (most notably as assistant to Baron von Stein, and later, from 1816 to 1823, as envoy to the Vatican), set about banning the Livian legends from the province of history. In their place he set a "history of Rome in broad, clear outlines, free from vexatious diversity, depicted with vivid truthfulness," as he expressed it in the second edition's dedication to King Frederick William III of Prussia. Of course Niebuhr, under the influence of the Homeric song theory of the philologist F. A. Wolf, admitted an unfortunate speculation by accepting the hypothesis of the existence of old Roman epic songs which had found expression in the Roman legends. Nevertheless, the progress signified by his Roman history was enormous. The earlier Roman history, a field which lacked great historical dynamism, offered in return great reward for methodical analysis. It was freed for the first time by Niebuhr from the coat of dust with which it had been covered by myth and a tradition reaching into the start of the 19th century. Under the hands of Niebuhr, the politician among scholars, Roman history came anew to light, in spite of the enormous time which separated the era of the Tarquinii from that of Napoleon. The influence of Niebuhr on 19th-century historical science is characterized by the words of his countryman, Theodor Mommsen: "Without exception, all historians—as far as they are worthy of the name—are Niebuhr's pupils, and not least those who do not profess to be of his school."

After Niebuhr's pioneering work, if one wanted to tackle a new synthesis of ancient Roman history, there were only two ways to make advances: by drawing on jurisprudence, which permits an interpretation of earlier conditions by inferences from later governmental institutions; and by inquiring into the direct evidence of the past, especially inscriptions. It is symbolic that one of the students listening to Niebuhr's lectures at the newly established University of Berlin was the legal historian Friedrich Karl von Savigny, whose advice the historian frequently followed in writing his Roman history.

The investigation of Roman law and its significance in the life of the Roman state, as well as the editing of Roman inscriptions, were the great tasks which Theodor Mommsen (1817–1903) set for himself. The imposing rise of German classical studies in the 19th century is inseparably bound up with his name. A driving urge toward the vivid realization of the past was native to Mommsen as to Niebuhr. From his experience of the Napoleonic era and from his belief in the reemergence of the Prussian state, Mommsen's great predecessor had drawn the strength for portraying Roman history. So also Mommsen, although primarily a scholar, remained deep in his heart always a politician, a fighter for right and freedom and the ideals of his youth—even when the foundation of the German empire by Bismarck seemed to have fulfilled his patriotic yearning. The soil of the Schleswig-Holstein borderland, the experience of the 1848–1849 battle for liberty in the northern frontier district, together with the knowledge of foreign countries gained by extensive travels in France and Italy, the gift of speaking and thinking in their languages—all this made Mommsen the man as he appears to us. He was a prince in the kingdom of knowledge, an ardent politician who never feared to swim against the current, a man with an awesome breadth of vision, created like no one else for the direction of a scholarly organization on a large-scale.

Mommsen's lifework always shows him as a lawyer, advancing through research in Roman law to a comprehensive conception of Roman antiquity. It was given only to him to place in the proper light the Roman achievements in law and statecraft, and thereby to do justice to the unique Roman achievement for human civilization. Among the educated, the fame of Theodor Mommsen rests above all on his *Römische Geschichte*, which appeared in three volumes in 1854–1856. It is a genuine document of politically oriented history, filled with sympathy and antipathy, illustrated with manifold parallels from his own time, and written in an unprecedentedly modern style. Here for the first time an investigator tried to answer the question why the Roman element became sovereign in Italy. Mommsen concluded that Rome had "more successfully, more seriously, and more luckily held fast to a unity of thought than any other Italic district," and that she owed her greatness to this absolute drive toward centralization.[3] The nature of his own times explains why Mommsen did not do justice to the role of the creative personality in constructing the Roman domination of the world—not even of so unique a personality as Caesar, whose portrait he painted in luminous colors, although in the final analysis he conceived of Caesar as a product of his environment.[4] The third volume of the *Römische Geschichte* ends with the battle of Thapsus (46 B.C.); a fourth volume never followed. In 1885, thirty years after the unfinished masterwork, Mommsen published a fifth volume, a description of the Roman provinces from Caesar to Diocletian. This volume documents its author's skill in making the inscriptions speak, thereby giving a unified cultural picture of a world for whose scientific exploration Mommsen's lifelong effort largely laid the groundwork.

Mommsen's significance as a scholar rests mainly on two achievements: the *Römisches Staatsrecht*[5] and the *Corpus Inscriptionum Latinarum* (abbr. *CIL*). Today many of Mommsen's works—the bibliography of Zangemeister and Jacobs lists 1513—might be forgotten, but the *CIL*, whose plan Mommsen laid out and carried through against determined resistance (with help from the Prussian Academy of Sciences), will remain. This monumental corpus of

---

[3] *Römische Geschichte* I, 100.

[4] *Ibid.*, III, 468.

[5] The three-volume work first appeared 1871–1888.

Latin inscriptions from the entire Roman world (in sixteen folio volumes, to which were added a series of supplementary fascicles) presents an enormous amount of material conveniently arranged by provinces and countries of the Roman Empire. The credit for it is due in first place to Theodor Mommsen, who had conceived the plan in 1845 during his meeting with the old master of Roman epigraphy, Count Bartolommeo Borghesi, and who remained true to it to the end of his life.

No codified constitutional law existed in ancient Rome. It was during the disorders of the Gracchan revolution that, for the first time in Rome, the constitution was discussed in order to use the results as a weapon in the day-to-day political struggle. Mommsen daringly extracted from ancient tradition—as W. Weber has said, with "the power of legal creativity of a real Roman"—Roman public law and systematized it. This was a decisive advance over the pre-Mommsen practice of simply collecting and registering legal and political facts of the ancient world. For the first time with legal precision Theodor Mommsen defined and set forth the significance of the magistracy and of the *imperium*. The very spirit of Rome seems here to have created a system of public law corresponding closely to Roman constitutional thinking. The *Römisches Strafrecht* supplements the *Römisches Staatsrecht*. In this work, finished very late in his life (1899), Mommsen pointed out that the basic pillar of Roman criminal law was the magistrate's power to inflict punishment (*coercitio*). Moreover, the work, especially the famous section on death penalties (pp. 911 ff.), is a significant contribution to cultural history.

Exploration of the entire ancient Roman world was the goal which Theodor Mommsen kept always before his eyes. Besides a *Römische Chronologie bis auf Cäsar* (1859) and a *Geschichte des römischen Münzwesens* (1860), his careful editions of later historians and legal sources broke the trail to a better knowledge of the transitional period from Antiquity to the Middle Ages. Jordanes, Cassiodorus, the *Chronica Minora*, the *Digest*, the *Codex Theodosianus* (published posthumously in 1904) are documents of this effort. Jurisprudence, epigraphy, and numismatics were freed from their roles as auxiliary sciences and were placed at the center of attention. Mommsen mastered their techniques as completely as he did those of philological interpretation.

Compared with his towering figure all other historians of the 19th century pale, with the one exception of Leopold von Ranke, whose life work was applied to other fields. Mommsen's work, however, remains the uncontested pinnacle in the study of Roman history; all modern research, including that which has developed beyond him, stands on his shoulders. It is primarily due to Mommsen that the study of Roman government and history, since the second half of the previous century, has undergone a decisive, methodological deepening, which distinguishes it even today so favorably from the often shakily constructed hypotheses in other provinces of ancient studies, especially in that of ancient Eastern history, and partly in that of Greek history.

In Mommsen's youth, in the first half of the 19th century, a serious transformation was effected in ancient studies. We see it today as a break with the classicistic-aestheticizing attitude to Antiquity, that is, with the attitude characterized by the intellecual movement for renewal of neohumanism. The Romantic movement created a new basis especially for a fruitful concern with the Orient. Already the 18th century had produced an extensive travel literature; it was the sign of a new feeling for life. The ardent desire, nourished by romantic currents, for the intellectual world of the East, the contacts which Napoleon's Egyptian expedition brought about, all contributed to the basic transformation of the one-sided, classical picture of Antiquity. The turn toward a new, history-based picture of the ancient world was proclaimed in the early work of a son of a Pommeranian pastor, Johann Gustav Droysen (1808–1884), especially in his *Geschichte Alexanders* (1833). New, even revolutionary, was Droysen's appreciation of Alexander, whom he viewed as one of the greatest bringers of civilization to mankind. Influenced by the Napoleonic experience, B. G. Niebuhr, on the contrary, had marked Alexander as a large-scale brigand and poseur. In the world movement begun by Alexander Droysen saw the embodiment of the creative genius (in Hegel's sense), the perfecter and enforcer of world law. Never before had the history of Alexander been seen from his own viewpoint. The judgment of the Macedonian kings Philip and Alexander by Demosthenes was and is, in spite of Droysen, still the authoritative view for part of the scholarly world, as is shown by the Englishman George Grote's *History of Greece* (see pp. 18 f.), Arnold Schaefer's erudite work *Demosthenes und seine Zeit* (ed. 2, 1885–1887), and even Werner Jaeger's *Demosthenes: The Origin and Growth of His Policy* (Berkeley 1938).

Undeterred, Droysen continued the same way in his *Geschichte des Hellenismus* (2 vols., 1836–1843). He did not, however, reach his goal, to bridge the era from Alexander to Caesar. Nevertheless, the description of the first century after Alexander's death—the work breaks off with 221 B.C.—is a landmark in the investigation of Antiquity. Droysen destroyed for the first time the framework of the classical age; the age of Hellenism—with which term Droysen, in opposition to the old usage, labeled the fusion of Greek with Oriental[6]—was recognized to be of equal historical rank and was appreciated for its world-wide effect on classical civilization. The bridge was laid from the world of classical Greece to that of the Roman Empire.

It is no accident that Droysen's early work belongs to a time when the bases for a methodical investigation of ancient Eastern languages were laid. This was achieved by the German Georg F. Grotefend, who presented to the Göttinger Gesellschaft der Wissenschaften on September 4, 1802, the first attempt at deciphering the old Persian cuneiform writing of the Achaemenids, and the Frenchman Jean François Champollion le Jeune (1790–1832), who worked out the bases of the system of hieroglyphic writing from a trilingual stone from Rosetta, which contained an Egyptian, priestly decree of 196 B.C. in hieroglyphics, demotic, and Greek.[7] Many decades of strenuous work in Babylonian-Assyrian and ancient Egyptian studies were needed before a sound scientific basis for these languages could be laid. In the study of cuneiform writing, in addition to the Briton Sir Henry Rawlinson, the German scholars Eberhard Schrader, Friedrich Delitzsch, Benno Landsberger, and Wolfram Freiherr von Soden, should be mentioned with respect. The Berlin school, under the direction of Adolf Erman (d. 1937), achieved decisive advances in the knowledge of the structure of the Egyptian language and its different periods.

The decisive impulse to overcome neohumanism was furnished by the systematic excavations. Gradually setting in during the first half of the 19th century, excavation activity received an enormous stimulus from the extraordinary success of the outsider Heinrich

---

[6] Droysen's term "Hellenism" is based on an erroneous interpretation of *Acts* 6.1, where the "Hellenists" (Ἑλληνισταί) are contrasted with the Hebrews. The "Hellenists" here are people of Greek culture and not, as Droysen thought, Oriental Greeks.

[7] *Lettre à M. Dacier*, Sept. 14, 1822.

Schliemann in Troy (Hissarlik), Mycenae, Tiryns, and Orcho-
menus (from 1871), as well as from the start of the excavations at
Olympia by the German government (from 1875). The monopoly
of philology on the study of Antiquity was thereby broken, and
archeological investigation took its place beside the interpretation
of classical texts. All civilized nations have increasingly taken part
in excavations. The findings have benefitted the prehistory and early
history of the Mediterranean area (e.g., this holds true especially
for the excavations of the British under A. Evans, from 1899, in
Knossos on Crete) and the history of the ancient East, as much
as they have our knowledge of Greco-Roman antiquity. The German excavations at Boghazköi in the loop of the Halys River (in
central Anatolia)—from 1906, first under the direction of Winckler,
then under Otto Puchstein; from 1932 under Martin Schede and
Kurt Bittel—introduced a new period to the study of the ancient
Near East: the find of the state archives at Chattušaš, the old capital
of the Hittite empire, and the recognition of the Indo-European
structure of the Hittite language by B. Hrozný (1915)[8] made it
possible to recognize the Hittite people and state as Indo-European
and to classify their civilization as a new component of the Near
Eastern history of the second millennium B.C. It was an especial
stroke of luck, in the decades which were decisive for transforming
and broadening the picture of the ancient world, that one investigator, after his preparatory training and qualification, was ready to as-
similate the new, amorphous findings and to formulate them into a
composite picture. This was the young native of Hamburg, Eduard
Meyer (1855–1930). The idea of a universal history of Antiquity
had already been advocated by others, such as the Tübingen historian, Alfred von Gutschmid, who was much advanced for his
time. But it was Eduard Meyer, with his *Geschichte des Altertums*,
which began to appear in 1884, who first tackled the great task of
writing a comprehensive history of the ancient world, based on
uniform, critical scrutiny of all source materials. The self-evident
demand for linguistic mastery of the written sources for classical
antiquity, Greek and Roman history, was carried over by Eduard
Meyer to the wide field of the ancient East. He thus became the

---

[8] Hrozný achieved an epoch-making discovery by the later famous sen-
tence: *nu-NINDA-an ezateni vadarma ekuteni*. All that was known was
NINDA, the Sumerian-Akkadian ideogram for "bread," and the accusative
ending *-an*. The translation is: "And ye eat bread and ye drink water."

real founder of the universal historiography of Antiquity. Admittedly he abandoned the work uncompleted; he could not portray, in the frame of his *Geschichte des Altertums*, the great change signified by the lives of Philip II of Macedon and his son.

Even the learning of Eduard Meyer had its limits: the results of investigation of the Hittite language came too late for him, and he never found the close relation to Assyriology which he had to Egyptology, the basic study from which his later work proceeded. Nevertheless, the scientific achievement of his *Geschichte des Altertums* is staggering. It was Eduard Meyer who laid the foundation, based on primary sources, for the periodization of Egyptian history, with its high points and its periods of decay; it was Eduard Meyer who was one of the first to recognize the significance of the Indo-European element in the Near Eastern world; and it was he, more competent than any other due to his intensive concern with questions of religious history, who pursued the great movements in the sphere of spiritual life and showed their place in ancient history.

In his last years Eduard Meyer recognized that it was the influence of B. G. Niebuhr which had pushed him toward the conception of the universal history of Antiquity. The key here was Niebuhr's *Vorträge über Alte Geschichte* (published by Niebuhr's son Marcus, 1847–1848), in which the creator of classical Roman history had given a sketchy presentation of the history of the classical world down to the battle of Actium (31 B.C.) based on the *Historiae Philippicae* of Pompeius Trogus.

The 1880's were of incisive significance for the development of the separate branches of ancient history. In 1886 appeared Julius Beloch's study of the population of the Greco-Roman world, in which for the first time with the help of modern methods important basic questions were discussed, such as the question of the size of population and its significance for the course of history. In the same decade appeared the first papyrological works of Ulrich Wilcken (1862–1944). They were precursors of many larger studies, including his *Griechische Ostraka aus Ägypten und Nubien* (1899). The subtitle, *Ein Beitrag zur antiken Wirtschaftsgeschichte*, indicates which field got the major benefit of his work.

Also in classical philology, at the end of the 19th century, the historical method personified by the towering figure of Ulrich von Wilamowitz-Moellendorff (1848–1931) carried off an uncontested victory over classicism. Here, too, the intention is now obvious: to

explain the creations of classical literature by a balanced considera-
tion of the entire tradition, even of the imposing monuments of
Antiquity.

The attempt to picture the ancient world has occasionally led to
distortions. Robert von Pöhlmann's *Geschichte des antiken Kom-
munismus und Sozialismus* (2 vols., 1893–1901), in the second and
third editions titled *Geschichte der sozialen Frage und des Sozialismus in Altertum*, shows how deeply the students of that generation
were enmeshed in contemporary aspirations and ideas, which they
believed to have rediscovered in the ancient world. The modernizing
trend is unmistakable also in the sometimes exceptionally emotional
altercation over ancient economic modes which grew up between
the economist from Leipzig, Bücher, and the historians Eduard
Meyer and Julius Beloch. This time the historians were modernizing, and they were frequently right. A document of the modern
(this is not to say "modernizing") conception of ancient history is
the *Griechische Geschichte* of K. J. Beloch (first ed. in 3 vols., 1893–
1904; second ed. in 4 vols., two parts to each, 1912–1927). A brilliant product of critical erudition, it is still the best foundation for
modern research—in spite of its often quite willful use of sources.

The constantly increasing material and the refined scientific work
being carried on in all civilized countries have caused it gradually to
become impossible for the single student to have a full view of all
of ancient history, or even of only Greek history or Roman history.
Not by chance did Beloch's *Griechische Geschichte*, which one
must praise for its almost complete presentation of source material,
close with the peace of Naupactus (217 B.C.), and the circumspect
Roman history of his Italian pupil Gaetano De Sanctis (*Storia dei
Romani*, 4 vols., 1907–1960) with the destruction of Numantia
(133 B.C.). Both therefore are incomplete. But they are among
the most significant results of ancient scholarship in the past half
century.

Since the middle of the 19th century non-German scholars have
come forth more frequently with significant works. The Englishman George Grote's 12-volume *History of Greece* (1846–1856)
is most nearly comparable to Niebuhr's Roman history. The breadth
of vision, the critical sharpness in discussing historical problems, but
above all an incorruptible sense of the realities of life make it one
of the most impressive historiographical documents of the past century, despite some one-sidedness caused by Grote's partisan political

views. The many-sided, exceptionally productive Frenchman, Gaston Maspero (1846–1916), provided a model for the investigation of ancient Eastern civilization. His brilliant *Histoire ancienne des peuples de l'Orient classique* (3 vols., Paris 1895–1899) is now wrongly relegated to oblivion. A whole series of archeologists and historians won their spurs at the French excavations on Delos and at Delphi, among them the excellent historians and epigraphers Maurice Holleaux (1861–1932) and Pierre Roussel (1881–1945). French, Italian, and English science can boast of many names on the field of Roman history; among them are E. Albertini, M. Besnier, J. Carcopino, A. Piganiol of France; G. De Sanctis, E. Pais, P. Fraccaro, A. Momigliano of Italy; F. E. Adcock, M. P. Charlesworth, H. Last, and R. Syme of England. In the study of the Hellenistic age the works of the American W. S. Ferguson (1875–1954) and the Briton W. W. Tarn (1869–1957) are important milestones. Social and economic classical history owe basic investigations to the American Tenney Frank and the Russian Michael Rostovtzeff (1870–1952). And in the history of religion the work of the Swede M. P. Nilsson (1874–1967) and the Belgian Franz Cumont (1869–1947) gave strong impulses, Cumont's especially for its knowledge of Iranism and its effect on the Western world.

Collections have become characteristic of recent historiography. Of these, first place goes to the *Cambridge Ancient History* (12 vols., 1924–1939), the first two volumes of which are now appearing fascicle by fascicle in a second edition. It covers the enormous period from the beginnings of ancient Near Eastern civilizations to Constantine the Great, and hence reaches to the beginning of the *Cambridge Medieval History*. Published by English historians, it makes use of a large, international staff. By contrast, almost exclusively French investigators were employed for the *Histoire Générale*, published by Gustave Glotz.

In opposition to the investigation of knowable and worth-knowing facts (embodied at its purest in Beloch's *Griechische Geschichte*), an orientation developed during the general intellectual crisis after World War I in Germany which attempted to extract the intellectual content of the classical world and to use it for constructing a new view of the world and a new ideal of personality. Classical Greece was given new life by this intellectual experience. Such a "neohumanistic orientation"[9] appeared in opposition to historicism,

[9] Cf. Werner Jaeger, *Humanistische Reden und Aufsätze* (Berlin 1937).

but it also pointed out new paths to the historical knowledge of Antiquity. All ancient studies, as well as ancient history, are indebted to Werner Jaeger for works of exceptional intellectual-historical insight, such as his *Aristoteles* (1923) and *Paideia* (3 vols., 1934–1947).

Characteristic of recent scholarship is the enormous broadening that the picture of the ancient world has undergone: the ancient civilizations of Iberia and Gaul, the civilizations of the Scyths and Sarmatians, the connections of the classical world with the Far East, with China and India, have been brought to the attention of scholars especially by the recent excavations. This larger picture has resulted in new perspectives and in some new methodological demands yet to be mastered. Now the incorporation of peripheral peoples and cultures will lead, just as once the discovery of the ancient East did lead, to a gradual transformation and enlargement of the study of ancient history.

In contrast to these clearly apparent universalist tendencies, there often appears a powerful urge to an intensive specialization, which has led nearly to rendering independent such separate areas of research as epigraphy, papyrology, and numismatics. General works have become rare: Gaetano De Sanctis' *Storia dei Greci dalle origini alla fine del secolo V* (1939), Martin P. Nilsson's *Geschichte der griechischen Religion*[10] (2 vols., 1941–1950), and Michael Rostovtzeff's *Social and Economic History of the Hellenistic World* (3 vols., 1941) sum up the lifework of these scholars, and will indicate the research of the coming generation. The task of today's students of Antiquity is not to lose sight of the forest for the trees and to preserve the underlying unity of ancient history.

BIBLIOGRAPHY

An older, comprehensive survey is K. J. Neumann, *Entwicklung und Aufgaben der Alten Geschichte* (Strassburg 1910); especially worthwhile among recent work is A. Momigliano, "Sullo stato presente degli studi di storia antica (1946–1956)," in *Relazioni del X Congresso Intern. di Scienze Storiche* VI (Rome 1955), 3 ff.; cf. further his "La formazione della moderna storiografia sull' Impero Romano," in *Contributo alla storia degli studi classici* (Rome 1955), 107–164 (first publ. 1936).

[10] In *Müller*. The third edition of volume one appeared in 1967, and the second of volume two in 1961.

STUDIES OF ANCIENT HISTORY IN THE RENAISSANCE: G. Voigt, *Die Wiederbelebung des klassischen Altertums* I (ed. 3, 1893; repr., 2 vols., Berlin 1960). Worthwhile for the history of the study of ancient history are the philological histories, among which are W. Kroll, *Gesch. d. klass. Philologie* (*Sammlung Göschen*, ed. 2, 1920), R. Pfeiffer, *History of Classical Scholarship* (Oxford 1968), from the beginnings to the end of the Hellenistic period, and U. v. Wilamowitz-Moellendorff, *Gesch. d. Philologie* (in *Gercke-Norden* I.1; ed. 2, 1960). Cf. also M. Wegner, *Altertumskunde* (*Orbis Academicus*, Freiburg i. Br. and Munich 1951): a collection of documents with related text, especially important for archeological study. Interesting is A. Momigliano, "Ancient History and the Antiquarian," in *Contributo alla storia degli studi classici* (Rome 1955), 67–106: note especially the connection of antiquarian studies with 17th century skepticism (Pyrrhonism).

On Niebuhr: U. Wilcken, *Gedächtnisrede auf B. G. Niebuhr* (Bonn 1931); E. Kornemann, "Niebuhr und der Aufbau der röm. Gesch.," *HZ* 145 (1931), 277 ff.; H. Bengtson, "B. G. Niebuhr und die Idee der Universalgeschichte des Altertums," *Würzberger Rektoratsrede 1960*; and S. Rytkönen, *B. G. Niebuhr als Politiker und Historiker* (Helsinki 1968).–On J. G. Droysen: F. Meinecke, in *Staat und Persönlichkeit* (Berlin 1933), 98 ff.; and H. Berve in the introduction to the new edition of Droysen's *Geschichte Alexanders* (*Sammlung Kröner*, Leipzig 1931; new ed. 1941).–On T. Mommsen: L. Wickert, *Theodor Mommsen* (2 vols., Frankfurt a. M. 1959–1964). Extraordinary is the codicil to Mommsen's will, recorded by him on September 2, 1899: H. Bengtson, *WG* 15 (1955), 87 ff.; see also A. Wucher, *Theodor Mommsen. Geschichtsschreibung und Politik* (Göttingen 1956), and A. Heuss, *Theodor Mommsen und das 19. Jahrhundert* (Kiel 1956), and the review of the latter by A. Momigliano, *Gnomon* (1958), 1 ff. Important for Mommsen as a scholar is *Mommsens Briefwechsel mit U. v. Wilamowitz* (Berlin 1935). For a catalog of Mommsen's correspondence see C. Zangemeister and E. Jacobs, *Th. Mommsen als Schriftsteller* (Berlin 1905).–On Eduard Meyer: H. Marohl, *Ed. Meyer, Bibliographie (mit Abdruck der Gedächtnisrede U. Wilckens)* (Stuttgart 1941); W. Otto, "Ed. Meyer und sein Werk," *ZDMG* N.F. 10 (1932), 1 ff.–On George Grote: A. Momgliano, "George Grote and the Study of Greek History," in *Contributo alla storia degli studi classici* (1955), 213–231.

THE DEVELOPMENT OF EGYPTOLOGY AND CUNEIFORM STUDIES: K. Sethe, *Die Ägyptologie: Zweck, Inhalt und Bedeutung dieser Wissenschaft und Deutschlands Anteil an ihrer Entwicklung (AO*

23.1; Leipzig 1921); B. Meissner, *Die Keilschrift* (*Sammlung Gös-chen* 708; ed. 3 by K. Oberhuber, Berlin 1967); older studies are noted in K. Wachsmuth, *Einleitung in das Studium der Alten Gesch.* (Leipzig 1895), 399 ff.; for recent work see E. Littmann, *Der deutsche Beitrag zur Wissenschaft vom Vorderen Orient* (Stuttgart and Berlin 1942), especially for the results of Semitic studies, and J. Friedrich, "Deutschlands Anteil an der Erschliessung der Keilschriftsprachen," in *Der Orient in deutscher Forschung*, ed. H. H. Schaeder (Leipzig 1944), 57 ff.

THE DEVELOPMENT OF ARCHEOLOGY: F. Koepp in *Müller* I (Munich 1939), 11 ff., which contains as a supplement a chronological survey of the most important excavations. For a character sketch of H. Schliemann cf. Ernest Meyer's edition of the *Briefe von Heinrich Schliemann* (Berlin and Leipzig 1936), and his *Heinrich Schliemann: Briefwechsel* (2 vols., Berlin 1953–1958). Worth reading also is Schliemann's autobiography (ed. 9, Wiesbaden 1961). The biography of Theodor Wiegand by C. Watzinger (Munich 1944) gives an interesting segment of the history of modern archeology. A readable summary of this history by an expert is A. Rumpf, *Archaeologie* I–II (*Sammlung Göschen* 538, 539; 1953). A popular treatment is W. Ceram (pseudonym for K. Marek), *Gods, Graves, and Scholars*, which has gone through numerous editions here and abroad. Among scholarly works cf. A. Parrot, *Découverte des mondes ensevelis* (Neuchatel-Paris 1952; tr. E. Hudson, New York 1955), and, on the archeological finds of the past 150 years, W. Wolf, *Funde in Ägypten* (Göttingen 1966).

EXCAVATIONS IN MESOPOTAMIA: V. Christian, *Altertumskunde des Zweistromlandes* I (Leipzig 1940), 1 ff., and J. Jordan, "Leistungen und Aufgaben der deutschen Ausgrabungen in Vorderen Orient," in *Der Orient in deutscher Forschung*, ed. H. H. Schaeder (Leipzig 1944), 228 ff.; A. Parrot, *Archéologie mésopotamienne* (2 vols., Paris 1946–1953).

III

The Fundamentals
of the Study of
Ancient History

I. CHRONOLOGY

Chronology, the science of reckoning time, has been called the "eye of history." All history takes place in time, and nothing has the same basic importance for the judgment and the historical classification of events as establishing their temporal sequence. Only when this is fixed can an event be included in a causative association. Whoever takes no account of temporal sequence violates a basic law of the science of history.

Chronology has two tasks: to determine the temporal relation which historical facts bear to each other (relative chronology), and to establish the distance of an historical event from the standpoint of the observer (absolute chronology). In historical judgment, for instance, it is of basic importance to know that the battles of Plataea and Mycale were fought in 479 B.C., and that the foundation of the Delian League occurred only in 478/477—the earlier battles are simply the historical prerequisite, the basis of that union. Their temporal relation, the relative chronology, is of fundamental significance. Another example from Greek history: the founding of the Corinthian League, that great Pan-Hellenic organization for peace effected by the Macedonian king Philip II in 338/337 B.C., and the beginning of the "Pan-Hellenic war of revenge" against Persia begun by Philip II in 336 B.C., are two events which only are placed in the right light by their relative temporal positions.

In order to determine the distance of individual events from his own standpoint (therefore, to ascertain the absolute chronology),

23

the historian, like anyone else, employs the current reckoning of time by years, months, and days. The difficulties begin when one transfers these terms of modern chronology to Antiquity.

Modern chronology is based on the Gregorian calendar, introduced in 1582 by Pope Gregory XIII and gradually accepted almost universally. Its structure goes back to the Julian calendar, named after C. Julius Caesar. Both calendars reckon the normal year at 365 days and add one day, an "intercalary" day, every four years. The novelty of the Gregorian calendar, in contrast to the Julian, is that in a space of 400 years three of these intercalary days are omitted (1600 was a leap year, but 1700, 1800, and 1900 were not). Thereby the modern calendar year almost exactly corresponds to an astronomical year, whose average length is 365.2420 days.

Did Antiquity also possess a system of chronology, a "calendar," which had gradually reached universal recognition, as has the Gregorian calendar? The question can be answered affirmatively for a part of Antiquity—and only for that part: during the course of the Roman Empire the Caesarian (Julian) calendar reform pushed out all other systems in the Latin West and in the Greek East.

Before Caesar's reform (it began January 1, 45 B.C.) we are faced with problems: there were almost as many calendars and "eras" (chronological systems which began their count from a fixed point) as there were peoples, states, and cities. The calendars were lunisolar ones determined empirically; the noteworthy exception is the ancient Egyptian calendar, oriented around the bright star Sirius.

Only the most important types of chronology in Antiquity can be mentioned here. The time-reckoning of the ancient Egyptians had the most far-reaching effect; even the Gregorian calendar—via the Julian calendar—goes back to it. The entire life of the ancient Egyptian peasants was determined by the Nile; it got its rhythm from the annual summer flooding of the Nile, caused by the monsoon-produced summer rainfall in Abyssinia and Equatorial Africa.[1] According to the Gregorian calendar the flood occurred in the middle of June. The "Bringer of the Nile" appeared to the ancient Egyptians to be the bright star Sirius, the star of Sothis, whose first rising in the dawn (heliacal rising) usually marked the onset of the flood-

[1] For the theories of Antiquity, see W. Capelle, *NJA* 33 (1908), 317 ff.; A. Rehm, *RE* XVII, 571 ff. s.v. "Nilschwelle."

ing of the Nile. One or two generations' observation of the flood's appearance could have led to ascertaining the "Nile year,"[2] which on the average amounted to 365 days. One modern school of research maintains in fact that at first the measure of time derived from astronomical observation of the rising of Sirius was secondary, to some extent as a corrective, to that derived from the observation of the flood.[3] Actually, however, there is scanty difference between the "civil" year of 365 days, based on observation of the Nile's flood, and the "Sothic" year of 365 1/4 days; nevertheless, in the course of lengthier periods of time the difference must have had a considerable effect. The day of the rising of Sirius, which corresponded at the beginning of astronomical observation with the appearance of the flood, passed through all the days of the year in a period of 1461 civil years, which correspond to 1460 Sothic years, which equal a Sothic cycle. Thus, the Sothic rising fell behind the civil year about one day in every four years, so that only in A.D. 140/143[4] and 1321/1318, 2781/2778, and 4241/4238 B.C.,[5] the beginning of the civil war coincided with the heliacal rising of Sirius. If one accepts an official introduction for the ancient Egyptian calendar—which, however, is not necessary—then it must have taken place at the beginning of a Sothic cycle, and specifically at a time when one may assume an already special knowledge of astronomy in Egypt. The year 4241, far back in Egyptian prehistory, is thus eliminated (in spite of Eduard Meyer, who to the end advocated this early date for the introduction of the Egyptian calendar). A. Scharff, above all others, has repeatedly favored 2781 (or 2776), the beginning of the next cycle.[6] This estimate appears to be the earliest legitimate one, especially because we now possess more Sothic dates

[2] For doubts about the acceptance of a Nile year, see H. E. Winlock, "The Origin of the Egyptian Calendar," *PAPhS* 83.3 (1940), 447 ff. and M. P. Nilsson, *Acta Orientalia* 19 (1941), 1 ff. On the other side see the reply of O. Neugebauer, *JNES* 1 (1942), 396 ff.

[3] O. Neugebauer, *Acta Orientalia* 17 (1938), 169 ff.

[4] According to Censorinus, *De die natali* 21.10, however, 139/142.

[5] The numbers according to Eduard Meyer's "cyclical" reckoning, among which are the astronomical estimates (which alone can be authoritative), differ a little. Following L. Borchardt, they are: 4236, 2776, 1318 B.C.; following J. Mayer, *Astron. Nachr.* 5906/07 (1932), 19: 4228, 2770, 1314 B.C.

[6] A. Scharff, *Grundzüge der ägypt. Vorgeschichte* (1927), 54 ff.; *HZ* 161 (1940), 3 ff. Similarly H. E. Winlock (*art. cit.*, n. 2) places the beginning of the Egyptian calendar in 2772 B.C.

from the Middle Kingdom, namely for the time after 2100 B.C. One cannot, however, entirely exclude the beginning of the next Sothic cycle, 1321/1318 B.C., the so-called era ἀπὸ Μενόφρεως.[7]

That the ancient Egyptians firmly held to their inconstant year, in spite of observing that it in no way coincided with the seasons— the Egyptian priesthood defeated a reform proposed by Ptolemy III in 238 B.C.—only underlines the tenacity with which the peasants and the protectors of their traditions, the priesthood, preserved the time-honored arrangements. This is an impressive example of the strength of tradition in the life of a nation of the ancient world.

It is mainly inscriptions which make the calendar of Athens in the classical and Hellenistic periods the best known of the many Greek calendars. There were two methods of reckoning the year in Athens: one was based on prytanies,[8] that is, on the "administrative year" of 366 days; the other was based on the moon, resulting in a 354-day civil year, whose adjustment with the true seasons, namely with the course of the sun, was made by intercalating a second month Poseideon.[9] The researches of W. K. Pritchett and O. Neugebauer[10] have shown that by making the prytany year equal the civil year (i.e., from the end of the fifth century B.C.), the prytany year was tightly controlled, while the length of each lunar month was set exclusively by observation of lunar phases. As long as Athens had ten phylae and ten prytanies, down to 307 B.C., the first through the fourth prytany each had 36 days and the fifth through tenth had 35 days each if the year was a regular one; or, if it was a leap year, they had 39 and 38 days respectively. It is clear that the discrepancy between the administrative year and the civil year in Athens was attended by a series of difficulties which the Athenians never really mastered—as, for example, the errors in inscriptions demonstrate. The institution of the 11th and 12th phylae in 307 B.C. in honor of the monarchs Antigonos Monophthalmos and Demetrius Poliorketes brought with it the great advantage that

---

[7] Cf. W. Struve, *Zeitschrift f. ägypt. Sprache* 63 (1928), 45 ff.

[8] In Athens the 50-man committee (of the Council of 500) which was in office for a tenth of the year was called a prytany.

[9] The Attic months were named Hekatambaion (c. July–August), Metageitnion, Boedromion, Pyanepsion, Maimakterion, Poseideon, Gamelion, Anthesterion, Elaphebolion, Munychion, Thargelion, and Skirophorion.

[10] *The Calendars of Athens* (Cambridge, Mass. 1947); cf. G. Klaffenbach, *Gnomon* (1949), 129 ff.

the administrative and civil years now ran parallel, and—except for a break during 223–201 B.C. when there were 13 phylae—did so until the time of the emperor Hadrian.

The Roman calendar of the pre-imperial epoch is, in its technical incompleteness, a testimony to the scant attention paid to science in ancient Rome. The year had 12 months (Martius, Maius, Quinctilis, and October with 31 days; Ianuarius, Aprilis, Iunius, Sextilis, September, November, and December with 29 days; and Februarius with 28) totaling 355 days. In the even years either 23 or 22 days were intercalated after the festival of the Terminalia on February 23. The four-year period resulted therefore in 355 + 378 + 355 + 377 = 1465 days, that is, an average of 366 1/4 days. Since, however, the correction was often arbitrarily made, the Roman Republican calendar "went neither with the sun nor the moon, but completely wild," as Mommsen said. When Caesar set the calendar in order in 46 B.C., 90 days had to be intercalated. Thus, when a date is given according to the unrevised, pre-Caesarian calendar, it can be equated with Julian dates—as far as it is possible at all—only by using empirical methods.

The various relationships between the chronologies and calendars of Antiquity are of great significance for cultural history. For example, the adoption of the so-called Octaëteris in Greece, an eight-year cycle of intercalation which had its origin in Babylonia, was momentous. Introduced probably as early as the seventh century B.C. through the influence of the Delphic priesthood,[11] this eight-year cycle of 99 months had great significance for the Greek calendar, insofar as through it the celebrations of the individual gods' festivals were fixed, thereby adding to the life of the Greek people an important element of unity in opposition to the centrifugal political splintering of ancient Greece. Also notable is the adoption of the Babylonian 19-year cycle of intercalation, the so-called Enneadekaëteris (of which seven of the 19 years were leap years: viz. 3, 6, 8, 11, 14, 17, 19), by Seleucus I. Although the acceptance of the neo-Babylonian (Chaldaean) calendar by the Diadochi may have been a question of external reasons of expediency, the influence of the East is incontestable. Unfortunately, the relationship of the well-known 19-year cycle of the Athenian Meton (432 B.C.) to the neo-Babylonian cycle cannot be determined; in addition, de-

[11] M. P. Nilsson, *Gesch. d. griech. Religion* I (ed. 3, Munich 1967), 645.

termination of the practical application of the Metonic cycle in Athens is out of the question.[12]

Because Caesar based his calendar reform on the Egyptian solar year, our present chronology goes back indirectly to the ancient Egyptians. The reason monarchs were at pains to establish a generally accepted calendar is easy to understand: the organization of the ruler cult with its sacrifices for the king binding equally on all subjects is practicable only when based on a unified calendar. Furthermore, and this applies especially to Caesar, the construction of a universal state requires above all a uniform administration, which is possible only with a uniform calendar.

Viewed from these standpoints, the ancient chronological and calendric systems are exceptionally meaningful for understanding cultural connections, as well as for understanding the political aims of their authors. This aspect of viewing ancient chronology has not been given the importance which it deserves.

We have four main possibilities for determining the date of historical events in Antiquity: (1) notices of celestial phenomena, especially solar and lunar eclipses, to the extent that one can successfully determine, with the help of modern astronomy, absolute dates; (2) synchronisms, that is, statements of the simultaneousness of events which took place at different places; (3) lists of rulers and eponyms; and (4) eras.

From the number of famous celestial phenomena noted in ancient sources, we might here mention two: the total lunar eclipse of August 27, 413 B.C., which in the final analysis caused the failure of the Athenians' Sicilian expedition by thwarting the departure of Nikias from Sicily, and that of September 20, 331 B.C., 11 days before the battle of Gaugamela (October 1). Here also belong the Egyptian Sothic dates, for they note on which day of the civil year the heliacal rising of Sirius was observed. The most famous Sothic date comes from a papyrus of Illahun in the Fayum. The document testifies to a date of the morning rising of Sirius in the seventh regnal year of a king of the XIIth dynasty, a specification which, according to Scharff, Winlock, *et al.*, relates to Sesostris III. If this is right, the beginning of the XIIth dynasty can be dated—with a minimal margin of two years—to 1991 B.C.

The cuneiform chronicles of Mesopotamia are rich in synchro-

---

[12] Cf. however A. Rehm, "Parapegmastudien," *ABAW* 19 (1941), 25; *NJA* (1941), 230.

nisms. For example, the "Synchronistic History," which comes from the palace library of King Assurbanipal in Nineveh (Kujundshik), gives a connected presentation of the wars and the conclusions of peace between Assur and Babel. In the "Babylonian Chronicle" we have, moreover, a history of Babylonia and Assyria from 745 to 668 B.C. Cuneiform tablets from the French excavations at Mari (Tell-el-Haridi) on the middle Euphrates have shown that King Hammurabi, the great lawgiver and ruler of the first dynasty of Babel, was a contemporary of the Assyrian king Šamšiadad I. Thus Hammurabi belongs to a time c. 1700 B.C. and not, as we used to think, to the 20th century B.C. This synchronism also does away with the gap in Near Eastern history which has played such an important role too in the history of the Hittite empire; and the gap between the Old and New Empire of the Hatti, which we formerly took to be more than two centuries, has shrunk by now to a few decades (c. 1530–1480 B.C.).

There also are numerous synchronisms in the historical literature of the Greeks and Romans. Polybius places the burning of Rome by the Gauls in the year of the peace of Antalkidas and the taking of Rhegium by Dionysius I, 19 years after the battle of Aigospotamoi, 16 years before the battle of Leuktra, that is, in 387–386 B.C. For 436 Livy mentions the outbreak of a plague at Rome (Livy 4.21 and 4.25), which can refer only to the famous epidemic of 430 described by Thucydides. The conclusion, that this Livian date is about six years too early, is compelling. One can view Livian dates for the fifth century B.C. perhaps only as the earliest possible dates, which can be reduced up to six years. Finally, some ancient synchronisms are only apparent, such as the notice that the battles of Salamis and Himera took place on the same day.[13] We are faced here not with a true synchronism, but a myth of coincidence, of which modern history, too, has numerous examples.

Lists of rulers and eponyms provide important chronological pegs. The Turin papyrus of the kings[14] stands first among the sources for the history of Pharaonic Egypt; it contains a list, unfortunately only partly preserved, of the Egyptian kings with their years of rule from Menes on. This list comes from the reverse of an account book from the XIXth dynasty. Modern research, however, mistrusts the dates for the early period (Ist to XIth dynasties). The

[13] The sources are in H. Bengtson, *Griech. Gesch.* (ed. 3, 1965), 178 n. 3.
[14] Ed. G. Farina, *Il papiro dei re restaurato* (Turin 1939).

kinglist of Chorsabad[15] is fundamental for the chronology of Assyrian rulers, for it establishes the whole series of Assyrian kings from 1430 to the end of the Assyrian empire, including the dates of rule of individual kings; for earlier chronology a difficulty remains, because the—clearly only brief—regnal dates of Assur-rabi I and Assur-nadin-naḫḫe I (shortly before 1430) have not been preserved.

From Roman imperial times we possess the so-called "Ptolemaic" royal canon ($\kappa\alpha\nu\grave{\omega}\nu$ $\beta\alpha\sigma\iota\lambda\epsilon\iota\hat{\omega}\nu$), a list for astronomical purposes of the regnal dates of Babylonian, Persian, and Ptolemaic kings and of Roman emperors from 747 B.C. to A.D. 160. Some manuscripts extend the list to A.D. 1453.[16]

The custom of designating individual years with the name of a personage comes from the ancient Orient, no doubt from Assyria. The eponyms, that is, the persons after whom individual years are named, are called *limmu* first in the cuneiform tablets of the Assyrian commercial colony of Kültepe in Cappadocia. Series of such *limmu* lists have been preserved from the new Assyrian empire. The Greeks adopted this custom from the ancient Orient (dating by archons in Athens, ephors in Sparta, stephanephoroi in Miletus, *et al.*), and in Rome we find individual years named for the consuls. Tied up with the eponymous lists are numerous chronological and historical problems, whose solutions are being sought by scholars. One of these problems is the reconstruction of the Attic archon lists of the Hellenistic era; in this connection the rule set up by the American W. S. Ferguson[17] of the succession of scribes—the scribes ($\gamma\rho\alpha\mu\mu\alpha\tau\epsilon\hat{\iota}\varsigma$ $\tau\hat{\eta}\varsigma$ $\beta\sigma\nu\lambda\hat{\eta}\varsigma$) in Athens follow one another annually in the official succession of phylae—has proved a valuable heuristic principle also for fixing the succession of archons.

In Roman history the credibility of traditional names in the consular *fasti*, especially before the Licinian-Sextian laws (367/366 B.C.), is under discussion. At present one can say that the radical scepticism about the older parts of the Roman consul list has today yielded to a constructive attitude.[18] With this basic problem, which

[15] A. Poebel, *JNES* 1 (1942), 247 ff.; 2 (1943), 56 ff.

[16] C. Wachsmuth, *Einleitung in das Studium der Alten Gesch.* (1895), 304 ff. Cf. E. J. Bickermann, *Chronology of the Ancient World* (1968), 81 f.

[17] *The Athenian Archons of the Third and Second Centuries B.C.* (*Cornell Studies of Classical Philology*, 1899); *Athenian Tribal Cycles in the Hellenistic Age* (1932).

[18] See e.g. the remarks of Ernst Meyer, *MH* 9 (1952), 176 ff.

no one can get around, are intertwined further problems, such as the historicity of the five-year *solitudo magistratuum* referred to by Livy (6.35.10) 15 years after the burning of Rome by the Gauls. It is viewed as historical by one group of modern students (O. Leuze) in opposition to B. G. Niebuhr and T. Mommsen.

The eras concern a continuous numbering of series of years which are reckoned from a specified point in time, the "epoch," even though this "epoch" may refer to a true or fictitious event. Thus the Seleucid era dates from Dios 1, 312 B.C. according to Macedonian reckoning, and from Nisan 1, 311 B.C. according to the Babylonian, whereas the Arsacid era is reckoned from the spring of 247 B.C. One of the Roman provincial eras was that of the province of Macedonia, whose "epoch" was 148 B.C. In addition there are the "freedom eras" of numerous Phoenician cities, which begin with their emancipation from the Seleucid empire.

Our present system was established by the Scythian monk Dionysius Exiguus, who equated the 532nd year of the era he reckoned *ab incarnatione Domini* with the 248th year of the Diocletianic era. In so doing he substituted for the era of the persecutor of the Christians a Christian era. Within just a few decades the new system found universal acceptance in the West.

In modern times Dionysius Petavius (1583–1652), the opponent of Scaliger (1540–1609), appears to have been the first scholar to use Dionysius Exiguus' Christian era also for the time before Christ's birth; since the 18th century we generally reckon with B.C. dates. Thereby a uniform chronology for world history has been acquired, which has the drawback for the time before Christ that the movement of history is connected with a reverse chronology.

Ancient chronography begins for us with the name of Eratosthenes of Cyrene (third century B.C.), and reaches a high point in late Antiquity with the Church father Eusebius (d. A.D. 338?). Ancient chronographic literature, however, is one great shambles. There is nothing left of Eratosthenes' *Chronographies* (Χρονογραφίαι) and *Olympionics* ('Ολυμπιονῖκαι) except an interesting short fragment in Clement of Alexandria[19] which acquaints us in broad outline with some salient points of Eratosthenes' chronology. Since the days of Scaliger and Petavius modern scholarship has worked at reconstructing the chronicle of Eusebius. It goes to A.D. 325, and

[19] *Stromateis* I.138.1–3 (*FGrH* 241.1).

was revised and continued to A.D. 378 by the Church father Jerome. Nevertheless, it is to be used with caution (cf. Jerome's saying on the *opus tumultuarium*).

Finally, ancient history is not very concerned with the new technique of radio carbon dating, inasmuch as it is based on observation of the decay of the carbon isotope C 14 and has a considerable margin of error. Although useful for prehistory, it has restricted application to historical times.

BIBLIOGRAPHY

There is no description of ancient Eastern and Greco-Roman chronology which even comes close to doing justice to the present standard of research. L. Ideler, *Handbuch der Chronologie* (2 vols., 1825–1826) and *Lehrbuch der Chronologie* (1831) are obsolete. F. K. Ginzel, *Handbuch der Chronologie* (Leipzig 1906–1914) is useful. A good orientation is given by the summary of E. J. Bikermann, *Chronology of the Ancient World* (London 1968).

M. P. Nilsson, *Primitive Time Reckoning* (Lund 1920) and *Die Entstehung und religiöse Bedeutung des griechischen Kalenders* (*Lunds Univ. Årsskrift*, N.F. Avd. I, Vol. 14, Nr. 21, 1918; ed. 2, Lund 1962) deal with the significance of ancient ways of reckoning time for cultural history.

The most recent compilation of all dates of ancient history is in the *Cambridge Ancient History* (12 vols., 1924–1939) in the tables at the back of each volume. Fascicle I.6 (1962) of the new edition of Volumes I and II, with the chronology of Egypt, western Asia, and the Aegean Bronze Age, is important. Modern works with chronological tables: for ancient Oriental history see A. Scharff and A. Moortgat, *Ägypten und Vorderasien im Altertum* (Munich 1950), 490 ff.; for Greek history see H. Bengtson, *Griechische Geschichte* (in *Müller*; ed. 4, Munich 1969) 573 ff.; for Roman history see E. Kornemann, *Weltgesch. des Mittelmeerraumes von Philipp I. von Makedonien bis Muhammed* (2 vols., Munich 1948–1949) and H. Bengtson, *Grundriss der römischen Geschichte mit Quellenkunde* (Munich 1964), 407 ff. See also E. Manni, *Fasti ellenistici e romani (323–31 a.C.)* (Palermo 1961).

ANCIENT EASTERN CHRONOLOGY: Fundamental for its time was E. Meyer, *Die ältere Chronologie Babyloniens, Assyriens und Ägyptens* (Supplement to Vol. I of *Gesch. des Altertums*, ed. 2, Stuttgart 1931). The modern arrangement for the chronology of the ancient East, especially for the third millennium but also for the first half of the second millenium B.C. is derived from the new assessment of Hammurabi (c. 1700 B.C.) and from the Assyrian kinglist of Chorsabad published by A. Poebel. Important modern works: For the shorter chronology (besides W. F. Albright): F. Cornelius, *Klio* 35 (1942), 1 ff.; E. F. Weidner, *AOF* 14 (1944), 362 ff.; Ernst Meyer, *Philologus* 97 (1948), 355 ff.; F. Schmidtke, *Der Aufbau der babylon. Chronologie* (*Orbis Antiquus* 7, Munster i. W. 1952); F. Cornelius, *AOF* 17 (1954–1956), 294 ff. (definitely idiosyncratic in the use of the Venus dates of Ammusaduqa, which, however, are not unequivocal).—The longer chronology still has its partisans, especially outside Germany: A. Goetze (for whom see below), B. Landsberger, *JCUN* 8(1954) 31 ff., 106 ff. (Hammurabi c. 1900); for an intermediate chronology see Sidney Smith, *Alalakh and Chronology* (London 1940); also M. B. Rowton, *JNES* 17 (1958), 97 ff. (Hammurabi 1792–1750). For criticism of the Assyrian kinglist see F. R. Kraus, *Könige, die in Zelten wohnten: Betrachtungen über den Kern der assyrischen Königsliste* (Amsterdam 1965). This study is important, for it has raised legitimate doubt, on the basis of the names, of the historicity of a part of the list.

The determination of ancient Egyptian chronology owes a great deal to the German scholar A. Scharff; see his essay on the so-called oldest date of world history, *HZ* 161 (1940), 3 ff., and his chronological disposition of the obscure intermediate period between the Old and Middle Kingdoms: "Der historische Abschnitt der Lehre für König Merikare," *SBAW* (1936), fasc. 8, pp. 39 ff.; also the more recent work of his student H. Stock, *Die erste Zwischenzeit Ägyptens* (in *Analecta Orientalia, Studia Aegyptiaca* 2; Rome 1949).—For the second intermediate period, the transition from the Middle to the New Empire, see H. Stock, *Studien z. Gesch. u. Archäologie der 13. –17. Dynastie Ägyptens* (Ägyptolog. Forsch. 12, Glückstadt 1942), whose estimates, however, should be reduced about three to four decades, inasmuch as Stock was not yet aware of the new estimate of Hammurabi. For the XIXth to XXth dynasties: J. v. Beckerath, *Tanis und Theben: Historische Grundlagen der Ramessidenzeit in Ägypten* (Ägyptolog. Forsch. 16, Glückstadt 1951), 103 ff.

All the material on the ancient Egyptian calendar can now be found in R. A. Parker, *The Calendars of Ancient Egypt* (Chicago 1951), whose acceptance of an original lunar-based calendar of the Egyptians, however, is hardly tenable; see e.g. E. Drioton and J. Vandier, *L'Égypte* (in the "Clio" series; ed. 3, Paris 1952), 15 ff.; J. v. Beckerath, "Der ägypt. Ursprung unseres Kalenders," *Saeculum* 4 (1953), 1–12.

CHRONOLOGY OF THE HITTITES: H. T. Bossert, *Altanatolien*

(Berlin 1942), 36 ff. The numbers there given are too high. Thus, the capture of Babylon by Muršiliš I should be placed not at c. 1600 (Bossert), but 1531. Telepinuš ruled c. 1480, so his birthday as reckoned by Bossert, c. 1570, is at least about a half century too early. A. Goetze, above all, advocates a chronology a full hundred years earlier (capture of Babylon 1651, not 1531): *BASOR* 122 (1951), 18 ff.; *ibid.* 146 (1957), 20 ff.; *JCUN* 11 (1957), 53 ff., 63 ff.; otherwise, cf. B. H. Otten, *MDOG* 83 (1951), 47 ff.

THE ASSYRIAN EPONYMS (LIMMU): Lists in *Reallexicon der Assyriologie* II, 412 ff. Neo-Babylonian chronology: Parker and Dubberstein, *Babylonian Chronology 626 B.C.–A.D. 75* (Providence 1956). Chronology of ancient Hebrew history: A. Jirku, *Gesch. des Volkes Israel* (1931), 20 ff.; E. R. Thiele, "The Chronology of the Kings of Judah and Israel," *JNES* 3 (1944), 137 ff.; *The Mysterious Numbers of Hebrew Kings* (ed. 2, Grand Rapids 1965). —The number of years of the "Judges" is often set much too high at 410. Frequently one has to reckon here with concurrent (instead of successive) rulerships, similar to the concurrence of two or more dynasties in ancient Babylonia. In any case the number should be reduced to barely 100 years.—For Lydian chronology: H. Kaletsch, *Historia* 7 (1958), 1–47.

ECLIPSES: F. Boll, *RE* VI, 2355; A. Steinbrüchel, *Tafel der Sonnen- und Mondfinsternisse, der Neu- und Vollmonde von 1265 v. Chr. bis 2345 n. Chr.* (Zurich 1937).

GREEK CHRONOLOGY: Important is the record of Olympic victors which begins with 776 B.C. The list of Olympic victors is contained in the chronicle of Eusebius, including also the Armenian version (ed. Karst, pp. 98 ff.). See L. Moretti, *Olympionikai, i vincitori negli antichi agoni olimpici* (Rome 1957). The ancient chronology of the Hellenistic era is based on the numbering of Olympiads (see e.g. the datings in the history of Polybius). A. Brinkmann, *RhM* 70 (1915), 622 ff., finally defended (in opposition to Beloch) the reliability of the list of Olympic victors, especially the older parts; cf. H. Bengtson, *Griech. Gesch.* (ed. 3, 1965), 70.—For the Attic calendar see B. D. Meritt, *The Athenian Year* (Berkeley and Los Angeles 1961).

With the help of Diodorus from the Augustan period, the Attic archon list from 480–302/1 B.C. can be reconstructed. For the later time inscriptions are a valuable help. A list for the classical period can be found in J. Kirchner, *Prosopographia Attica* II, 631 ff.; for the Hellenistic period, W. K. Pritchett and B. D. Meritt, *The Chronology of Hellenistic Athens* (1940), which is not yet definitive; and for the Roman Empire, *Hesperia* II (1942), 82 ff.

ROMAN CONSULS OF THE REPUBLIC: *Corpus Inscriptionum Latinarum* I (ed. 2) and *Inscriptiones Italiae* XIII.1; consuls of the Empire are listed in A. Degrassi, *I fasti consolari dell'Impero Romano (30 av.–613 d. Cr.)* (Rome 1952). T. R. S. Broughton, *The Magistrates of the Roman Republic* (2 vols., *Philological Monographs publ. by the American Philological Association* 15; 1951–1953; Supplement, 1960) is valuable.

RULER LISTS: T. C. Skeat, *The Reigns of the Ptolemies* (*Münchener Beitr. z. Papyrusforsch.* 39, 1954); also the older work of H. Gauthier, *Livre des Rois d'Égypte* (5 vols., Cairo 1907–1917), which dates everything according to the Egyptian kings from the first dynasty to the Emperor Decius, is still useful, although a new edition is desirable.—New Seleucid dates: H. Bengtson, *Historia* 4 (1955), 113–114.

ERAS: For the Seleucid era and the "freedom eras" see E. J. Bickermann, *Chronology of the Ancient World* (London 1968), 70 ff., and in *Berytus* 8 (1944), 73 ff., where there are also new remarks on the Arsacid era.

THE ROMAN CALENDAR AND ROMAN CHRONOLOGY: T. Mommsen, *Röm. Chronologie* (ed. 2, 1859); O. Leuze, *Die röm. Jahrzählung: Ein Versuch, ihre geschichtl. Entwicklung zu ermitteln* (Tübingen 1909), has important conclusions; Agnes K. Michels, *The Calendar of the Roman Republic* (Princeton 1967).

ANCIENT CHRONOGRAPHY: C. Wachsmuth, *Einl. in das Stud. d. Alt. Gesch.* (1895), 127 ff.; E. Kornemann, *Die röm. Kaiserzeit* (in *Gercke-Norden* III.2; ed. 3, 1933), 157.—For the chronicle of Eusebius (out-of-date edition of A. Schoene, 2 vols., 1875, 1866; Armenian version by Karst, 1911) see R. Helm, *Die Chronik des Hieronymus* (ed. 2, Berlin 1956); E. Schwartz, *RE* VI, 1376 ff.; H. Lietzmann, *Gesch. d. alten Kirche* III (1938), 155 ff. (tr. B. Woolf, New York 1949–1950).

For the conversion of ancient dates (note the advice in E. J. Bickermann, *Chronology of the Ancient World* (London 1968), 80 ff.) see P. V. Neugebauer, *Hilfstafeln zur technischen Chronologie* (Kiel 1937); for the Roman Empire see H. Lietzmann, *Zeitrechnung* (*Sammlung Göschen* 1085; ed. 3 by K. Aland, Berlin 1956).

All dates for Antiquity are given as Julian and not Gregorian ones; there was no year zero. Hence it follows that in calculating periods of time which extend from B.C. to A.D. dates, one year must always be subtracted. For example, Augustus was born Sept. 23, 63 B.C. and died Aug. 19, A.D. 14. His life span amounted to 75 (not 76!) years, 10 months, 27 days.

2. GEOGRAPHY

In Antiquity history and geography were not divided. Thus for Herodotus geography and ethnology were indissolubly bound up with history, just as "research" ($i\sigma\tau o\rho\epsilon\hat{\iota}\nu$) for writers of ancient history expressed itself especially in travel and becoming acquainted with strange lands and peoples, whose customs were thoroughly described. Belief in the mutual relationship of people and environment was so strong in ancient man that he could not allow the geographic factors in an historical portrayal to be left aside. It is true that the underlying unity, as Herodotean history presented it, later was often dispensed with; at present the geographic comments stand beside the historical, and there lead a positive, independent life as periods of rest in the narration of events. Furthermore, history and geography were originally bound up with each other also in the modern process of teaching and research, until in the 19th century geographic science turned to problems explicitly of natural science, and loosened its bond to history. In no wise, however, is geography an auxiliary to history; rather it is prerequisite to all historical perception, for all history takes place in space, and geography affects the historical roles of all nations and individuals.

It is not enough for the historian of Antiquity to know the lands with which his research is concerned. An ability to visualize historically the geographic background must accompany the historical imagination which is indispensable to the historian. The student of history must be able, by his knowledge of the earth's history, to imagine accurately an event's scene of action. This is not possible without knowledge of the facts decisive for topographic changes. Helmuth von Moltke once called locale "the left-over bit of the reality of a long past event." The historian must be aware that this assertion holds true only with qualifications.

Natural events and artificial alterations by man are in like manner responsible for changes in the earth's surface. Thus even in Antiquity (as in modern times) destructive earthquakes affected wide sections of the Mediterranean world, especially Greece, the Greek islands, Asia Minor, and Syria. Particularly well-known is the earthquake of 464 B.C. in Sparta; it caused the Spartans heavy casualties, thus triggering the great helot revolt. The notorious destruction of the Peloponnesian cities Helike and Bura in 373 B.C. is possibly connected with seismic phenomena: Bura was swallowed by a gaping chasm, while Helike reputedly slid into the sea. Also, the earthquake of 227 (or 226) B.C. which afflicted Rhodes, causing the collapse of the city's landmark, the Colossus of Helios, was one of the great natural catastrophes of Antiquity.

In the history of ancient settlement the manifold changes of river courses and of coastlines, as well as volcanic activity, are to be considered. For example, the change of the landscape at Thermopylae in central Greece caused by the alluvial deposits of the Spercheios River in the Malic Gulf[20] is well known. Another example is in the deep south of modern Iraq where a new land formation, altering that of Antiquity, has been created by the deposits of the Tigris and Euphrates Rivers, which now join to form the Shatt-al-Arab before entering the Persian Gulf. Coastal changes also have often affected the fate of particular settlements. Thus, when the harbors of Aquileia and Ravenna silted up, the cities were robbed of their maritime importance; other cities, such as Trieste, the ancient Tergeste, were likewise changed. Noteworthy also is the progressive, eustatic rising of the sea, which has caused many changes in the Mediterranean landscape since Antiquity.

To natural changes, which sometimes could be postponed but never—at least in Antiquity—completely checked, may be added man-made alterations of whole landscapes or particular settlements. The fertility of the Nile valley and of ancient Babylonia depended above all on the maintenance of many canals, through which precious water in larger or smaller courses was led to the productive land. Man here constructed a system of waterways whose upkeep was, and even today partly is, of greatest significance for the welfare of the inhabitants. Their joint labor on the canal network strongly promoted the drive for political unification—although it would be an exaggeration, for example, to label the Nile the creator of the ancient Egyptian state.

Of special significance for the topographic character of particular regions are alterations which human beings have effected. One example is the deforestation of ancient Italy, which, however, surely also is tied up with the decrease of underground water and with the drying up of sources in historic time.[21] Apropros here are the

[20] S. Marinatos, *Berichte des VI. Internat. Kongr. f. Archäologie in Berlin 1939* (1940), 333 ff.

[21] H. v. Trotta-Treyden, "Entwaldung in den Mittelmeerländern," *Petermanns Mitteil.* 62 (1916), 248 ff., 286 ff.

economic changes during the Punic wars, in whose course the great latifundia with their extensive pasture economy were introduced in place of the native, yeoman Italian population, and finally brought about even physical changes.

The cultural level of every district is reflected in the construction and number of its settlements, of villages and above all of cities, whose geographic and geopolitical setting often gives valuable data about the political, economic, and cultural circumstances dominant at their foundation. Formerly, in connection with Thucydides' statements (1.7), the view has been occasionally taken that without exception Greek settlements came into being on the heights, turned away from the sea; only later did they to some extent descend and face the sea.[22] Modern studies have shown, however, that already by the middle of the second millennium B.C., Greek cities may have existed in immediate proximity to the sea.[23] Cities in such locations probably can be explained by the fact that already in this early age a measure of safety was available beside the sea. This observation, in turn, allows us to draw inferences regarding the overall political relationships and the trade conditions of that early epoch.

In Antiquity no less than in modern times, political factors influenced the site of settlements. It was no accident that during their dominion over Egypt (from c. 1680 to 1560 B.C.) the Hyksos, those peculiar outsiders, established a capital in the Delta city Avaris (Tanis) instead of in Memphis or in Upper Egypt in Thebes. In fact, Avaris was the appropriate center of the Hyksos empire, which besides Egypt included at least parts of Syria.[24] Finally, political and strategic grounds led to the foundation of Constantinople in A.D. 330 on the site of the old, dilapidated Byzantium. Constantine's foundation of this important fortress on the Bosporus signifies the displacement of the center of gravity of the Roman Empire from Rome to the East, a process which had started during the course of the third century; Diocletian already had resided for an extended period at Nicomedia in Bithynia.

The notion that the formation of a people's character heavily depends on geographic factors was widely held in Antiquity. Thus,

[22] G. Hirschfeld, "Zur Typologie griech. Ansiedlungen," in *Historische u. philologische Aufsätze Ernst Curtius gewidmet* (Berlin 1884), 353 ff.

[23] K. Lehmann-Hartleben, "Die antiken Hafenanlagen des Mittelmeeres," *Klio-Beiheft* 14 (1923), 6 ff.

[24] See, e.g., P. Montet, *Le drame d'Avaris* (Paris 1940).

this view is mirrored in the tract Περὶ ἀέρων, ὑδάτον, τόπων from the Hippocratic corpus[25] and especially in the works of the great polymath Poseidonius of Apamea (c. 130–50 B.C.), above all in his treatise Περὶ ὠκεανοῦ.[26] Modern geographic research has taken the ancient suggestions and in its turn has scrutinized the connection of mankind with its environment.[27]

Undeniable interactions exist between geographic and political configurations. The shape of the land—the territory and its limitations by mountains, rivers, and the sea—contains a profusion of political and cultural development for men. In many cases one can say that some areas are conducive to the movements of peoples. Thus a land like ancient Hellas, by its division into many geographic units, separated from one another mostly by mountains, seems almost predestined for political fragmentation. Historically the extensive division of Greece was a blessing and a curse—a blessing owing to the intensification of the inner life of the particular states, a curse because the geographic division prevented the formation of larger states. The extensive subdivision of Hellas into tiny cantons, as well as the ubiquity of the sea, must be taken into account for even such a characteristic and complex phenomenon as Greek colonization at the end of the Mycenaean period (c. 1100–900 B.C.) and in the eighth to sixth centuries B.C.—even if other factors must be considered: such as the relative overpopulation of the homeland and, for the second period of colonization, also the internal wars between aristocrats and tyrants. Furthermore, the climate of the new lands was decisive in the emigrants' choice of new areas of settlement outside Greece. For only exceptionally did the Greeks settle outside the zone of the mild Mediterranean climate, like the north and east shores of the Black Sea; in these areas commercial interests were at stake.[28] Generally, however, the underlying connection of Greek colonization with the special climatic conditions confirms the hypothesis that the aspiration for new land was an important motive for colonial expansion; indeed, the Greeks settled almost exclusively in areas which allowed cultivation of the vine and of olive trees. Cer-

[25] The treatise comes from the last decades of the fifth century B.C.; cf. H. Diller, "Wanderarzt und Aitiologe," *Philologus Suppl.-Bd.* 26.3 (1934), 69.

[26] Fragments in *FGrH* 87.74 ff.

[27] Cf. F. Ratzel, *Anthropogeographie oder Grundzüge der Anwendung der Erdkunde auf die Geschichte* (ed. 3, 1909).

[28] H. J. Schultze, "Zur Gesch. d. altgriech. Kolonisation," *Petermanns Mitteil.* (1941), 7 ff.

tainly, from the beginning the intention of winning new room for settlement was bound up with other motives, especially commercial ones.

Undoubtedly the climate, which in Greece promotes outdoor life, contributed to forming a distinct feeling of community and to promoting participation in affairs of common concern to an extent unparalleled in Antiquity. The participation of the Greek in the business of his usually tiny state is an outstanding characteristic of Greek history.

Under the influence of climatic conditions different from those at home, the Greeks, who in the Hellenistic age expanded over all the Near East as far as India, took on new forms of life and to some extent adapted themselves to those of the natives. In assessing the decline of the Hellenistic states of the East and of Hellenistic culture, this is always too lightly considered.

From the time when the Indo-European immigrants mixed with the Mediterranean population in Hellas (i.e., from the first half of the second millennium B.C.), the presence of the sea, which enticed the daring to new and exotic adventures, made the Greeks excellent sailors. Those who live inland are usually led onto the sea only by compulsion. So, for example, when the Assyrians and Persians advanced from the Iranian highland and from the middle Tigris region to the Mediterranean Sea, they tried to shift the burden of naval warfare to the expert seamen inhabiting the Phoenician cities and Cyprus. The Persians chose the Greeks of Asia Minor, the Carians and others, to man their fleets.

The geographic situation often determines the relation of particular nations with their neighbors. Thus ancient Egypt, which on the east and west was blocked by an uninhabitable fringe of wasteland, appears naturally much less open to foreign influences than does ancient Mesopotamia, which time and again was exposed to the intrusions of nomads from the Iranian plateau and Syria.

Like nations and states, the individual is governed by geographic factors. Great political and strategic plans, which so often have created a new regime for the world, depend on geographic conditions; without a satisfactory idea of geographic conditions one cannot devise such plans, much less put them into effect. For example, whoever speaks of the last plans of Alexander, which were aimed at the conquest of the West, or of Caesar's plan for the Parthian expedition, must know that these plans imply a clear picture of the world. The plan of Darius I for the Scythian expedition miscarried ultimately because of insufficient geographical knowledge.[29]

Knowledge of the geographic background, therefore, is the chief assumption for the judgment of historical events by the creative historian. He must know that in this connection Alexander's expedition was epochal in the history of man, and that Caesar's conquest of Gaul and his passage to Britain were exceptionally important for broadening ancient geographic knowledge. Guided by Hugo Berger's *Geschichte der wissenschaftlichen Erdkunde der Griechen*, we can get a general view of changes in the ancient image of the earth. The history of the discoveries of Antiquity, which stretch from the voyages to Punt of the ancient Egyptians under queen Hatshepsut to the periploi (accounts of coasting voyages) of Greek and Carthaginian seafarers down to late Antiquity, is significant also for the general history of the ancient world. These explorations reveal different, often opposed motives as the driving force: yearning for unknown, fabulous, far-away places; thirst for gold and treasures; scientific aspiration to discover; plans for political power; and whatever else stirs the heart of man. Here the student can demonstrate whether he is able to meet the demand on him for an especially sensitive, sympathetic understanding of the thoughts and intentions of ancient men.

The geographic science of Antiquity sprang from practical requirements. Commercial intercourse, which took place early between the Far East and the areas settled by the Greeks,[30] gave the first impulse to describing shipping routes, that is, coastlines, and likewise to the design of maps of the world; apparently they were first made available to the Ionians by the Babylonians.[31] The many sea and land descriptions and itineraries typical of the Romans served practical necessities. A good idea of these itineraries is conveyed by the so-called *Tabula Peutingeriana*. Although our surviving copy of it comes from the Middle Ages (12th to 13th centuries), it derives from the world map of M. Vipsanius Agrippa.

The founder of scientific geography in Antiquity was Eratosthenes of Cyrene (c. 285–205 B.C.), the creator of ancient chro-

---

[29] Cf. E. Meyer, *Dareios d. Gr.*, in eds. E. Marcks and K. A. von Müller, *Meister der Politik* I (ed. 2), 25.

[30] Cf. H. Schaal, *Vom Tauschhandel zum Welthandel* (1931), 56.

[31] B. Meissner, "Babylonische und griechische Landkarten," *Klio* 19 (1923), 97 ff.

nography. He was the first to be concerned with geodesy. All later
students stand on his shoulders, including Strabo of Amasea in
Pontus (the Augustan period); Eratosthenes' geographic work
(Γεωγραφικά) summarized in seventeen books, unfortunately only
partly preserved, the scholarly achievements to his time. In spite
of its weaknesses, the work is worthy of the universal task which
Strabo took as a theme and which consisted of describing all the
then-known lands of the *oikumene*. Some 150 years after Strabo,
an Alexandrian Greek, Ptolemy, collected the geographic knowledge of his time in his Geography (Γεωγραφικὴ ὑφήγησις). This
work, which gave the latitude and longitude of more than 8000
places, set for centuries thereafter the geographic image of the
earth; it was not until the era of exploration that the geographer
Mercator (1512–1594) established a new map in place of Ptolemy's.
Offshoots of ancient geographic science were the *Topographia
Christiana* of Kosmas Indikopleustes (from the era of Justinian)
and the work of the Ravenna Cosmographer, a huge geographic
index of names of the seventh century A.D.

BIBLIOGRAPHY

The study of ancient geography was founded anew by the learned
Philipp Cluver (Cluverius) of Danzig (1580–1622) with his *Italia
Antiqua* (Leiden 1624). Following Cluver was a series of 19th-
century German investigators: Heinrich Kiepert (1818–1899), Karl
Müllenhoff (1818–1884), Hugo Berger (1836–1904), and Carl
Neumann (1823–1880). The history of the investigation of ancient
geography has been described by K. J. Neumann, *Entwicklung
und Aufgaben der Alten Gesch.* (Strassburg 1910), 70 ff.

No comprehensive presentation of ancient geography and of
geographic knowledge in Antiquity corresponds to the present state
of knowledge. A. Forbiger, *Handbuch der Alten Geographie* (3
vols., Hamburg 1842–1843; ed. 2 of vol. 1, 1877) is out of date.
For scientific geography: Hugo Berger, *Gesch. d. wissensch. Erdkunde der Griechen* (ed. 2, Leipzig 1903); F. Gisinger and F. Boll,
"Geographie," in *RE* Suppl. IV (1924), 521–685, s.v. "Geographie"; A. Rehm, "Exacte Wissenschaften," in *Gercke-Norden* II.5
(1933); J. O. Thomson, *History of Ancient Geography* (Cambridge 1948).

THE MOST IMPORTANT WORKS ON MAPS: H. and R. Kiepert,
Forma Orbis Antiqui (Berlin 1893–1914; maps with critical text
and references): a basic, admirable work, unfinished and long in

need of revision; H. Kiepert, *Atlas antiquus* (ed. 12, 1902); K. Spruner, W. Sieglin, M. Kiessling, *Histor. Handatlas* (Gotha 1893 ff.; incomplete). In process is the *Tabula Imperii Romani*, of which to date only single pages have appeared, among them page 32 (Mainz). For Gaul: *Gallia: Carte archéologique de la Gaule romaine* (Paris 1931 ff.). For Romain Britain: *Map of Roman Britain, publ. by the Ordnance Survey* (ed. 3, Southampton 1956). An excellent map (with critical text) of ancient Italy has been drawn up by P. Fraccaro in *Grande Atlante Geografico* (ed. 4, Novara 1938).—Modern small-scale maps may be found in the *Grosse Historische Weltatlas des Bayerischen Schulbuch-Verlages* (ed. 4, Munich 1963), Part I: Prehistory and Antiquity (with "Commentaries" in German in the same volume), by H. Bengtson, V. Milojčič, and others; *Atlante storico*, by M. Baratta, P. Fraccaro, L. Visintin (repr. Novara 1954); *Westermanns Atlas zur Weltgeschichte* (repr. Braunschweig 1968), eds. H. E. Stier and E. Kirsten.

SPECIAL WORKS: Changes of the earth's surface by natural causes: T. Wiegand in *Müller* I (1939), 74 ff.—Earthquakes in Antiquity: O. Weismantel, *Die Erdbeben des vorderen Kleinasien in geschichtlicher Zeit* (Diss. Marburg 1891); A. Sieberg, *Untersuchungen über Erdbeben und Bruchschollenbau im östl. Mittelmeer* (Jena 1932), 180 ff.; W. Capelle, "Erdbeben im Altertum," *NJA* (1908), 603 ff.; *ibid.*, *RE* Suppl. IV (1924), 344 ff. s.v. "Erdebenforschung." Changes of coast line: e.g. S. Casson, *Macedonia, Thrace, and Illyria* (1926), 14 ff.: on the change of the Thermaic Gulf in the area of the mouth of the Haliakmon and Axios.—Deforestation in the Greek and Hellenistic world: Theophrastus, *Hist. Plant.* 3–5, on which M. Rostovtzeff, *Social and Economic History of the Hellenistic World* III (Oxford 1941), 1613 f.—Eustatic rise of the sea: D. Hafemann, in *Deutscher Geographentag in Berlin 1959, Tagungsberichte u. wiss. Abhandlungen* (Wiesbaden 1960), 218 ff.

HISTORY OF SETTLEMENTS: (a) Basic works: E. Kornemann, "Polis und Urbs," *Klio* 5 (1905), 72 ff.; *ibid.*, "Stadtstatt und Flächenstaat des Altertums in ihren Wechselbeziehungen," *NJA* 21 (1908), 233 ff.—On the origin and development of Greek cities and their precursors: A. von Gerkan, *Griechische Städteanlagen* (Berlin 1924); F. Tritsch, "Die Stadtbildungen des Altertums und die griech. Polis," *Klio* 22 (1929), 1 ff.; E. Kirsten, *Die griech. Polis als historisch-geographisches Problem des Mittelmeerraumes* (Bonn 1956), with copious bibliography. (b) More important detailed studies: F. Bilabel, *Die ionische Kolonisation (Philologus Suppl.-Bd. 14.1, 1920)*; V. Tscherikower, *Die hellenistischen Städtegründungen von Alexander d. Gr. bis auf die Römerzeit (Philologus Suppl.-*

Bd. 19.1, 1927); A. H. M. Jones, *The Cities of the Eastern Roman Provinces* (Oxford 1937) and *The Greek City from Alexander to Justinian* (Oxford 1940)—both works unfortunately have only incomplete documentation; E. Kornemann, *RE* IV, 511 ff. s.v. "Coloniae"; F. Vittinghoff, *Röm. Kolonisation u. Bürgerrechtspolitik unter Caesar und Augustus* (*Abhandlungen d. Mainzer Akad.*, Wiesbaden 1952). Cf. in addition the section "Special Geographic Studies," p. 46.

LAND AND PEOPLE: R. v. Pöhlmann, *Hellenische Anschauungen über den Zusammenhang zwischen Natur und Geschichte* (Leipzig 1879), out of date but still worth reading; on Poseidonius: K. Reinhardt, *Poseidonios* (Munich 1921), 67 ff.—Especially instructive for the problem in question are the concluding chapter of the history of Herodotus (on which see. F. Egermann, *NJA* (1938), 245) and, from Hellenistic literature, the *City Portraits* of Herakleides (so-called Pseudodikaiarchos): Περὶ τῶν ἐν Ἑλλάδι πόλεων: F. Pfister, "Die Reisebilder des Herakleides," *SAWW* 227.2 (1951), with translation and detailed commentary.—In Antiquity the problem of the influence of a maritime site on a people's character was often discussed, among others by Plato, Aristotle, Cicero: see R. v. Pöhlmann, *op. cit.*, 62 ff.

GEOGRAPHY AND HISTORY: the most important modern literature is noted in H. Hassinger, *Die geographischen Grundlagen der Geschichte* (*Geschichte der führenden Völker* II: ed. 2, Freiburg i. Br. 1953). From the geographic side the problem is illuminated by S. Passarge, "Ägypten, Irak, Turan, eine vergleichende geschichtsgeographische Betrachtung," *F&F* (1954), 41–48. A survey: M. Cary, *The Geographic Background of Greek and Roman History* (London 1948), on which see J. Vogt, *Gnomon* (1951), 208 ff. Among important works for the ancient historian are: W. M. Ramsay, "The Geographical Conditions Determining History and Religion in Asia Minor," *GJ* 20 (1902), 257 ff., on which also C. Bosch, "Das Anatolische in der Geschichte," *Veröff. des 2. Türk. Geschichtskongr.* (1937); for Greece: V. Ehrenberg, "Griechisches Land und griechischer Staat," in *Polis und Imperium* (Zurich 1965), 63 ff., on which see the *Einleitungen der Griech. Gesch.* by K. J. Beloch and H. Berve; for Italy: A. v. Hofmann, *Das Land Italien und seine Geschichte* (Berlin and Stuttgart 1921); J. Vogt, "Raumauffassung und Raumordnung in der röm. Politik," *Orbis* (1960), 172 ff.

CLIMATE: In general: K. Sapper, "Über die Grenzen der Akklimatisationsfähigkeit des Menschen," *Geogr. Zeitschr.* 38 (1932), 385 ff.; *Klima, Wetter, Mensch*, ed. H. Woltereck (Leipzig 1938), with essays by E. Breznia, W. Hellpach, *et al.* The theories of E. Huntingdon about climatic deviation have caused a stir in the last decades especially for Antiquity: *Civilization and Climate* (1927); "Climatic Pulsations," in *Hyllningsskrift till Sven Hedin* (Stockholm 1935); and *passim*. According to Huntingdon periods of wetness alternated with dry ones. To the former ostensibly belong the years 450–250 B.C., with reservation also the period from 121 B.C. to A.D. 120, and above all the third century A.D.; and these wet periods coincide with periods of political and cultural flowering. With good reason M. Rostovtzeff, *The Economic History Review* 2.2 (January 1930), 209 ff., has contested this theory; cf. also N. H. Baynes, *Byzantine Studies and Other Essays* (1955), 86 ff. The theory of climatic deviations (for the second millennium B.C.) has been taken up again by O. Paret, *Das neue Bild der Vorgeschichte* (Stuttgart 1948). Recently Rhys Carpenter, *Discontinuity in Greek Civilization* (Cambridge 1966) has tried to show that the period 1200–850 B.C. was one of drought and famine.—For the influence of climate on a people's character with regard to the work Περὶ ἀέρων, ὑδάτων, τόπων (see p. 39), cf. A. Philippson, *Das Klima Griechenlands* (Bonn 1948), 203 ff. Full bibliography in S. Lauffer, *Gnomon* (1950), 107 ff.

ALEXANDER'S IDEA OF THE WORLD: H. Berve, *Gestaltende Kräfte der Antike* (ed. 2, eds. E. Buchner and P. Franke; Munich 1966), 333 ff., and V. Burr, *Würzb. Jahrbücher* 2 (1947), 91 ff.

HISTORY OF ANCIENT EXPLORATION: R. Hennig, *Terrae Incognitae* I (The ancient world to Ptolemy: ed. 2, Leiden 1944) and II (A.D. 200–1200: 1937) contain translations of ancient sources with references to important literature, to be used critically for particulars but on the whole a useful accomplishment; M. Cary and E. H. Warmington, *The Ancient Explorers* (London 1932; rev. with additional bibliography, Baltimore 1963, Penguin Books).—For the geography of ancient Italy: E. Wikén, *Die Kunde der Hellenen von dem Lande und den Völkern der Apenninenhalbinsel* (Lund 1937), on which see R. Güngerich, *Gnomon* (1942), 217 ff.

STRABO AND ANCIENT GEOGRAPHY: R. Honigmann, *RE* IV A (1931), 76 ff.; edition of Strabo by A. Meineke (Leipzig 1852–1853). A modern, thorough commentary on Strabo (with maps) is one of the most urgent tasks of ancient history. For the ancient geography of Greece, the geographic description of Pausanias (Περιήγησις τῆς Ἑλλάδος, composed c. A.D. 150) is indispensable; cf. the edition with commentary and maps of H. Hitzig and H. Blümner (3 vols., Leipzig 1896–1910), and the English translation and commentary of J. G. Frazer (1913); further information by E. Pernice in *Müller* I (1939), 244 n.3; in addition see Ernst Meyer, *Pausanias:*

Beschreibung Griechenlands, neu übersetzt mit Einleitung u. Anmerkungen (Zurich 1954).—The editions of minor Greek and Latin geographers are important: C. Müller, *Geographi Graeci Minores* (2 vols., Paris 1882), of which a new edition is needed; A. Riese, *Geographi Latini Minores* (Heilbronn 1878; repr. Hildesheim 1964). On the periploi see R. Güngerich, *Die Küstenbeschreibung in der griech. Literatur* (*Orbis Antiquus* 4, Münster i. W. 1950).—Ptolemy of Alexandria and his Γεωγραφικὴ ὑφήγησις: a modern complete edition is lacking. A partial treatment by O. Cuntz, *Die Geographie des Ptolemaios (Galliae, Germania, Raetia, Noricum, Pannonia, Illyricum, Italia)* (Berlin 1923). Further literature in James O. Thomson, *History of Ancient Geography* (1948), 230 n. 1.—Kosmas Indikopleustes: E. O. Winstedt, *The Christian Topography of Cosmas Indicopl.* (Cambridge 1909).—The so-called Cosmographer of Ravenna: edition in the *Itineraria Romana* II (Leipzig 1940) by J. Schnetz; in addition, *ibid., Untersuch. über die Quellen der Kosmographie des anonymen Geographen von Ravenna* (*SB* Munich 1942) and *Ravennas Anonymus* (Uppsala 1951; German translation).—The *Tabula Peutingeriana*: Editio princeps by Marcus Welser (Venice 1591; complete, Amsterdam 1598); still important is K. Miller, *Die Weltkarte des Castorius* (Ravensburg 1887–1888) and *Die Peutingersche Tafel* (ed. 2, Stuttgart 1929), although reservation is necessary about his hypotheses of the history of the origin of the *Tabula Peutingeriana*. See also James O. Thomson, *History of Ancient Geography* (1948), 379 ff.

SPECIAL GEOGRAPHIC STUDIES: Comprehensive works which correspond to the present state of knowledge are lacking for Egypt, Mesopotamia, Iran, and Asia Minor; the modern literature is discussed in H. Hassinger, *Geogr. Grundlagen der Geschichte* (ed. 2, Freiburg i. Br. 1953). For Egypt, K. Baedeker, *Ägypten und Sudan* (ed. 8, rev. by G. Steindorff, Leipzig 1928), offers a survey with constant reference to the conditions of Antiquity. Syria: R. Dussaud, *Topographie Historique de la Syrie antique et médiévale* (*Bibl. archéol. et hist.* 4, Paris 1927), which today naturally is somewhat out-of-date; more recent is Emma Brunner-Traut and Vera Hell, *Ägypten. Studienreiseführer mit Landeskunde* (Stuttgart 1962); F. M. Abel, *Géographie de la Palestine* (2 vols., Paris 1933–1938).

GREECE: A significant achievement for its time was Conrad Bursian, *Geographie von Griechenland* (2 vols., Leipzig 1862–1872); see also: C. Neumann and J. Partsch, *Physikalische Geographie von Griechenland* (Breslau 1885); A. Philippson, *Das Mittelmeergebiet* (ed. 4, Berlin and Leipzig 1922); O. Maull, *Griechisches Mittelmeergebiet* (Breslau 1922); J. Béquignon, *Grèce* (*Guides Bleus*, Paris

1935); E. Kirsten and W. Kraiker, *Griechenlandkunde: Ein Führer zu klassischen Stätten* (ed. 5, Heidelberg 1967). For particular Greek districts: F. Stählin, *Das hellenische Thessalien* (Stuttgart 1924); W. Judeich, *Topographie von Athen* (ed. 2, in *Müller*, Munich 1931), of which a revised edition is planned; W. Wrede, *Attika* (Athens 1934); H. Lehmann, *Landeskunde der Ebene von Argos und ihrer Randgebiete* (Athens 1937); Ernst Meyer, *Peloponnesische Wanderungen* (Zurich 1939), on Arcadia and Achaea; *ibid.*, *Neue peloponnesische Wanderungen* (Bern 1957). H. Schaal, *Die Insel des Pelops* (Bremen 1943). Worth reading also is the book of the archeologist Ernst Reisinger, *Griechenland: Schilderungen deutscher Reisender* (ed. 2, Leipzig 1923), with a survey of the modern travel literature from Ciriaco of Ancona on; cf. also M. Wegner, *Land der Griechen: Reiseschilderungen aus 7 Jahrhunderten* (ed. 3, Berlin 1955); a distinguished work is A. Philippson (d. 1953), *Die griechischen Landschaften* (4 vols. in 8 parts, Frankfurt a. M. 1950–1959), with additions by E. Kirsten in the first volumes.—A rich source for the historical geography of the Greek (and also Roman) world are the volumes of inscriptions, the *Inscriptiones Graecae* (*IG*) and the *Corpus Inscriptionum Latinarum* (*CIL*); also the relevant articles in the *RE* and the archeological excavation reports, which formerly appeared e.g. annually in the "Archäol. Anzeiger" of the *JDAI* and in the *AOF*.

ITALY: H. Nissen, *Italische Landeskunde* (2 vols., Berlin 1883–1902); O. Richter, *Topographie von Rom* (in *Müller*, Munich 1913); H. Jordan and C. Hülsen, *Topographie der Stadt Rom im Altertum* (3 vols., Berlin 1878–1907); S. B. Platner and T. Ashby, *A Topographical Dictionary of Ancient Rome* (Oxford 1929); E. Nash, *Bildlexicon zur Topographie des antiken* Rom (2 vols., Tübingen 1961–1962). Modern literature on particular regions of Italy is provided by H. Hassinger, *Geogr. Grundlagen* (ed. 2, 1953). Especially outstanding is T. Ashby, *The Roman Campagna in Classical Times* (London 1927). The Istituto di Studi Romani publishes the series "Forma Italia" and "Italia Romana."

BIBLIOGRAPHIC AIDS: J. Bérard, *Bibliographie topographique des principales cités grecques de l'Italie méridionale et de la Sicile dans l'antiquité* (1941), which is a supplement to Bérard, *La colonisation grecque de l'Italie méridionale et de la Sicile dans l'antiquité* (1941; ed. 2, 1957); H. Gauthier, *Dictionnaire des noms géographiques contenus dans les textes hiéroglyphiques* (7 vols., Cairo 1925–1931). Also, A. H. Gardiner, *Ancient Egyptian Onomastica* (2 vols. of text, 1 of tables, Oxford 1947) and *The Wilbour Papyrus* (2 vols. of text, 1 of tables, Oxford 1941–1948); especially the latter contains a wealth of toponymic material from the era of Rameses.

We have only begun to study historical geography in Antiquity, for the material is too fragmentary. The following works may be mentioned: E. Forrer, *Die Provinzeinteilung des assyrischen Reiches* (Leipzig 1921); U. Kahrstedt, *Syr. Territorien in hellenistischer Zeit* (Berlin 1926), to be used critically; O. Leuze, *Die Satrapieneinteilung in Syrien und im Zweistromlande von 520 bis 320 (Schriften der Königsberger Gelehrt. Gesellsch.*, Halle 1935), on which cf. H. Bengtson, *Gnomon* (1937), 113 ff.; P. J. Junge, "Satrapie und Nation," *Klio* 34 (1941), 1 ff., on the historical geography of the Achaemenid empire. For Asia Minor: W. M. Ramsay, *The Historical Geography of Asia Minor* (London 1890) and *The Cities and Bishoprics of Phrygia* (2 vols., Oxford 1895–1897); Ernst Meyer, *Die Grenzen der hellenistischen Staaten in Kleinasien* (Zurich 1925), is outstanding; A. Erzen, *Kilikien bis zum Ende der Perserherrschaft* (Diss. Leipzig 1940), on which cf. H. Bengtson, *Gnomon* (1942), 208 ff.—Egypt: H. Gauthier, *Les nomes d'Égypte depuis Herodot jusqu'à la conquête arabe* (Cairo 1935); J. Ball, *Egypt in the Classical Geographers (Ministry of Finance Survey of Egypt*, Cairo 1942); H. Kees, *Das alte Ägypten: Eine kleine Landeskunde* (ed. 2, Berlin 1958).—Republican Italy: A. Afzelius, *Die röm. Eroberung Italiens (340–264 v. Chr.) (Acta Jutlandica* 14.3, Copenhagen 1942). Imperial Italy: R. Thomsen, *The Italic Regions from Augustus to the Lombard Invasion (Classica et Mediaevalia*, Diss. 4; Copenhagen 1942).—Iberian Peninsula: A. Schulten, *Iberische Landeskunde* I (Strassburg-Kehl 1955).—Byzantium: E. Honigmann, *Die Ostgrenze des byzantinischen Reiches, 363–1071* (1935); A. Philippson, *Das byzantinische Reich als geographische Erscheinung* (Leiden 1939).

3. ANTHROPOLOGY

Time and space are the precincts in which the activity of man develops. Man himself, however, is the subject and object of history; and when history is called on to declare the ultimate goal of its endeavor, the only answer can be that it aims at men, at piercing their nature and at discerning, understanding, and doubting their feelings, decisions, and passions. In this sense history is the science of men; it is an open book which registers their deeds and misfortunes.

Modern anthropology, the "science of man" (strictly speaking), is an exact science; it works with calipers and a tape measure. Its task consists of investigating the history of the development of *homo sapiens* and of differentiating from one another as separate entities, as races, certain groups of men related by bodily characteristics. As an exact science anthropology is a child of the 19th century, although its beginnings are more remote. There was a time when the schematic grouping of the great Swedish scholar Karl von Linné (1707–1778) found much approval;[32] and even today the five races of mankind of the Göttingen anatomist J. F. Blumenbach (1752–1840)—Caucasian, Mongolian, Ethiopian, American, Malayan—form for many the basis of all anthropological knowledge. Pioneering work in modern anthropology was done by the ethnologist Felix von Luschan and the geographer Friedrich Ratzel. Luschan correctly warned against the apparently ineradicable confounding or blending of the concepts of race and nation (*Volk*): nations are social groups, races are groups of men tied together by anatomical attributes. It must be left to natural science, especially genetics, to decide to what extent intellectual, in contrast to physical, characteristics are passed on within certain groups of men.

Although in Antiquity no anthropology like the exact science of today existed, there was no lack of attempts to categorize human beings into homogeneous groups. In *Genesis* the differentiation of mankind is based on Noah's sons, Shem, Ham, and Japhet. As a general principle, however, anatomical features were less decisive for classifying ancient man than were other criteria, such as geographic and social environment, or membership in a political community or linguistic family. Especially the dichotomy between Hellenes and barbarians comes to mind; it was decisive in political history, and with the same sharpness also in the cultural sphere.[33] There is a concrete basis, however, for the ancient awareness of the difference between Romans and Germans, which found its finest statement in Tacitus' *Germania*.

Although in Antiquity national and allied cultural differentia-

---

[32] Linné's characterization is striking: "The American is reddish, choleric, upright; the European white, sanguine, industrious; the Asiatic yellow, melancholy, tenacious; the African black, phlegmatic, sluggish. The American is obstinate, contented, free; the European versatile, intelligent, resourceful; the Asiatic cruel, ostentatious, stingy; the African sly, lazy, indolent. The American is covered with tattoos and ruled by custom; the European is covered with well-fitting clothes and ruled by laws; the Asiatic is enveloped by loose robes and ruled by opinions; and the African is smeared with grease and ruled by arbitrariness."

[33] J. Jüthner, "Hellenen und Barbaren. Aus der Geschichte des National-bewusstseins," *Das Erbe der Alten* 8 (1923).

tions were well-known and had found literary expression, one really cannot speak of a conception of anthropological, racial differences. There is no reason to believe that the ancient antitheses ever attained effective historical consequence in the antagonisms of power politics. Racial antagonisms did not determine the war between Rome and Carthage[34] or the resistance of the Jewish Maccabees to the forced Hellenization under the Syrian king Antiochus IV in the 160's B.C.,[35] and it is even a matter of debate how far the antagonisms in Ptolemaic Egypt between Hellenes and natives were politically significant. What ancient men noted were clearly perceptible differences in national characteristics, customs, beliefs, and worship —factors important in wars between Jews and Greeks in Roman Alexandria.[36]

Although the trained anthropologist is not prevented by this insight from investigating and determining ancient racial groups, he must remain conscious that he is working with modern categories of thought alien to ancient men.

An idea of the unsteady ground on which are based hypotheses about the ancient significance of racial diversity should here be interposed. We possess from Antiquity only a tiny amount of anthropological material. The stock of tolerably preserved and scientifically analyzed skeletons consists of a few chance finds. Furthermore, the soft parts of the human body are as significant for anthropological inferences as are the bony parts.

In the face of this negative finding the historian will console himself with the awareness that pure racial types exist only in theory and that they are found as rarely in ancient as they are in modern history. Examinations of the graveyards of pre-Roman Switzerland, of the so-called *La Tène* period, have shown for example that long skulls and short skulls occur in a happy jumble. The Celtic Helvetians thus were not a definite, physically homogeneous race; on the contrary, this pre-Roman population of Switzerland resulted from a mixing process which apparently also found expression in bodily characteristics.[37] Analyses of the extant material from the

---

[34] M. Gelzer, "Der Rassengegensatz als geschichtlicher Faktor beim Ausbruch der römisch-karthagischen Kriege," in *Rom und Karthago*, ed. J. Vogt (Leipzig 1943), 178 ff.; the title of the study is unfortunate.

[35] See E. Bickermann, *Der Gott der Maccabäer* (Berlin 1937).

[36] H. I. Bell, *Juden und Griechen im römisch. Alexandreia (Beihefte z. Alt. Orient 9, 1926)*.

[37] F. Stähelin, *Schweizer Beitr. z. Allg. Gesch.* 1 (1943), 11.

excavations in the Athenian Kerameikos (Potters' Quarter)[38] have shown that in Attica (in the period c. 1150–1000 B.C.) no pure "Nordic" population existed. Rather, the ancient Greeks resulted from a fusion of the Indo-European immigrants with the earlier, Mediterranean (often called "Carian" or "Asia Minor") population of Greece. The degree of blending was perhaps different for each of the Greek tribes: the conclusion from skeleton finds in the Spartan burials of 403 B.C. in the Athenian Kerameikos[39] is that the Spartans were more purely "Nordic" than were, for example, the Ionians (to whom belong the Athenians).[40] In any case, the complete absorption of one population by a superimposed one must be viewed as a rare historical occurrence.[41] Miscegenation has nothing to do with degeneration. The specific talent of the Greek people resulted from a process of fusion, which with the help of archeology and linguistics we can follow in detail. The same holds true for the Italic peoples, and generally for all peoples who have played a role in world history.[42] The historian also must take into account racial changes even in the absence of those caused by external influences. B. G. Niebuhr has correctly pointed out that the bodily form of a people may not be so constant as is usually assumed. What is true for a people's physical character holds true also, within limits, for its intellectual character; the number of possibilities is inexhaustible.

Additionally, it might be noted that portraiture, which next to skeletal remains is the most important anthropological evidence for Antiquity, often is strongly schematized. We are not always so fortunate as to have a representation like that of the Syrian prisoners or exiles in the grave of Pharaoh Haremhab of the XIXth dynasty. "Nordic" features also appear among them;[43] these features are often associated with the Indo-European upper class of the Mitanni. Conversely one may refer to the anthropological appearance of the Etruscans. In Etruria, modern Tuscany, one now encounters a type whose distinguishing characteristic is a convex nose (cf. the portrait

[38] E. Breitinger, in K. Kübler, *Kerameikos* I (1939), 223 ff.; cf. K. Kübler in *Das Neue Bild der Antike* I, ed. H. Berve (1942), 35 ff.

[39] E. Breitinger, *AA* (1937), 200 ff.

[40] W. Otto, *Antike Kulturgeschichte* (*SBAW* 6 [1940]), 16.

[41] H. Bengtson, *Gnomon* (1942), 211.

[42] M. P. Nilsson, "Über Genetik und Geschichte," *Opusc. selecta* II (1952), 964 ff.

[43] M. Semper, "Zur Rassengeschichte der Indogermanen Irans," in *Festschr. f. Herman Hirt* I (1936), 341 ff.

of Dante). To conclude from this characteristic, however, that
the ancient Etruscans belonged to a certain racial type (or even,
as E. Fischer would have it, to a "Nordic," so-called "aquiline"
type[44]), which supposedly had been superimposed by a thin layer
of Near Eastern, Armenoid immigrants, would be wrong—as is
shown by the fact that the whole culture of ancient Etruria belonged
not to the "Nordic" cultural sphere, but to the Mediterranean.
Sound arguments of style controvert Fischer's hypothesis of an
"aquiline" race: ancient portraits show convex noses, which he connected with the "aquiline" type, at the earliest in the fourth century
B.C. This means that the representations were conditioned by
stylistic considerations,[45] and thus are to be used for anthropological
inferences only with caution.

The basic question in using such representations as anthropological evidence is to what extent can they be considered portraits.
For the earlier periods of Pharaonic Egypt A. Scharff has denied the
existence of real portraiture,[46] and so is opposed to Julius Wolf,[47]
who has used the methods of modern physiognomic science to
draw anthropological conclusions from the relief-portraits of King
Narmer and others of the first dynasty. In Greek art real portraiture
begins late: the former consensus on the fourth century B.C. as the
beginning of the art of individual portraiture is too late an estimate,
in the light of the newly discovered portrait-herm of Themistocles
at Ostia.

However valuable the information (about individuals and groups
of ancient men) which an historian can get from ancient anthropological material, the nation (*Volk*) as such is the principal object of
historical research. Regardless of how we may conceive of "nation,"
it should be viewed as a group of individual humans who have
grown together into a unit of historical significance by a common
political destiny, and often also by a common language.[48] Here, just
as with the formation of a tribe, the crucial element is the voluntary
political act of individuals or of groups, whatever the motives. Perhaps an instructive modern example is the formation of India and

[44] E. Fischer, *SDAW*, *phys.-math. Kl.* 25 (1938), and *F&F* (1939), 101 ff.
[45] F. Matz, *Klio* 35 (1942), 314 ff.
[46] *Müller* I (1939), 501.
[47] *Physiognomie u. Völkergeschichte* (Berlin 1935).
[48] Jacob Grimm's definition, that a nation (*Volk*) is an aggregate of human
beings who speak the same language, is not comprehensive enough.

Pakistan, in which the religious differences above all contributed to the final political determination.

Nevertheless, it would be an error to assume a "nation" at the start of every historical development. Nations develop and nations pass away, and even this process is the object of the science of history, whose special task is to determine which national elements have contributed to the formation of a political union (which is not always identical with a nation). It must penetrate the process of amalgamation and explain in detail how the separate national units grew together into a larger political organism, for example as happened in ancient Italy under Roman leadership by the formation of the great Italian military partnership, the shocks of the Gracchan revolution, and the Social War of 91–88 B.C. Language played a part in the formation and preservation of nationhood, as was recognized in Antiquity; indeed the Assyrians, systematically and irrespective of ethnic affiliation, mixed subjugated nations, in order to "make them of one mouth"[49] as the Assyrians put it. One might here recall the language policy of the Romans, granted that to some extent it has been contested.[50] Latin increasingly prevailed in Italy under the Roman political hegemony of the second and the beginning of the first century B.C., until by Sulla's time it had attained uncontested dominance in Italy; this fact of cultural history is significant for Pan-Italian consciousness.

Language and nationality do not constitute an indissoluble unity. As Hugo Schuchardt said, "Language is a function, the nation is its carrier; the carrier can change the function, not vice versa." Changes of language have occurred always, even in Antiquity. Thus, conclusions about nationality or race based on language are inadmissible —a fact that has often been misunderstood. The most dissimilar factors can be decisive in forming new languages. For example, the development of Romance languages in the late Roman Empire was the result of drastic social and national changes throughout the empire; the fact that the connection of the provinces with Rome, the imperial capital, gradually slackened and came undone must have been especially significant for this process. In addition, however, regional variations in nationality, varying degrees of Romanization, the Germanic invasions of the empire, and many other factors have

[49] B. Meissner, *Könige Babyloniens und Assyriens* (Leipzig 1926), 169.
[50] J. Göhler, *Rom und Italien* (Breslau 1939), 23 ff.

to be taken into account. Finally, new nations are not always born with the newly developed languages: there is a Provençal and a Catalan language, but no Provençal or Catalan nation.

For Antiquity it is important to determine to what extent language was felt to be a unifying and binding force. For example, it is forever surprising that in Greece the existence of a common literary language (which is to be distinguished from the many dialects of spoken language) never took effect as a decisive factor in politics. It was much more the active will of Sparta and Athens, the most important Greek states, which united the Greeks in a defensive war against the Persian danger of 481/480 B.C.; and so, the idea of the cultural and national unity of the Greeks was consciously employed in the service of politics.

Instructive from the cultural and political viewpoint is the formation of personal and place names in Antiquity (just as in the modern world). In early times the Greeks lacked a common name. Their designation as "Ionians" ("Ιωνες, Ἰάϝονες) originated in the East, where it appeared first in the eighth century B.C.[51] The peoples of the Near East named the Greeks after the tribe which was in closest geographical and cultural contact with them (cf. the French name "Allemands" for the Germans). In the seventh century B.C. the term "Panhellenes" first came into being as a common name for the Greeks. Later they called themselves "Hellenes," which primarily characterizes the contrast with non-Greeks, namely barbarians. Interesting for cultural history is the gradual extension of the significance of "Italia."[52] From the deepest south of the Apennine peninsula the term traversed the country, finally stopping at the foot of the Alps. The extension of the name kept pace with the political development which terminated under the Second Triumvirate in 42 B.C. with the incorporation of Cisalpine Gaul into the area of Roman citizenship. It might be added that from the formation of the Lombard empire the term "Italia" stuck especially to upper Italy: the "Regnum Langobardorum" was practically equated with "Italia."

One school of modern scholarship (including Eduard Meyer)

[51] H. Bengtson, *Philologus* 92 (1937), 148 ff.; E. Schwyzer, *Griech. Grammatik* I (1939), 77.
[52] The etymological meaning of "Italia" as "Cattleland" (from *vitulus*), which was advocated by the ancients, has been accepted by modern scholarship.

has distinguished between the terms *Volk* and *Nation*, and has considered *Nation* to embody a higher, ideal political unity (cf. the English term "nation-state") or cultural unity. Since the terms *Volk* and *Nation* are synonymous in German usage, they seem unsuited to characterize different entities. The infelicitous distinction should therefore be abandoned.

What about the problem of "national consciousness" in Antiquity? If this term is understood to express a people's awareness that it feels itself to be a "national unit" consciously set apart from other peoples, then only seldom in Antiquity—and even then only for brief periods—is an explicit nationalism discernible: in Hellas during the Persian Wars, in Rome and Italy under the rule of Augustus. Witnesses to nationalism are, for example, the *Persai* of Aeschylus and later the history of Herodotus;[53] in Rome Vergil's *Aeneid*, Horace's *Odes*, and Livy's historical works. There never developed an Hellenic or Italian nation in the sense of a nation-state or of a cultural unit (*Kulturvolk*). Political reasons hindered this: in Greece the independence of the *poleis*, in Rome the opposition between Italy and the provinces. In Antiquity only the Israelites (in the politically glorious days of the kings) and the ancient Egyptians can be labeled genuine nations, national units in the political and cultural sense. In fact, among the Egyptians a development almost without foreign influence brought unity to every area of intellectual life: to art, to literature, to religion, to the way of life. This national unity, which for almost three millennia the people had preserved in spite of temporary conquests by foreigners (Hyksos, Assyrians, Persians), was menaced most heavily by the incorporation of Egypt into Alexander's empire. The underlying unity was gradually eroded by the social antagonism, latent at first but later increasingly apparent, between the Egyptians and the politically and economically dominant foreigners, both Hellenes and others. Greek culture appeared alongside the Egyptian, and soon large groups of Egyptians adopted it.

To comprehend the character of a people, the historian will pursue the influences, positive and negative, which have affected the formation of a particular, national individuality. For example, the problem of the Hellenistic influence on Italy and the East, or of the significance of Babylonian civilization for its neighbors, deserves

[53] Cf. especially Herodotus 8.144.

special attention: the one problem with regard to the development of Romano-Italian civilization, the other with regard to the formation of the intellectual and spiritual life of the Hittites and Israelites.

The classification of the linguistic families of Antiquity into the Indo-European and Semitic groups (the remaining groups, especially the Aegean-Asia Minor and Hamitic, are less involved in the present problem) must not divert us from the principle that nations are the primary objects of historical study. The principle of linguistic division, including the classification of Indo-European languages into *centum* and *satem* groups, has no practical significance for historical judgment. In particular, the concepts of "Indo-European" or "Semitic culture," which are based on linguistic kinship, are not very fortunate. 19th-century scholarship was the first to create the notions of Romanic and German nations. There has never been a real Romanic or Germanic feeling of solidarity. What the speaker of a peculiar language senses is rather the complete foreignness of his own tongue to that of another, whether that tongue belongs to a near relative or a stranger in the pedigree of languages. This is not to gainsay that an ideology of solidarity can be constructed by educated men based on knowledge of linguistic kinship; nevertheless, such an ideology never existed in Antiquity because the scientific assumptions for it were lacking. The degree of linguistic kinship between two nations plays no role (or only a very subordinate one) in the development of a feeling of solidarity; more decisive is membership in the same cultural sphere. Thus, to Western European civilization belong, in addition to the nations of Indo-European speech, the Basques, Magyars, and Finns, who speak non-Indo-European languages. Perhaps historically even more instructive is the fact that nations of basically different languages belong to the Islamic cultural sphere: Arabs, Persians, and Turks. Arab is a Semitic, Persian an Indo-European, and Turkish a Ural-Altaic tongue. Therefore, one should limit the terms "Indo-European culture" and "Semitic culture," if one uses them at all, to the earliest period of the Indo-Europeans and the Semites—when each group must have lived in a restricted area. Moreover, it is characteristic of Antiquity that nations of different languages belonged to the same cultural community. Hellenism, which tied the numerous nations of the ancient world into a great community, and the Babylonian civilization, which left its stamp on the features of the whole Near East, are only two especially obvious examples of this.

The unity of a civilization depends as much on a common script as on a common tongue; in the *Imperium Romanum* it was Latin (in addition, in the eastern Empire Greek was in use as a second official language), in the Hellenistic world the Greek language and script, and in the Near East under Hammurabi Babylonian and cuneiform. The influence of a foreign culture shows itself by the absorption of foreign words into the national language, a process of great general and cultural historical significance.

Finally, languages arise from a complicated intellectual process of amalgamation just as peoples do from a corresponding anthropological process. Some examples from the Greeks illustrate this: it has been established that nouns in *-nthos*, *-assos*, and *-issos* (e.g. Korinthos, Parnassos, Illissos) and many others belong to a pre-Greek stratum.[54] This determination of linguistic history is also significant for cultural history. It demonstrates that the Greek people was produced by the fusion of Mediterranean and Indo-European elements. The Greek for "I marry," ὀπυίω, exemplifies an amalgamation of different peoples; linguistics connects it with the Etruscan, therefore probably Aegean, *puia*, "woman."[55] In this word, therefore, the process of national and social amalgamation seems transparent. It perhaps would be possible to explain the ancient Mediterranean (Aegean) substratum in the Greek language only by the adoption of ancient Aegean cultural values, without at the same time accepting an extensive ethnic fusion; the strong survival of ancient Mediterranean traditions in Greek religion,[56] however, is an unimpeachable testimony for the ethnic fusion of the immigrants and the already settled population.

Corresponding processes are assumed for the other peoples of the ancient world. From the common life of immigrants and natives was often developed a new nationality, which for its part experienced changes caused by influences from without and within. Social regrouping, wars, and peaceful relations with neighboring peoples are some frequent causes of national transformations. Thus, the na-

---

[54] P. Kretschmer, *Einleit. in die Gesch. d. griech. Sprache* (1896); E. Schwyzer, *Griech. Grammatik* I (1939), 60 ff.
[55] Hammarström, *Glotta* 11 (1921), 212; E. Schwyzer, *op. cit.*, 62.
[56] M. P. Nilsson, *Gesch. d. griechischen Religion* I (ed. 3, 1967), 256 ff.

tionality and advanced culture of the old Babylonians grew from
an amalgamative process between the Sumerians, whose anthropological determination is not yet certain, and the Akkadians, Semites who immigrated to southern Mesopotamia from the west.
Even so, Babylonian civilization first got its characteristic cast from
the addition of a third element, the Amorites (also called East
Canaanites), who, like the Akkadians, were Semitic. The population
of ancient Asia Minor and the Indo-European Hittites formed the
characteristic Anatolian type of man; and in northwest India there
arose a new breed of men based on the fusion of Indo-Europeans,
who immigrated there probably about the middle of the second
millennium or somewhat later, with the indigenous elements. In Italy
the immigration of Indo-European groups from the north in the
late second millennium and their amalgamation on the peninsula with
peoples of Mediterranean origin again created special national and
cultural conditions, which we can study in detail with the help of
archeology and linguistics. Insight into the complicated questions
relating to population warns the investigator to be cautious with
conclusions about national character or about the bases of specific
talents.

Many peoples, in their travels, encounter an alien environment.
For example, the Indo-European immigrants who invaded what later
was called Hellas came south into the zone of Mediterranean civilization, just like the Thracians and Illyrians. The Hittites, Iranians,
Indians, Phrygians, and Armenians likewise appear as erratic elements in what to them was the strange world of the Near East;
and the Tocharians even penetrated the Sino-Buddhistic cultural
sphere. Many of these nations moved from one cultural complex
into another, different one. Thus the Armenians were partly Hellenized, and later became one of the Christian peoples of the Near
East. An important problem of historical knowledge is the assessment of peoples' contacts with alien cultures.

If the many overlappings of nations are considered, the assumption of a sharp demarcation between the Indo-European and the
Near Eastern worlds cannot be justified. Historical research based
on such an antithesis ignores historical life, which cannot be squeezed
into categories, least of all anthropological ones. Of course the historian is justified who, from his standpoint surveying thousands of
years, views ancient history as a single, gigantic altercation between
East and West—an idea which was familiar even to ancient thinkers,

as is witnessed by Herodotus' work. The main contrast here, of course, is not one of race, but one of ideals.

A section on the anthropological bases of ancient history should include a few fundamental remarks about the problem of "the individual and the multitude," for historical events are rooted in the reciprocal relationship between the two. It is undeniable that ancient history can be viewed and written from the viewpoint of a partisan of a personality cult (J. G. Droysen) as well as from that of an advocate of collectivism (K. J. Beloch). Nevertheless, for many, if not for most, eras of Antiquity a solution of the problem is impossible, for the source material does not suffice to determine the role of the individual. With some exceptions this holds true for the entire history of the ancient East, in which we perceive as individuals only solitary figures of rulers like Hammurabi and Darius I, and a few personalities of kings and prophets from Israelite history. It is similar with Greek history, in which our first recognizable personalities are Hesiod, Archilochus, and Solon; and the history of the individual in Rome begins for us as late as Scipio Africanus Maior (d. 183 B.C.) and Cato the Censor (d. 149 B.C.). Only for Cicero, Caesar, and the emperor Julian (ruled A.D. 361–363) has sufficient biographical material survived to allow us a true picture of their characters.

The question of the historical significance of the individual in ancient history can be answered only by examining each case. For example: the expedition of the 10,000 Greeks portrayed by Xenophon permits us to recognize, especially in the march back, a common inner determination of such a kind that the commanding officers recede into the background; and the history of the Punic wars teaches that the bulk of the Carthaginian mercenary army was given inner unity by the genius of Hamilcar Barca and Hannibal. The same is true for the relation of Caesar to his soldiers.[57]

The interrelations between the individual and the multitude form a fundamental theme of historical knowledge. With regard to this, ancient propaganda should be taken into account, for even the ancients understood how to influence politically the masses, although with other, slower-working methods than those of today: pamphlets, inscriptions, and portraits and legends on coins provide primary material which still awaits intensive working.

[57] J. Vogt, "Cäsar und seine Soldaten," *NJA* (1940), 120 ff., reprinted in *Orbis* (1960), 89 ff.

The student of the essence of the masses and their assessment in Antiquity will find much to ponder particularly in the *Histories* and the *Annals* of Tacitus.[58] Nevertheless, his often one-sided verdicts show that this "historian of the upper 10,000" makes no secret of a negative attitude toward the *profanum vulgus*.

The study of ancient population figures, on which anthropological research is based, is just beginning. The conclusions of this study, however, will probably never be as certain for Antiquity as they are for the modern world, where adequate statistical material is available.

BIBLIOGRAPHY

CONNECTIONS BETWEEN RACE, NATIONALITY, AND SPEECH: Eduard Meyer, "Elemente der Anthropologie," in *Gesch. d. Altert.* I.1 (ed. 3, 1910), 73 ff.; also e.g. A. Debrunner, *NJA* 41 (1918), 433 f.—Discussion about the connections between race and speech has nowhere achieved certain results; properly sceptical is the Indo-Europeanist H. Krahe, *Indogerm. Forsch.* 56 (1938), 43 ff.; 58 (1942), 83. Some new points of view in V. Pisani, "L'elemento razza nella evoluzione linguistica," *Rev. étud. indoeuropéenes* 4 (1947), 266 ff. and "Linguistica e antropologia," *Paideia* 5 (1950), 20 ff.—A noted example against assertions of the congruence of race and language is modern India, which has almost 200 principal languages and more than 500 dialects, so the languages do not at all coincide with the races.

Epoch-making for the study of the races of Antiquity were the works of Felix von Luschan; see his *Völker, Rassen, Sprachen* (1922). Together with the geographer H. Kiepert, F. von Luschan first recognized and scientifically established the exceptional anthropological position of the people of Asia Minor. A rich fund of material is furnished, especially for modern times, by E. Frhr. v. Eickstedt, *Die Forschung am Menschen* (3 vols., Stuttgart 1940–1963). Methodologically important are B. Lundman, *Umriss der Rassenkunde des Menschen in geschichtl. Zeit* (Copenhagen 1952) and *Stammeskunde der Völker* (Uppsala 1961).

INDIVIDUAL STUDIES: C. U. Ariens Kappers and Leland W. Parr, *An Introduction to the Anthropology of the Near East in Ancient and Recent Times* (Amsterdam 1934); W. M. Krogmann, *Racial Types from Tepe Hissar Iran from the Late 5th to the Early 2nd Millennium* (*Verhandl. der Akad. d. Wiss.*, Amsterdam 1940). Also worth reading is P. E. Newberry, *Ägypten als Feld für anthropologische Forschung* (tr. G. Roeder; *AO* 27.1, Leipzig 1927), al-

---

[58] H. F. Seiler, *Die Masse bei Tacitus* (Diss. Erlangen 1936).

though the title does not correspond to the contents. For Cyprus: C. M. Fürst, *Zur Kenntnis der Anthropologie der prähistorischen Bevölkerung der Insel Cypern* (*Lunds Univ. Arsskrift*, N.F. Avd. 2, XXIX Nr. 6; 1933).—Early Greek anthropological material is evaluated among others by C. M. Fürst (*Lunds Univ. Arsskrift*, N.F. Avd. 2, XXVI Nr. 8; 1930); by E. Fischer in Georg Karo, *Die Schachtgräber von Mykenai* (Munich 1930–1933), 320 ff.; and by E. Breitinger in *Kerameikos-Werkes* I (Berlin 1929), 223 ff. Important studies have been done by the American J. L. Angel, e.g. "Skeletal Material from Attica," *Hesperia* (1945), 279 ff., which deals with all the skeletal material of Attica from the beginning of history to the decline of Antiquity; "A Racial Analysis of the Ancient Greeks, an Essay on the Use of Morphological Types," *Amer. Jour. of Phys. Anthropology* N.S. 2 (1944), 329 ff.; and, on the human remains in Troy, *Troy, Suppl. Monograph* I (Princeton 1951).—Numerous more recent works for ancient Anatolia are given in A. Goetze, *Kleinasien* (ed. 2, 1957), 8–12.

BROADER COMPREHENSIVE WORKS: Aubrey Diller, *Race Mixture among the Greeks before Alexander* (*Illinois Studies in Language and Literature* 20. 1–2, 1937). Alexander the Great's "policy of amalgamation" has been often debated, e.g. by W. Kolbe, *Die Weltreichsidee Alexanders d. Gr.* (*Freiburger Wiss. Ges.* 25, 1936) and by H. Berve, *Klio* 31 (1938), 135 ff., whose view, that Alexander himself was aware of the racial kinship of the Macedonians and Persians, is not tenable.—For the *Orbis Romanus*: M. P. Nilsson, "The Race Problem of the Roman Empire," *Hereditas* (Lund) 2 (1921), 370 ff. (*Opuscula Selecta* II, Lund 1952), 940 ff. I have not yet seen A. Sherwin-White, *Racial Prejudice in Imperial Rome* (Cambridge 1967). Interesting evidence for the intrusion of foreign elements into Italy at the time of the transition from Republic to Principate has been furnished by inscriptions from Minturnae: details in F. Zucker, *Hermes* 78 (1943), 200 ff.

The so-called "structural investigation" is important for the knowledge of national individualities; on this cf. B. Schweitzer, *NJA* (1938), 162 ff. An example of its use: A. Moortgat, *Die bildende Kunst des Alten Orients und die Bergvölker* (Berlin 1932) and *Bildwerk und Volkstum Vorderasiens zur Hethiterzeit* (*Sendschr. d. Deutsch. Orientges.* 8, Leipzig 1934).

Detailed works: Important for the anthropology of Egypt in Roman times are the mummy portraits; cf. H. Drerup, *Die Datierung der Mumienporträts* (Paderborn 1933); K. Parlasca, *Mumienporträts und verwandte Denkmäler* (Wiesbaden 1966). Nevertheless, they represent without exception the portraits of urban upper classes, i.e. of a "social elite." Further, the conscious stylization of the portraits must be taken into account for anthropological use. The same is true for the *Bildnisse der antiken Dichter, Redner und Denker*, which K. Schefold has assembled (Basel 1943). Cf. also K. Schefold, *Griechische Dichterbildnisse* (Zurich 1965). On the herm of Themistocles from Ostia see e.g. H. Sichtermann, *Gymnasium* 71 (1964), 348–381.

"VOLK" AND "NATION": For the concept of *Volk*, see E. Meyer, *Gesch. d. Altert.* I.1 (ed. 3, 1910), 77 ff.; opposed H. E. Stier, *Grundlagen und Sinn der griech. Geschichte* (Stuttgart 1945), 73, 107, 110, 113, etc. Stier's view, that there was generally no Greek people (*Volk*), but only separate Greek nations (*Nationen*), underestimates the unifying forces of Greek history in favor of the divisive ones. Stier (*op. cit.* p. 100) slights the Herodotean passage (8.144) which speaks emphatically for a Pan-Greek consciousness at the time of the Persian Wars. Cf. also Herodotus' opinion (8.3) which designates the quarrels between Greeks as στάσις ἔμφυλος, i.e. as "internal discord"; cf. Xenophon, *Hellenika* 3.2.21 f., concerning which see H. Bengtson, "Rastloses Schaffen," in *Festschrift für F. Lammert* (Stuttgart 1953), 31 ff. Further, see H. Bengtson, "Hellenen und Barbaren," in *Unser Geschichtsbild*, ed. K. Rüdinger (Munich 1954), 25 ff.; H. Schaefer, *Relazioni del X Congr. Intern. di Scienze stor.* VI (Rome 1955), 677 ff.—Worth notice is Herakleides' concept of Hellenes in his *City Portraits*, fr. 3.2: they are those who trace their ancestry to Hellen and who speak Greek.—On H. E. Stier see also F. W. Walbank, "The Problem of Greek Nationality," *Phoenix* 5 (1951), 41 ff. A good survey is E. Lommatzsch, *Patria* (Griefswald 1922); cf. also L. Krattinger, *Der Begriff des Vaterlandes im republikanischen Rom* (Diss. Zurich 1944).

As yet there is no history of national consciousness in the ancient world; a preliminary study is the dissertation of A. Heubeck, *Das Nationalbewusstsein des Herodot* (Erlangen 1936).

THE ROLE OF THE INDIVIDUAL PERSONALITY IN THE HISTORY OF ANTIQUITY: Besides the significant general statements of F. Meinecke in the introduction to the compilation *Menschen, die Geschichte machen* I (ed. 2, Vienna 1933), see: Ernst von Stern, *Staatsform und Einzelpersönlichkeit im Klassischen Altertum* (*Hallische Univ.-Reden* 20, Halle 1923); on Scipio Africanus Maior, H. Bengtson, "Scipio Africanus: Seine Persönlichkeit und seine weltgeschichtl. Bedeutung," *HZ* 168 (1943), 487 ff. The small book of W. v. Soden, *Herrscher im Alten Orient* (Berlin 1954), is an attempt to comprehend the rulers of the ancient Orient as personalities.

THE SIGNIFICANCE OF THE MASSES IN ANCIENT HISTORY: The most important sources are the collections of inscriptions, inasmuch as the literary material acquaints us as a rule only with the socially elevated classes. Examples of studies: Helen H. Tanzer, *The Common People of Pompei* (*The Johns Hopkins University, Studies in Archaeology* 29; Baltimore 1939). Also cf. A. Maxey, *Occupations of the Lower Classes in Roman Society* (Chicago 1938). A colossal amount of socioeconomic historical material is included in Tenney Frank, *Economic Survey of Ancient Rome* (1933–1940, repr. 1959) and in the works of M. Rostovtzeff, *Social and Economic History of the Roman Empire* (1927; ed. 2 by P. M. Fraser, Oxford 1957) and *Social and Economic History of the Hellenistic World* (Oxford 1941).—The studies of ancient slavery, which were carried out under the direction of J. Vogt and with the assistance of the Mainz Academy, are significant for knowledge of the social, economic, religious, and humanitarian conditions of Antiquity.

ANCIENT PROPAGANDA: See as examples of modern studies: Kenneth Scott, "Octavian's Propaganda and Antony's de sua ebrietate," *CPh* 24 (1929), 133 ff. and "The Political Propaganda of 44–30 B.C.," *MAAR* 11 (1933), 7 ff.; M. P. Charlesworth, *The Virtues of a Roman Emperor. Propaganda and the Creation of Belief* (*PBA* 23, London 1937). The studies of the idea of the monarch in the Hellenistic period (above all by W. Schubart, *APF* 12 (1937), 1 ff.) and in the Late Antique (J. Straub, *Vom Herrscherideal in der Spätantike* (Stuttgart 1939)) are important preliminary works for a wide-ranging study of ancient propaganda. Also worth mentioning are the peculiar *Historia Augusta*, in which the figure of Julian the Apostate is glorified in the person of Severus Alexander, and the so-called contorniates (from the Italian "contorno" = outline; a type of coin with a groove on the rim), which were used as a weapon against Christianity by the pagan aristocracy at Rome in the fourth and fifth centuries A.D.: A. Alföldi, *Die Kontorniaten: Ein verkanntes Propagandamittel der stadtrömischen heidnischen Aristokratie* (Budapest 1943).

SIZE OF POPULATIONS: K. J. Beloch concerned himself with this basic problem. The results of his penetrating studies, however, are far from certainty; authentic material is available only since the Renaissance. Besides Beloch's *Die Bevölkerung der griechisch-römischen Welt* (1886), one should know the volumes which appeared after his death (1929), *Bevölkerungsgeschichte Italiens* (Berlin 1937–1940; there is a new ed. of vol. 2, and a third vol. appeared in 1959). For an instructive example of Beloch's method, see his inaugural lecture as professor of ancient history at Leipzig, "Die Volkszahl als Faktor und Gradmesser der historischen Entwicklung," *HZ* 111 (1913), 321 ff., which shows this sharp-witted historian's undervaluation of historical imponderables and of the irrational in history. For contrast see a work like Ernst von Stern,

Volkskraft und Stattsmacht im Altertum (Halle 1916). Cf. the
notable compilation of data from Antiquity by E. Meyer in *Handwörterbuch der Staatswissenschaften* II (ed. 2, 1899), 674 ff., s.v.
"Bevölkerungswesen III." See also the so-called "Bevölkerungs-
Ploetz": E. Kirsten, *Raum und Bevölkerung in der Weltgeschichte*,
Part I: *Von der Vorzeit zum Mittelalter* (Würzburg 1956); naturally the numbers given here are hypothetical.

An instructive special problem: A. W. Gomme, *The Population
of Athens in the Vth and IVth Centuries B.C.* (Oxford 1933), together with the criticism of G. De Sanctis, *RFIC* (1937), 288 ff. and
Gomme's reply with the counter-reply of De Sanctis, *ibid.* (1938),
169 ff.—Methodologically interesting is the problem of numbers in
the Persian Wars: see the basic tabulations of Hans Delbrück, *Die
Perserkriege und die Burgunderkriege* (1887) and also the essay of
R. v. Fischer, *Klio* 25 (1931), 289 ff. On the problem of numbers
in Caesar's *Bellum Helveticum*: Ernst Meyer, *Zeitschr. f. Schweiz.
Geschichte* 29 (1949), 65 ff.—The *formula togatorum* ("list of
armed men") of Polybius 2.24, which is given for 225 B.C., is fundamental for reckoning the population of ancient Italy; modern cal-
culations based on this list, however, are contradictory. For Roman
census figures see e.g. A. H. M. Jones' lecture, "Ancient Economic
History" (1948), 3 ff.—Methodologically instructive is F. G. Maier,
"Römische Bevölkerungsgeschichte und Inschriftenstatistik," *Historia* 2 (1953/54), 318 ff., which correctly refers to the insufficiency
of statistical material and of the conclusions based thereon.—A. E. R.
Boak has tried to prove that the scarcity of men may have caused
the fall of the Western Roman Empire: *Manpower Shortage and
the Fall of the Roman Empire in the West* (Ann Arbor 1955); on
which, however, see e.g. H. Bengtson, *BO* (1957), 58–59 and M. I.
Finley, *JRS* 48 (1958), 156–164.

The great common diseases in Antiquity have so far received too
little attention; they are significant for judging the problems of
ancient population and for the intellectual development of ancient
men. Modern studies: G. Sticker, *Festschrift Bernh. Nocht* (1937),
597 ff., which concentrates on the epidemics of Antiquity; B. v.
Hagen, "Die sog. Pest des Thukydides," *Gymnasium* 49 (1938),
120 ff., which identifies the plague as a combined spotted-fever and
smallpox epidemic; *ibid.*, *Die Pest im Altertum* (Jena 1939). See
also P. Fraccaro, "La malaria e la storia degli antichi popoli classici,"
in *Opuscula* II (Pavia 1957), 337 ff. The "pathological perspective"
of Antiquity is stretched too far, especially for Late Antiquity, by
F. Kaphahn, *Zwischen Antike und Mittelalter: Das Donaualpenland
im Zeitalter St. Severins* (Munich 1947).

___ IV ___

The Sources

___

Every student of Antiquity must first concern himself with the study and criticism of the sources. The significance of sources, as the word implies, is that they are original and genuine. Just as pure water flows from a spring, so true testimony from the past is drawn from the sources.

In a wide sense, everything preserved from Antiquity is a source for the history of Antiquity. These sources include writings of both literary and documentary character, architecture and art, objects from intellectual and material pursuits—in short, everything bearing on the life of people in ancient times. So regarded, the sources are of enormous diversity, and nobody can master a part of them, much less all. The pyramids of the Old Kingdom, the buildings of Periclean Athens, the Ara Pacis of Augustus—all are sources just as important as the narratives of the Westcar Papyrus from the Middle Kingdom, the books of the Old Testament, the Athenian Tribute Lists, and the *Commentaries* of Caesar.

One can easily see, however, that there is a fundamental difference between two categories of sources. The first includes buildings and works of art, which are expressions of their age and as such are important for the historian. The second category includes all written records, and it is with this category that we begin.

I. LITERATURE AND DOCUMENTS

Written records are of two types: (1) works shaped by the literary tradition, the most important being the ancient historians' writings but including all other forms of literature as well; (2) primary materials such as documents, letters, and speeches, which give us direct testimony about events and are themselves a part of history, whereas literary works transmit the past as interpreted by the writer. Because we have only fragments of the ancient tradition the modern scholar must be prepared to use whatever is preserved, both documents and histories, as well as all forms of poetry and prose. Nevertheless he should always remember the special importance of primary materials.

Unfortunately only a small part of the documentary material has been preserved. That documents were as important in Antiquity as in medieval and modern times has been demonstrated by a number of finds such as the Amarna Tablets (discovered in Middle Egypt in 1887–1888, including archives of Amenophis III and IV of the 14th century B.C.), the Hittite state archive (discovered at Boghazköi, central Anatolia), the rediscovery of the Palace Library of Assurbanipal (died c. 631 B.C.) in old Nineveh, which includes many works in classical Babylonian script, and finally the administrative records and documents preserved by ancient inscriptions and by papyri found in the Egyptian desert. Yet all of this is only a tiny fragment of the enormous mass of material from 3500 years, most of which has been lost because of fire, flood, war, and accident.

Therefore we must consider a special gift of fortune the recent discovery of many Aramaic documents, among them ten letters of the Persian satrap Arsames dating from 411 to 408 B.C. They are a valuable addition to the Aramaic documents found some years ago in Elephantine, Egypt.

Through the discoveries of Hebrew texts in Qumran on the Dead Sea made since 1947 we have gained new and surprising insight into the intellectual world in which Jesus and the Apostles lived. Even though there is still disagreement on many details, much knowledge has been gained concerning the textual history of the Old Testament (among the scrolls is a manuscript of Joshua and a commentary on Habakuk) and the thought of Palestinian Judaism, especially the Jewish sects (from a manual of discipline and an eschatological writing, "The War of the Sons of Light against the Sons of Darkness").

All writings are characterized by the use of a particular script and a particular language. Script and language are therefore of basic importance to the historian who surveys several millennia. The historical development of the Egyptian script from hieroglyphic to cursive to demotic (during which hieroglyphic continued to be used as a monument script until almost the end of Antiquity, down to

Theodosius I),[1] the development of the Mesopotamian scripts from the so-called pictographic of the early dynastic period to the classical cuneiform of the New Assyrian empire down to the script of the Achaemenid inscriptions, and finally the development of the Greek epigraphic script during the archaic, classic, and Hellenistic periods—all these aspects of the history of writing are of great historical significance. The same is true of the changes undergone by individual languages, such as the transition from the Old Latin of the Lapis Niger found in the Roman Forum or of the Twelve Tables, to the classical Latin of Cicero and Caesar, the Silver Latin of Seneca and Tacitus, vulgar Latin, and finally Romanic; or the changes in the Greek language from literary Attic to the Hellenistic *Koinē*, to Byzantine, and then to modern Greek.

Especially significant historically is the use of a language or script by peoples to whom these are foreign. The fact that the correspondence in the Amarna Archive between the kings of Egypt and the rulers of the Near East was carried on in Babylonian cuneiform and language indicates the central importance of the Babylonian script and of Babylonian culture in general.[2] Similarly the fact that the Hittites also used not only the so-called Hittite hieroglyphic (decipherment of which has entered a new stage with the discovery of a bilingual text in Cilicia)[3] but also used cuneiform to write both their own language and other languages of Asia Minor indicates the cultural dominance of Old Babylonia in the Near East during the second millennium B.C. The appropriation of a foreign script and its adaptation for a new language allow conclusions about the special achievements of both the originator and the recipient; a well-known example is the use of the North Phoenician consonantal script by the Greeks and its transformation into an alphabet suited to the Greek language.[4]

Great interest—and not only among scholars—was aroused by the decipherment of the Cretan script, Linear B,[5] as a result of which

---

[1] The last hieroglyphic inscription is dated A.D. 394 and is on the Gate of Hadrian at Philae.

[2] B. Meissner, *Könige Babyloniens und Assyriens* (1926), 82.

[3] Discovered by H. Bossert; cf. H. Güterbock, *Eranos* 47 (1949), 93 ff., and P. Meriggi, *Athenaeum* n.s. 29 (1951), 25 ff.

[4] R. Harder, "Die Meisterung der Schrift durch die Griechen" in *Kleine Schriften* (1960), 89 ff.

[5] M. Ventris and J. Chadwick, *JHS* 73 (1953), 84–103; cf. their *Documents in Mycenaean Greek* (1956).

the language used in a number of Greek archives from the Mycenaean Age has been identified as an archaic Achaean dialect. Recently, however, such serious criticisms have been advanced[6] that the
decipherment cannot yet be considered secure.

After this digression, let us take up primary historical materials
again, and let us first note certain categoric divisions which will
enable us to use the material better. Documents include all writings
except literary works (history, poetry, novels, etc.), and they can
be divided into documents of public and of private life. In the first
group are international treaties, administrative documents and records, magistrates' edicts—in short, all writings connected with public
life.

Let us begin with the basic source for the study of diplomacy,
treaties. The most important for the history of the ancient Near
East are those from the Hittite archive.[7] All treaties of Antiquity
are to be published in a series sponsored by the Munich Commission
for Ancient History and Epigraphy, and volume two has already
appeared, covering the period 700–338 B.C.[8] It includes the document of the so-called "King's Peace" (Peace of Antalkidas) of 387/
386 B.C., which the Persian king Artaxerxes II "granted" to the
Greeks.[9] From Roman history it includes the treaties between Rome
and Carthage, the dates of which are still unsettled, especially that
of the first, which Polybius ascribes to the first year of the Republic.[10]

Scholars were recently surprised by the discovery and publication
of a fragment of the treaty of 212 B.C. between Rome and Aetolia.[11]
The discussion of this treaty and the many new problems it has
raised, among others the question of Polybius' dependability, still
continues.

Historical and legal analysis of treaties has in many cases illumi-

[6] E. Grumach, *Orientalist. Literatur-Zeitung* (1957), 293 ff.; A. J. Beattie,
Mitt. d. Instituts für Orientforschung [Berlin] 6 (1958), 33–104. For the other
side see J. Chadwick, *The Decipherment of Linear B* (Cambridge 1958).

[7] A. Götze, *Kulturgeschichte des Alten Orients: Kleinasien* (ed. 2, 1957),
91 ff.

[8] *Die Verträge der griechisch-römischen Welt von 700 bis 338 v. Chr.*, eds.
H. Bengtson and R. Werner (Munich 1962).

[9] U. Wilcken, "Über Entstehung und Zweck des Königsfriedens," *Abh.
Preuss. Akad. d. Wiss.* 1941, no. 15.

[10] J. Vogt, *Römische Geschichte* in *Gercke-Norden* III.2 (ed. 3, 1933), 40;
but cf. E. Kornemann, *Römische Geschichte* I[5] (Kröner Verlag edition,
1964), 84 and 96.

[11] G. Klaffenbach, *SDAW* 1954, no. 1.

nated the characteristics of ancient politics. The work of V. Korošec is especially important; he has shown that the Hittites concluded
two distinct types of treaty, treaties of alliance and treaties of vas-
salage, and so has provided us with a new basis for the analysis of
Hittite domestic and foreign policies.[12] In Roman studies the view
of Theodor Mommsen and Eugen Täubler, that the Romans regarded any state not covered by a treaty as *ipso facto* an enemy, has
been disproved by A. Heuss,[13] leading to new insights into Roman
diplomacy. Only the student familiar with these matters will be
able to grasp the mentality behind the policies which enabled Rome
to master the world.

Just as treaties illuminate diplomacy, so the legal systems of nations are revealed by laws, codes, and legal documents, and we have
many of these from the ancient Near East, Greece, and Rome.
These documents tell us much about the history of law in Antiquity;
they also give more general insight into ancient civilization, society,
and class structure; they show the close connection between ideas
of justice and divinity; and they give us an understanding of the
minds of great lawgivers such as Hammurabi, Draco, and Solon.
Especially important both for comparative law and for our knowledge of Babylonian civilization in the period 2,000–1,500 B.C. is
the Code of Hammurabi. It was discovered by French archeologists
on a diorite block in Susa, where it had been brought by Elamites
from Babylon.[14] Another code, about 1700 years more ancient, is
the Code of Lipit-Ishfar from Isin.[15] Whereas the legal documents
of ancient Mesopotamia, especially those of the Assyrians, reveal a
spirit of pitiless harshness, as expressed in numerous provisions for
degrading mutilations, the fragments of Hittite law[16] are notable
for unusually humane punishments.[17] Many Greek legal documents
have been preserved, most of them in the form of inscriptions, and
usually showing no distinction between public and private law.
Thus an inscription in Ionic dialect dating from c. 575 B.C. was

[12] V. Korošec, *Hethitische Staatsverträge: Ein Beitrag zu ihrer jurist. Wer-
tung (Leipzig. Rechtswiss. Studien* 60, 1931).
[13] E. Täubler, *Imperium Romanum* I (1913); A. Heuss, *Die völkerrecht-
lichen Grundlagen der römischen Aussenpolitik in republikanischer Zeit,
Klio-Beiheft* 31 (1933).
[14] W. Eilers, "Die Gesetzesstele Chammurabis," *AO* 31 (1932), nos. 3–4.
[15] A Falkenstein and M. San Nicolò, *Orientalia* 19 (1950), 103 ff.
[16] J. Friedrich, *Die hethitischen Gesetze* (Leiden 1959).
[17] A. Goetze, *op. cit.*, 114–115.

found on a stone column in Chios.[18] The inscription is a constitutional law, and in its form as a "law column" is clearly to be connected with the slightly earlier κύρβεις (pyramid tablets) of Athens on which extracts from Solon's laws were inscribed. Solon laid the foundations of Attic law, which in Hellenistic times became the model for the whole Greek world. From Dorian lands comes the Code of Gortyn, found on Crete; its discovery has been well described by E. Fabricius.[19]

The remains of Roman law begin with the Lapis Niger inscription and the Twelve Tables, and are vast and diverse. Roman civilization was especially oriented toward law, and its achievements in this field are unsurpassed. In the late medieval period Roman law was revived (the "Reception"), and so its influence has continued to the present. This applies especially to the codes of the Later Empire, the *Codex Theodosianus* issued in A.D. 438 by Theodosius II and Valentinian III,[20] the *Codex Iustinianus* of A.D. 534,[21] and the collection of laws issued subsequent to the latter by Emperor Justinian, the *Novellae*.[22] These works, together with the *Institutiones* of Justinian, a "beginner's textbook," and the *Digesta*, a collection of extracts from the older jurists, form a monumental structure of law unique in history.[23]

Administrative documents abound; only a few can be mentioned here. At the courts of the ancient Near East official record was kept of the more important events in palace and empire. These "court journals" (called βασιλικαὶ διφθέραι by the Greeks) were documents which were used primarily for control of the bureaucracy. We find them at the court of the Persian king as well as the king of Israel,[24] later at the court of Alexander the Great (the so-called Ephemerides). This material is lost, but we can form an idea of what the "court journals" were like from surviving extracts on papyrus from bureaucratic "administrative journals."[25] Roman ad-

[18] M. N. Tod, *Greek Historical Inscriptions* I (ed. 2, 1946), no. 1.

[19] J. Kohler and E. Ziebarth, *Das Stadtrecht von Gortyn* (Göttingen 1912); E. Fabricius, "Eine Forschungsreise in Kreta vor 60 Jahren," *NJA* (1941), 161 ff.

[20] Eds. Th. Mommsen and P. M. Meyer, 1905.

[21] *Corpus Iuris Civilis* II, ed. P. Krüger (ed. 10, 1929).

[22] *Ibid.* III, eds. R. Schoell and W. Kroll (ed. 5, 1928).

[23] *Institutiones, Digesta,* and *Novellae* published in *Corpus Iuris Civilis* I, eds. P. Krüger and Th. Mommsen (ed. 15, 1928).

[24] E. Täubler, *Tyche* (Leipzig and Berlin 1926), 218 and 221.

[25] U. Wilcken, "Ὑπομνηματισμοί," *Philologus* 53 (1894), 80 ff.

ministration had an analogous institution in the *commentarii* of magistrates.[26] Administrative lists also played an important role in Antiquity; for example, we have a document called the "Court and State Calendar" of King Nebuchadnezzar,[27] we have lists of Attic archons and Roman consuls, and from the beginning of the fifth century A.D. we have a complete manual of the civil and military dignitaries of the Later Roman Empire, the *Notitia Dignitatum*.

A related group of documents are "administrative directives," known to us mainly from papyri. Thus we have from Tebtunis (P. Teb. III.703) the directives issued at the end of the third century B.C. by the Ptolemaic minister of finances, the dioiketes (διοικητής) to a subordinate, probably an oikonomos (ὀικονόμος). This important document has been compared with the directive issued by the Vizier Rechmire of the XVIIIth dynasty.[28] Equally well known is the extract from the directives issued to the Idios Logos, a high imperial finance official in Roman Egypt, under Antoninus Pius or Marcus Aurelius.[29] Similar documents are known from the Hittite culture.[30]

In the hieratic Wilbour Papyrus published by A. H. Gardiner[31] we have a priceless document from the age of Rameses V (c. 1150 B.C.) describing the measurement and taxation of Egypt's cultivated land. This document is equally important for the administrative and social history of ancient Egypt, and raises the question of how far related institutions of the Ptolemaic period (e.g., the διαγραφὴ σπόρου) were influenced by those of the Pharaonic period.

Among the "administrative documents" of the Roman Empire are the letters of Pliny the Younger to Emperor Trajan and his replies, published as book ten of Pliny's *Letters*.[32] They reveal much

[26] A. v. Premerstein, *RE* IV, 732 ff.
[27] E. Unger, *Theologische Literatur-Zeitung* 50 (1925), 481 ff.
[28] K. Sethe, "Die Einsetzung des Vezirs unter der 18. Dynastie," *Untersuchungen zur Geschichte* Ägyptens V.2 (1909).
[29] W. Schubart, *Ägyptische Urkunden aus den staatlichen Museen zu Berlin* (*BGU*), vol. V.1 (1919); W. Graf Uxkull-Gyllenband, *ibid.*, vol. V.2 (1934: commentary).
[30] E. V. Schuler, *Hethitische Dienstanweisungen für höhere Hof und Staatsbeamte* (Graz 1957).
[31] A. H. Gardiner, *The Wilbour Papyrus* (2 vols. of text, 1 vol. of plates, Oxford 1941–1948).
[32] Cf. Plinius Minor, *Opera*, ed. M. Schuster (Leipzig 1958).

about imperial problems and illuminate the spirit of imperial administration in the provinces. The basic decision made by Trajan
on the handling of Christians (*Ep.* X. 96, 97) was of fundamental
historical importance.[33]

Mention of Pliny's *Letters* brings us to a group of writings which
illuminate politics and which may be considered either documentary
or literary in character, according as one regards form or content.
These writings are "primary materials of official nature" even though
they are not addressed to rulers or ministries but rather to private
persons, mostly persons connected with official life. Included in
these writings are speeches, memoirs, political pamphlets, and the
like. They all have in common the fact that they arise out of
political struggles and preserve for us the spirit of those struggles.
Usually they have a definite political purpose, such as the self-
justification of a retired statesman or the support of a party's pro-
gram in an anonymous pamphlet, so that these writings are to some
extent political propaganda.

In the category of speeches, memoirs, and pamphlets we are again
confronted with a mass of fragments. From the ancient Near East
there are many inscriptions which one may call memoirs in a wider
sense. Examples are the Assyrian royal inscriptions and the biographic inscriptions of Later Egypt[34]; in the autobiographic inscription of King Idrimi of Alalach on a statue we have a valuable contemporary document of the 15th century B.C. These and similar
inscriptions, however, are only a small fraction of what originally
existed. Similarly, the rich memoir literature of the fifth century B.C., which begins with the work of Ion of Chios entitled
Epidemiai ("Travel Diary"),[35] is represented only by slight remains. In the Hellenistic age the genre was especially cultivated, and
the memoirs of King Pyrrhus and the Aetolian statesman Aratus
are well known because of their use by Plutarch in his biographies
of them. The Romans took over memoir-writing, and examples
were left by Sulla, Cicero, Caesar, and others. Military affairs play
a major part in memoir literature because of the character of the
men who wrote them. In general memoirs follow their own rules

[33] W. Weber, "Nec nostri saeculi est," *Festgabe für K. Müller* (Tübingen
1922), 24 ff.

[34] E. Otto, *Biographische Inschriften des ägyptischen Spätzeit* (Leiden
1954).

[35] *FGrH*, 392; and F. Jacoby, *CQ* (1947), 1 ff.

of style; they do not belong to the grand tradition of historical writing, but are rather modeled on official forms such as the military logbook and the administrative journal. The precision found in such documents, combined with the graces of literary style such as one finds in Xenophon's *Anabasis* and Caesar's *Commentaries*, gives memoirs a fresh and genuine charm usually found only in oral accounts.

Classical rhetoric, which lived on in the trial speeches of the Romans, developed along two main lines: forensic oratory and political oratory. Rhetoric developed in Greece under the influence of Sophism, and it must be judged as an art form. The high aesthetic sensibility of the Athenian public of the fourth century B.C. is indicated by the fact that the surviving speeches of the popular orators Isocrates and Demosthenes are marked by elegance of style and the subtle use of rhythm, and remain unsurpassed classical models of oratory.

The speeches as given were revised for publication. Nevertheless the forensic and political speeches which survive give us the key to a concrete historical situation, and that is what is of interest to the historian. The great political speeches of Demosthenes, for example, are somewhere on the border between oratory and political propaganda. The theory that many of Demosthenes' speeches were never delivered in the form in which they survive, but instead were issued as political pamphlets and indeed were never speeches, is probably correct. The same is true of the political essays of Isocrates, including his *Philippos*[1] 346 B.C. and *Panathenaikos* (completed 339 B.C.).

Roman oratory is derived from Greek. The great opponent of Greek culture, Cato the Censor (234–149 B.C.), was in fact the man who brought Greek oratory to Rome. He was the first to include actual speeches (his own) in his historical work *Origines*, although this was contrary to traditional rules of style. With M. Tullius Cicero (106–43 B.C.) Roman oratory reached its acme, and it is because of Cicero's speeches (and letters) that we know more about the last years of the Roman Republic than about most other periods of ancient history. Cicero's speeches include some which were never delivered, the most important being the five books of the *actio secunda* against Verres and the *Second Philippic* against Mark Anthony. Although we must assume that all fifty-eight surviving speeches of Cicero have been revised, they are nevertheless almost

without exception primary documents of great importance. For
example, whatever we know about the taxation of Sicily and provincial administration in general under the Republic is based almost
entirely on Cicero's *Verrines*. The atmosphere of the great struggle
which erupted at Caesar's death is present in Cicero's *Philippicae*,
modeled after the speeches of that name delivered by Demosthenes
to rouse his fellow-Athenians to resist Philip II of Macedon. Ciceros'
Philippicae recapture the political battles during the months from
September, 44, to April, 43 B.C. The valuable historical material in
Cicero's speeches was recognized in Antiquity, and a thorough
commentary on them was written under Nero by Q. Asconius
Pedianus. Asconius' work was a counterpart to the commentary on
Demosthenes' speeches written under Augustus by Didymus of
Alexandria, part of which has been preserved on papyrus.

The orations of the Roman Empire, both Latin and Greek, are
also valuable sources for the historian, even the sometimes unattrac-
tive type of "ceremonial speeches." Important examples include:
Pliny the Younger's *Panegyric*, which is addressed to Trajan (with
thrusts at the dead tyrant Domitian); the orations of the prominent
Bithynian philospher Dio Chrysostom, especially the first and third
on monarchy, in which Trajan is praised as an exemplar of the
Cynic-Stoic true ruler, and that on the Borysthenites of Olbia; and,
finally, the prize speech by Aelius Aristides on Rome, which gives
important insights into social conditions in the Empire c. A.D. 150.
Some of these speeches have only recently been studied for their
historical value, but all are valuable additions to the authentic historical source materials. Of course the scholar must use them with
careful attention to the contemporary documents, and due allow-
ance must be made for the way in which conditions are seen through
the eyes of a rhetorician, as has long been done with the Attic orators. The manner in which an oration can be drawn upon as an
historical source has been beautifully demonstrated by M. Rostovtzeff and J. H. Oliver in their use of Aelius Aristides' prize speech.[36]

Another literary genre in Antiquity was the letter. Here it is difficult to distinguish official letters from literary ones—that is, letters
which ought to be regarded as essentially part of ancient literature.

[36] M. Rostovtzeff, *Social and Economic History of the Roman Empire*
(ed. 2, ed. P. Fraser, Oxford 1957), 130–134; J. H. Oliver, *The Ruling Power*
(*Transaction Am. Philos. Society*, new series vol. 43, no. 4; Philadelphia
1954.).

This is partly because even the official letter was composed according to particular rules of style, rules which we are only now learning to recognize through comparison with documents on stone and papyrus.

The status of the letter as a recognized literary genre helps explain why many forged letters, both single and collections, were circulated in Antiquity. Just how hard it is to identify what is and what is not genuine is shown by the long debates on the letters of Plato, Demosthenes, and Isocrates; no firm conclusions have yet been reached. It was in this field, incidentally, that modern philology won its first triumphs. The brilliant proof that the "letters of Phalaris" were forgeries (as well as the letters of Themistocles and the Socratics), which the English scholar Richard Bentley (1662–1742) advanced, was and remains one of the pioneer achievements of philological criticism. His conclusions, it is true, have had to be revised in the case of the Socratic letters; E. Bickermann and J. Sykutris have demonstrated through thorough linguistic and historical analysis that the thirtieth letter of the Socratic Corpus, the letter of Speusippos to Philip II of Macedon, is genuine and corresponds to the political developments of 342 B.C.[37] It is a veritable mine of untouched treasure for the ancient historian, and the fact that it is constantly being increased ensures that there will always be new problems to solve.

The ancient pamphlets take us into the world of political controversy. They were often published in the form of an "open letter," and were very common in Antiquity, especially in epochs of political change such as at the end of the Roman Republic and during the struggle between the Roman Empire and Christianity. Often it is difficult in individual cases to draw the line between pamphlet, letter, and oration. To the category of pamphlets in a wider sense one should add political satires such as those written at Rome by Lucilius under the Republic and by Seneca (*Apocolocyntosis Divi Claudii*) under the Empire. They share with pamphlets the object of criticizing existing political and social conditions and of developing from this viewpoint, on occasion, suggestions for

---

[37] E. Bickermann and J. Sykutris, *Speusipps Brief an König Philipp* (*Berichte über die Verhandlungen der Sächsischen Akademie der Wissenschaften, phil.-hist. Klasse*, vol. 80, no. 3; Leipzig 1928); cf. R. Harder, *Philologus* 85 (1930), 250 ff., and J. Sykutris, *Die Briefe des Sokrates und der Sokratiker* (*Studien zur Geschichte des Altertums* 18; Paderborn 1933).

improvement. Works such as the *Constitution of the Athenians*, written by an unknown author during the first years of the Peloponnesian War, or the two *Epistles to Caesar*, supposedly written by Sallust, are worthy of attention not so much because of their specific suggestions as for their quality as documents of contemporary history, which they mirror directly.

Finally, the category of "primary sources" also includes the mass of inscriptions and papyri, which gives us valuable information on the population, economy, social conditions, religion, and cults of Antiquity. This material will be discussed below under "basic disciplines."

BIBLIOGRAPHY

PRIMARY SOURCES: There exists no modern collection of ancient primary sources. Our knowledge of the history of the ancient Near East rests almost entirely on such sources, historiography as understood in the West never having developed there. Basic information is provided in modern narrative works, particularly Eduard Meyer's *Geschichte des Altertums*, which has extensive discussions of the sources of ancient Near Eastern history. For Egyptian sources see E. Drioton and J. Vandier, *L'Égypte* (ed. 3, 1952: in the "Clio" series). A useful work is the translated collection of sources edited by J. B. Pritchard, *Ancient Near Eastern Texts Relating to the Old Testament* (ed. 2, Princeton 1955). Egyptian documents are collected and translated in J. H. Breasted, *Ancient Records of Egypt* (4 vols., Chicago 1906–1907); this work is useful both for Egyptologists and for laymen, though the original texts must be used for historical and philological research.

FOR MESOPOTAMIA there is the old collection of the cuneiform texts edited in the 19th century, *Keilinschriftlichen Bibliothek* I–III (1889–1892) ed. E. Schrader, IV (judicial and commercial texts) ed. Peiser, V (Amarna tablets, now replaced by Knudtzon's edition) ed. H. Winckler, VI (mythic and epic texts) ed. P. Jensen. This work has been rendered obsolete in large part by later research, and has been replaced by volumes in the series *Vorderasiatischen Bibliothek*, in particular: I.1 (1907): *Die sumerischen und akkadischen Königsinchriften*, ed. F. Thureau-Dangin; IV (1912): *Die neubabylonischen Königsinschriften*, ed. S. Langdon; VI (1914): *Babylonische Briefe aus der Hammurapidynastie*, ed. A. Ungnad. Besides, see G. A. Barton, *The Royal Inscriptions of Sumer and Akkad* (New Haven 1929). An important publication is the series *Neu-*

babylonische Rechts- und Verwaltungsurkunden, eds. M. San Nicolò and A. Ungnad (Leipzig, since 1928). The texts from Mari have been by now partly edited: *Archives royales de Mari* I–VIII, eds. G. Dissin, C. F. Jean, J. R. Kupper, J. Bottéro, *et al.* (Paris 1946–1957).

ASSYRIAN SOURCES: Collected and translated by D. D. Luckenbill, *Ancient Records of Assyria and Babylon* (2 vols., Chicago 1926–1927), but the work is not entirely trustworthy. Important text editions include: *Die Inschriften der altassyrischen Könige* [up to Salmanassar I], eds. E. Ebeling, B. Meissner, and E. F. Weidner (Leipzig 1926); *Une rélation de la 8me campagne de Sargon*, ed. F. Thureau-Dangin (Paris 1912); *Die Inschriften Assarhaddons, Königs von Assyrien*, ed. R. Borger (*Archiv für Orientforschung*, Beiheft 9, Graz 1956); *Assurbanipal und die letzten assyrischen Könige* (3 vols., ed. M. Streck, *Vorderasiatische Bibliothek* 7.2, 1916), and Th. Bauer, *Das Inschriftenwerk Assurbanipals* (*Assyriol. Bibliothek*, new series, vol. 2, 1933); C. Gadd, *The Fall of Nineveh* (London 1923: end of the Assyrian empire in 612 B.C.); D. J. Wiseman, *Chronicles of Chaldean Kings (626–556 B.C.) in the British Museum* (1956); R. C. Watermann, *Royal Correspondence of the Assyrian Empire* (Ann Arbor 1930–1935); R. H. Pfeiffer, *State Letters of Assyria (722–625 B.C.) (American Orient Series* 6, Philadelphia 1935).

HITTITE MATERIALS: Those available up to 1957 are surveyed in the excellent work of A. Goetze, *Kulturgeschichte des Alten Orients, Kleinasien* (ed. 2, 1957), 82 ff. The most important editions include: *Keilschrifttexte aus Boghazköi* (14 vols., eds. Figulla, Forrer, Weidner, Hrozný, Otten, *et al.*, Leipzig 1916–1921, 1954–1963) abbreviated *KBO*; *Keilschrifturkunden aus Boghazköi*, 39 vols., published by the Berlin *Staatliche Museen* (1921–1963), abbreviated *KUB*. A brief review of the sources for the Achaemenid empire is given by A. Christensen in *Kulturgeschichte* (ed. 1, 1933), 205 ff. Important text editions include: *Keilinschriften der Achämeniden*, ed. F. Weissbach, in the above-mentioned *Vorderasiatische Bibliothek* III (1911); E. Herzfeld, *Altpersische Inschriften* (Berlin 1938); R. G. Kent, *Old Persian: Grammar, Texts, Lexicon* (ed. 2, New Haven 1953); *Persepolis Treasury Tablets*, ed. G. G. Cameron (Chicago 1948); G. Posener, *La première domination perse en Égypte* (Cairo 1936), with a collection of hieroglyphic documents related to Persian rule.

HEBREW HISTORY: A useful survey of the sources is given in B. A. Jirku, *Geschichte des Volkes Israel* (1931), 13 ff.

GREEK HISTORY: The standard guides to the sources and general introductions do not sufficiently distinguish between primary sources and other material. Thus, for example, the chapter "Documentary and Monumental Sources" in C. Wachsmuth's *Einleitung in das Studium der alten Geschichte* (1895), 241 ff., is unsatisfactory. A limited selection is given by M. Cary, *The Documentary Sources for Greek History* (Oxford 1927).

For a survey of the available primary materials see the appendices to the *Cambridge Ancient History* and H. Bengtson, *Griechische Geschichte* in *Müller* III.4 (ed. 3, 1965). A new survey, based on a sharp distinction between the different categories, would be welcome. For further information see the section below on basic disciplines.

ROMAN HISTORY: We have an excellent manual, A. Rosenberg, *Einleitung and Quellenkunde zur römischen Geschichte* (Berlin 1921), in which a clear distinction is made between primary documents and works of history. Excellent surveys are contained in *Gercke-Norden* III.2 (ed. 3, 1933) by Joseph Vogt on the Republic (pp. 34–45) and E. Kornemann on the Empire (pp. 147–149 and 167 ff.); these are the best summaries available. Another valuable work is A. Piganiol, *Histoire de Rome* (ed. 5, Paris 1962).

EDITIONS AND STUDIES: The Amarna Tablets have been published by J. A. Knudtzon, *Die El-Amarna-Tafeln* (Leipzig 1915), and commented upon by Ed. Meyer, *Geschichte des Altertums* II (ed. 2), 334 ff., and by Br. Meissner, *Könige Babyloniens und Assyriens* (1926). For more recent discoveries see A. Götze, *Hethiter, Churriter und Assyrer* (Oslo 1936), 47.

NEW ARAMAIC DOCUMENTS: G. R. Driver, *Aramaic Documents of the 5th Century B. C.* (Oxford 1954); E. G. Kraeling, *The Brooklyn Museum Aramaic Papyri: New Documents of the 5th Century B.C. from the Jewish Colony at Elephantine* (New Haven 1953). For older documents see A. E. Cowley, *Aramaic Papyri of the 5th Century B.C.* (Oxford 1923).

DEAD SEA SCROLLS: Out of the large literature only a few selected items can be noted: H. Bardtke, *Die Handschriftenfunde am Toten Meer* (Berlin 1952), and O. Eissfeldt, *Einleitung in das Alte Testament* (ed. 2, Tübingen 1956), 788 ff. Good introductions are M. Burrows, *The Dead Sea Scrolls* (New York 1955), and *More Light on the Dead Sea Scrolls* (New York 1958). Other recent literature is listed in Chr. Burchard, *Bibliographie zu den Handschriften vom Toten Meer* (1957).

HITTITE TREATIES: E. F. Weidner, *Politische Dokumente aus Kleinasien: Die Staatsverträge in akkadischer Sprache aus dem*

Archiv von Boghazköi (*Boghazköi-Studien* 8–9, 1923); J. Friedrich, *Staatsverträge des Hattireiches in hethitischer Sprache* I (*Mitt. d. Vorderasiatisch-Ägyptischen Gesellschaft* 31.1, 1926) and II (*ibid.* 34.1, 1930).

LIBRARY OF ASSURBANIPAL: It contains copies of all surviving works of Sumerian and Babylonian literature, including mythology, magic, astronomy, medicine, and history. See the surveys by O. Weber, *Die Literatur der Babylonier und Assyrer* (Leipzig 1907), 27 ff., and C. Bezold, pp. 95 ff. in *Rahmen der Weltgeschichte*, ed. J. V. Pflugh-Hartung (Berlin 1910).

HISTORY OF WRITING: The best introduction is by F. W. v. Bissing and A. Rehm in *Handbuch d. Archäologie* I, ed. W. Otto, (1939), 147 ff. and 182 ff. See also K. Sethe, *Vom Bild zum Buchstaben: Die Entstehungsgeschichte der Schrift* (*Unters. zur Geschichte u. Altertumskunde Ägyptens* 12, 1939), ed. S. Schott; S. Schott, *Hieroglyphen* (*Abh. Akad. Mainz* 24, 1950); G. R. Driver, *Semitic Writing from Pictograph to Alphabet* (ed. 2, London 1954). Very impressive is the monograph of J. Friedrich, *Entzifferung verschollener Schriften und Sprachen* (Berlin 1954).

LANGUAGE: On Egyptian see H. Grapow, *Vom Hieroglyphischen-Demotischen zum Koptischen* (*SB Preuss. Akad.* 1938, no. 28); on Greek see P. Kretschmer, in *Gercke-Norden* I (ed. 3, 1927), 66 ff.; ed. Schwyzer, *Griechische Grammatik* I (1939), 45 ff.; on Latin see G. Devoto, *Storia della lingua di Roma* (Bologna 1940) and V. Pisani, *Manuale storico della lingua latina* (vols. 2–4, Turin 1950–1953). An important work is E. Norden, *Die antike Kunstprosa* (2 vols., ed. 2, Leipzig and Berlin 1909); it surveys the development of literary language in Greece and Rome from the beginning down to the Renaissance.

CULTURAL SIGNIFICANCE OF LANGUAGE: W. von Soden, *Zweisprachigkeit in der geistigen Kultur Babyloniens* (*SAWW* 235, no. 1, 1960); L. Hahn, *Rom und der Romanismus im griechisch-römischen Osten* (1906); L. Hahn, *Zum Sprachenkampf im römischen Reich bis auf die Zeit Justinians* (*Philologus*, Supplement 10, 1907), 675 ff.; H. Zilliacus, *Zum Kampf der Weltsprachen im oströmischen Reich* (Diss. Helsinki 1935).

ANCIENT TREATIES: Besides the works mentioned in the text, see F. Hampl, *Die griechische Staatsverträge des 4. Jahrhunderts v. Chr. Geb.* (Leipzig 1938), with review by F. Wüst, *Gnomon* 1938, 367 ff. An example of a juristic study is A. Heuss, "Abschluss und Beurkundung des griechischen und römischen Staatsvertrages," *Klio* 27 (1934), 14 ff., 218 ff. On Greek documents see A. Wilhelm, *Beiträge zur griechischen Inschriftenkunde* (Vienna 1909), 227 ff., and G. Klaffenbach, *Bemerkungen zum griechischen Urkunden-wesen* (*SDAW* 1960, no. 6).

LAW: For the ancient Near East these works are particularly important: A. Scharff and E. Seidl, *Einführung in die ägyptische Rechtsgeschichte bis zum Ende des Neuen Reiches* I (*Ägyptolog-ische Forschungen* 10, 1929); E. Seidl, *Ägyptische Rechtsgeschichte der Saiten- und Perserzeit* (*ibid.* 20, 1956); E. Seidl, *Ptolemäische Rechstgeschichte* (ed. 2, Glückstadt 1962); M. San Nicolò, *Rechts-geschichtliche Beiträge im Bereich der keilschriftlichen Rechtsquel-len* (Oslo 1931); P. Koschaker, "Keilschriftrecht," *ZDMG*, series 2, vol. 14 (1935), 1 ff. Collections of legal documents from the ancient Near East include: A. Falkenstein, *Die neusumerischen Gerichtsurkunden* (*Abh. Munich, phil-hist. Kl.*, ser. 2, nos. 39, 40, 44; 1956–1957); G. Driver and J. Miles, *The Babylonian Laws* (2 vols., 1955–1956), and *Assyrian Laws* (Oxford 1935). For Hellenic law see H. v. Prott and L. Ziehen, *Leges Graecorum sacrae* (2 vols., 1896–1901); P. Meyer, *Juristische Papyri* (Berlin 1920), excellent also as an introduction to legal papyri in general. We do not yet have a general survey of Greek law, but important monographs in-clude: K. Latte, *Heiliges Recht* (Tübingen 1920); E. Weiss, *Grie-chisches Privatrecht* I (Leipzig 1923); J. Partsch, *Griech. Bürg-schaftsrecht* I (Leipzig 1909); F. Pringsheim, *The Greek Law of Sale* (Weimar 1950); H. Lipsius, *Das attische Recht und Rechts-verfahren* (3 vols., Leipzig 1905–1915); H. Weber, *Attisches Prozessrecht in den attischen Seebundstaaten* (Paderhorn 1908). For the relations between Greek and Roman law the fundamental work remains L. Mitteis, *Reichsrecht und Volksrecht in den östlichen Provinzen des römischen Kaiserreichs* (Leipzig 1891); an interesting work is W. Kunkel, *Herkunft und soziale Stellung der römischen Juristen* (Weimar 1952).

Roman legal sources are available in several collections. C. Bruns and O. Gradenwitz, *Fontes Iuris Romani* (2 vols., ed. 7, Tübingen 1909) with *Additamenta* (2 vols., 1912); P. Girard, *Textes de droit romain* (ed. 6, Paris 1937); G. Baviera, C. Ferrini, G. Furlani, and V. Arangio-Ruiz, *Fontes Iuris Romani Anteiustiniani* (3 vols., Flor-ence 1940–1943), outstanding for bibliography. On the codes of the later Empire (Theodosius II and Justinian) the best historical account is by E. Kornemann, "Die römische Kaiserzeit," in *Gercke-Norden* III.2 (ed. 3, 1933), 166–167.

Roman legal sources are surveyed by Th. Kipp, *Geschichte der Quellen des römischen Rechts* (ed. 4, Leipzig 1919), a good intro-duction; L. Wenger, *Die Quellen des römischen Rechts* (Vienna 1953). A useful survey is B. Kübler, *Geschichte des römischen*

Rechtes (Leipzig 1925). The characteristics of Roman law are discussed by F. Schulz, *Principles of Roman Law*, tr. M. Wolff (Oxford 1936), reviewed by M. Gelzer, *Gnomon* (1935), 1 ff.; also by W. Otto, *Antike Kulturgeschichte* (*SB Munich* 1940, no. 6), 35 ff.; P. Koschaker, *Europa und das römische Recht* (Munich 1947). For Roman private law see Jors, Kunkel, and Wenger, *Römisches Privatrecht*, based on the work of P. Jors (ed. 3, Berlin 1949); M. Kaser, *Römisches Privatrecht* (2 vols., Munich 1955–1959), with extensive references to sources and studies. Historians will find useful H. Berger, *Encyclopedic Dictionary of Roman Law* (*Trans. Am. Philosophical Society*, n.s., vol. 43, no. 2; Philadelphia 1953).

ADMINISTRATIVE DOCUMENTS: Court journals of the Achaemenids are cited in *Ezra* 4.15, 6.2; *Esther* 2.23, 6.1; Diodorus 2.33.4 (Ctesias). Alexander's Ephemerides are discussed by H. Berve, *Das Alexanderreich auf prosopographischer Grundlage* I (Munich 1926), 50; F. Altheim, *Weltgeschichte Asiens im griechischen Zeitalter* I (1947), 1115 ff.; L. Pearson, *Historia* 3 (1954–1955), 429 ff. The *Notitia Dignitatum* has been edited by O. Seeck (1876), discussed by A. Piganiol, *Histoire de Rome* (ed. 5, 1962), 476 and 590, also by H. Nesselhauf, *Die spätrömische Verwaltung der gallisch-germanischen Länder* (*Abh. Berlin, phil.-hist. Kl.*, 1938, No. 2), 37 ff. For the general history of late Antiquity, not just for Church history, the documents of the General Councils are of great importance, and they should be studied in the editions of Eduard Schwartz, which are discussed by A. Rehm, *E. Schwartz' wissenschaftliches Lebenswerk* (*SB Munich* 1942, no. 4), 74 and 41 ff.

MEMOIRS: Surveyed by G. Misch, *A History of Autobiography in Antiquity* (2 vols., London 1950). For the Idrimi inscription see S. Smith, *The Statue of Idri-mi* (London 1949), reviewed by H. Bengtson in *Der Aquädukt C. H. Beck 1763–1963* (Munich 1963), 48 ff. Memoirs of Pyrrhus are in *FGrH* 229 (but one should not doubt their authenticity, as does Jacoby), those of Aratus are in *ibid.*, 231, discussed in F. Walbank, *Aratos of Sicyon* (Cambridge 1933). The older Roman memoirs, including those of Cicero, have been lost; among the authors of such works were M. Aemilius Scaurus (consul 109 B.C.) and P. Rutilius Rufus (consul 105 B.C.), on whom see G. Hendrickson, "The Memoirs of Rutilius Rufus," *CP* 28 (1933), 153 ff. In the Sullan age memoirs were written by Q. Lutatius Catulus (*Liber quem de consulatu et de rebus gestis suis scripsit*) and by Sulla himself; he left a work of 22 books (*Commentarii rerum gestarum*). Cicero composed a work in Latin and Greek about the high point of his life, his consulate of 63 B.C. Extant are the military memoirs of Caesar, the *Commentarii rerum gestarum*

Galliae (7 books) which were completed in 51 B.C. to which Hirtius, his friend and comrade, later added an eighth book; also Caesar's *De bello civili* (3 books), on which see K. Barwick, "Caesars Bellum Civile," (*SB Leipzig* 99, no. 1, 1951); K. Abel, *MH* 15 (1958), 56 ff.; J. Collins, *AJP* 80 (1959), 113–132. Their clarity and originality make Caesar's military works a valuable source. According to Hirtius (*B. Gall.* 8, praef. 5) Caesar wrote the *Commentarii* in order to give historians knowledge of the events; that is, Caesar did not regard the *Commentarii* as examples of history in the great tradition, but rather as preliminary works.

See the comments of Cicero, *Brutus* 75.26; cf. U. Knoche, "Caesars Commentarii, ihr Gegenstand und ihre Absicht," *Gymnasium* (1951), 139–160; F. Bömer, "Der Commentarius," *Hermes* 81 1953), 210 ff. On Caesar's writings see A. Klotz, *Cäsarstudien* (Leipzig 1910); E. Howald, *Vom Geist antiker Geschichtsschreibung* (Munich 1944), 113 ff.; A. Kappelmacher, "Das Wesen der antiken commentarii und der Titel von Cäsars Gallischem Kriege," *Wiener Blätter* 1 (1922), 2 ff. The successive publication of the *Commentarii* has recently been again argued, convincingly, by K. Barwick, *Caesars Commentarii und das Corpus Caesarianum*, (*Philologus*, Supp. 31, no. 2, 1938). His view can at least be regarded as a good working hypothesis, and it also explains the introduction of ethnographic and geographic excursus in the *Bellum Gallicum*; cf. F. Beckmann, *Geographie und Ethnographie in Cäsars Bellum Gallicum* (Dortmund 1930), reviewed by H. Fuchs, *Gnomon* (1932), 241 ff. On the reliability of Caesar see G. Walser, *Caesar und die Germanen* (*Historia, Einzelschrift* 1, Wiesbaden 1956); M. Rambaud, *L'art de la déformation historique dans les Commentaires de César* (Paris 1952), is certainly too negative.—The *Corpus Caesarianum* includes three other works: *Bellum Alexandrinum, Bellum Africum, Bellum Hispaniense*; the first was written by A. Hirtius, the other two by unknown officers of Caesar. For the editions see *Schanz-Hosius* I (ed. 4, 1927), 348 ff. A good discussion of the main problems is given by V. Stegemann, *Gaius Julius Caesar: Der Gallische Krieg* (ed. 2, 1956), with German translation and commentary.

Many memoirs were written during the imperial period, briefly reviewed by E. Kornemann in *Gercke-Norden* III.2, 148. Augustus wrote an autobiography; fragments in E. Malcovati, *Caesaris Augusti Imp. Operum Fragmenta* (ed. 3, Turin 1948); his well known *Res Gestae*, generally called *Monumentum Ancyranum* since the most important copy was found at Ankara (the ancient Ancyra), was published in a classic edition by Th. Mommsen, *Res gestae divi*

Augusti (ed. 2, Berlin 1883); new discoveries have rendered it obsolete, and the best editions are those of J. Gagé, *Res gestae divi Augusti* (Paris 1935 and 1950), and of H. Volkmann, *Bursians Jahresbericht* 276, *Supp.* (1942). See too Volkmann's edition in *Kleine Texte* 29/30 (1957).—Tiberius' autobiography: its existence was doubted by C. Cichorius, *Römische Studien* (Leipzig 1922), 388 ff. Further material is given in H. Peter, *Die geschichtliche Literatur über die römische Kaiserzeit* I (Leipzig 1897); it is dated, but as a survey not yet replaced.

ORATORY: For Greek history in the fourth century B.C. the speeches of Isocrates, Demosthenes, Aischines, and others are a basic source. Modern works, especially the *Griechische Geschichte* of K. Beloch, have used the speeches to reconstruct the course of events. Historical use in modern times has been furthered above all by the work of P. Wendland, *Beiträge zur athenischen Politik und Publizistik des 4. Jahrhunderts* (*SB Göttingen* 1910); also important are the works of U. Wilcken, e.g., *Philipp II von Makedonien und die panhellenische Idee* (*SB Berlin* 1929, no. 18); A. Momigliano, *Filippo il Macedone* (Florence 1934), and the many articles noted therein; P. Treves, *Demostene e la libertà greca* (Bari 1933); W. Jaeger, *Demosthenes* (Berlin 1939). An important study is E. Buchner, *Der Panegyrikos des Isokrates* (*Historia, Einzelschrift* 2, 1958). —The older work by F. Blass, *Die attische Beredsamkeit* (3 vols., ed. 2, Leipzig 1887–1898), is useless for historical studies. On the other hand a mine of information is to be found in A. Schaefer, *Demosthenes und seine Zeit* (3 vols., ed. 2, Leipzig 1885–1887). Much remains to be done.

The most important editions: full collections include *Oratores Attici*, ed. I. Bekker (5 vols., Paris 1823–1824); eds. G. Baiter and H. Sauppe, (2 vols., Zurich 1839–1843). Both editions are outdated. Individual editions include: *Antiphon*, eds. F. Blass and Th. Thalheim (Leipzig 1914) and ed. L. Gernet (Paris 1923); *Andokides*, eds. Blass and Fuhr (ed. 4, Leipzig 1918), and see F. Ferckel, *Lysias und Athen* (Diss. Würzburg 1937); *Isokrates*, ed. E. Drerup (1906, but only vol. 1 published), and the older edition of Benseler-Blass (1889–1898, reprinted), and see K. Münscher in *RE* and P. Treves, *Isocrate, il Panegirico, con introd. e note* (Turin 1932); *Demosthenes*, eds. Fuhr and Sykutris (incomplete), along with the *OCT* edition of Butcher-Rennie (1903 ff.); also edition with commentary of the 2nd and 3rd Philippics by P. Treves (Naples 1936); *Aischines*, ed. Blass (Leipzig 1908), along with the edition of Schultz (1856), important for its Scholia, and the recent edition of V. Martin and G. de Budé (Paris 1927); *Hypereides*, ed. Jensen (ed. 2, Leipzig 1917); *Demades*, ed. De Falco (Pavia 1932); *Isaios*, ed. P. Roussel (Paris 1922 and 1960); *Lykurgos*, ed. F. Durrbach (Paris 1932).

The fragments of the speeches of Roman orators have been collected by E. Malcovati, *Oratorum Romanorum Fragmenta* (Turin 1930–1955). Cicero's speeches have been edited by A. Clark and W. Peterson (Oxford 1900–1910), and also in the Teubner series (1918 ff.). Revision of the speeches before publication is discussed by J. Humbert, *Les plaidoyers écrits et les plaidoiries réelles de Cicéron* (Paris 1925); see too the remarks of E. Bickel, *Geschichte der römischen Literatur* (Heidelberg 1937), 368 ff. on *notae Tironianae*, the ancient shorthand. Asconius has been edited by Giarratano (1920); on his personality see G. Wissowa, *RE* II, 1524 ff., *Schanz-Hosius* II (ed. 4, 1935), 731 ff. Pliny's panegyric of Trajan has been edited by M. Durry, *Pline le Jeune: Panégyrique de Trajan* (Paris 1938).

Greek rhetoric under the Empire: Dio Chrysostom of Prusa (c. A.D. 40–120) has been edited by H. v. Arnim (1893–1896) and G. de Budé (1916–19). An important work for the historian is H. v. Arnim's *Leben und Werke des Dio von Prusa* (Berlin 1898).— Aelius Aristides (A.D. 117–189) from Hadrianutherai in Mysia: edition by B. Keil, but only vol. 2 (Berlin 1898, repr. 1959), otherwise the outdated edition of W. Dindorf (Leipzig 1829). On the prize speech *To Rome* see the older studies given in *Schmid-Stählin* II.2 (ed. 6, 1924), 706; also M. Rostovtzeff, *Social and Economic History of the Roman Empire* (ed. 2, 1957), 130–134; J. Oliver, *The Ruling Power* (*Transactions Am. Philos. Soc.*, n.s., vol. 43, no. 4; Philadelphia 1954). For general studies see A. Boulanger, *Aelius Aristide et la sophistique dans la province d'Asie au IIe siècle de notre ère* (Paris 1923); U. v. Wilamowitz-Moellendorff, *Der rhetor Aristeides* (*SB Berlin* 1925), 333 ff.—Libanius of Antioch (314–c. A.D. 394), ed. R. Foerster (1903–1927); important recent studies by P. Petit, *Libanius et la vie municipale à Antioche au IVme siècle apr. J.-C.* (1956), and *Les étudiants de Libanius* (1956).— Themistius (c. A.D. 317–388), edited by W. Dindorf (1832); on his career see W. Stegmann in *RE*.—On the historical role of late Greek orators see R. Laqueur, "Über die Beeinflussung der Reden des Themistios durch die Kaiser," *Probleme der Spätantike* (Stuttgart 1930), 27 ff., and especially J. Straub, *Vom Herrscher-Ideal in der Spätantike* (Stuttgart 1939).—An interesting document is the speech of Synesius, later bishop of Cyrene, "On Kingship," delivered in A.D. 399 before Emperor Arcadius in Constantinople, in which among other things much is said against the growing influence of Germans at court; cf. O. Seeck, *Geschichte des Unterganges der antiken Welt* V, 315 ff.; J. Pando, *The Life and Times of Synesius of Cyrene* (Washington 1940); C. Lacombrade, *Le discours sur la royauté de Synésios de Cyrène* (Paris 1951).

EPISTOLOGRAPHY: Surveys: H. Peter, *Der Brief in der römischen Literatur* (*SB Leipzig* 20, No. 3, 1901, repr. 1965); O. Seeck, "Der antike Brief," *Deutsche Rundschau* (1907), no. 1, 5 ff. An excellent synthesis is J. Sykutris, "Epistolographie," *RE*, Supp. V (1931), 185 ff. On forged collections see F. Dornseiff, *Echtheitsfragen antik-griechischer Literatur* (Berlin 1939), 36: the forgeries aimed to portray an individual's personality as seen in his relations with others, the form is "semi-dramatic."—Editions: an old collection of the Greek material is R. Hercher, *Epistolographi Graeci* (Paris 1873). Cicero's letters have been edited by L. Purser (Oxford 1901–1903) and H. Sjögren (Leipzig 1914 ff.). Chronological arrangement makes useful the edition of R. Tyrrell and L. Purser (7 vols., London 1890–1901, partly in second or third editions), and of L. Constans and J. Bayet, *Cicéron: Correspondence* (5 vols., CB, Paris 1934–1964), as yet extending only to March 25, 49 B.C. For discussion see O. Schmidt, *Der Briefwechsel des Cicero von seinem Prokonsulat in Cilicien bis zu Cäsars Ermordung* (Leipzig 1893). Excellent historical use of the letters figures in E. Meyer, *Cäsars Monarchie und das Principat des Pompeius* (ed. 3, 1922); see more recently M. Gelzer, *RE* VII A.1, 827 ff. The work of J. Carcopino, *Les secrets de la correspondance de Cicéron* (2 vols., Paris 1947), is as stimulating as his other works, but his hypothesis—that the collection was made in 34–32 B.C. with Octavian in mind, and was published by Atticus, Tiro, and young M. Cicero—cannot be proved, and is indeed unlikely.—The letters of Pliny the Younger have been edited by M. Schuster (Leipzig 1958). For the chronology see T. Mommsen, *Gesammelte Schriften* IV (1906, repr. 1966), 366 ff.; W. Otto, *SBAW* 1919, No. 10; R. Syme, *Tacitus* II (1958), 656 ff.; Otto argues against Mommsen, Syme supports him. For late Antiquity we can only refer to the letters of Symmachus (c. A.D. 340–402) in Latin, edited by O. Seeck, *MGH, AA* 6.1 (1883); and as a document of the Greek East the letters of Libanius (see above under Oratory).

BENTLEY'S CRITICISM: Boyle's edition of the letters of Phalaris in 1695 caused Richard Bentley to write his polemical work, *Dissertation on the Epistles of Phalaris, Themistocles, Socrates, Euripides, and others, and the Fables of Aesopus* (London 1697). Boyle replied with *Dr. Bentley's Dissertation on the Epistles of Phalaris and the Fables of Aesopus* (1698), and to this Bentley then countered with the work for which he is best known, *A Dissertation upon the Epistles of Phalaris with an Answer to the Objections of the Hon. Ch. Boyle* (1699), also published in Bentley's *Opuscula philologica* (Leipzig 1781), translated by W. Ribbeck (Leipzig 1857).

OTHER CONTROVERSIES: Of the many works concerned with the letters ascribed to Plato we shall note only one: G. Pasquali, *Le lettere di Platone* (Florence 1938), with full references. On the letters attributed to Demosthenes see U. v. Wilamowitz, *Hermes* 33 (1898), 496 ff., and H. Sachsenweger, *De Demosthenis epistulis* (Diss. Leipzig 1935). An important source for Ptolemaic Egypt is the letter of Aristeas to Philocrates, which gives the legendary story of the translation of the Jewish Torah into Greek under Ptolemy II Philadelphus. The name of the author as well as that of the addressee are both false, and the letter surely dates from the end of the second century B.C. It has been edited by P. Wendland (Leipzig 1900), more recently by Moses Hadas, *Aristeas to Philocrates* (New York 1951); cf. H. I. Bell, *Cults and Creeds in Graeco-Roman Egypt* (Liverpool 1953), 44–45.

ANCIENT PAMPHLETS: *The Constitution of the Athenians* by "Pseudo-Xenophon" has been edited with translation and commentary by E. Kalinka (Leipzig 1913); more recent literature includes K. Gelzer, *Die Schrift vom Staate der Athener* (*Hermes, Einzelschrift* 3, 1937), on which see review of H. Diller, *Gnomon* (1939), 113 ff.; E. Rupprecht, *Die Schrift vom Staate der Athener* (*Klio*, Beiheft 44, 1939); H. Frisch, *The Constitution of the Athenians* (Copenhagen 1942), with good bibliography including German studies, among them M. Volkening, *Das Bild des attischen Staates in der pseudoxenophontischen Schrift vom Staate der Athener* (Diss. Münster 1940).

LUCILIUS: Edited by F. Marx (1904–1905); see studies of C. Cichorius, *Untersuchungen zu Lucilius* (Berlin 1908); F. Münzer, "Lucilius und seine Zeitgenossen," *NJA* (1909), 180 ff.; N. Zerzaghi, *Lucilio* (Turin 1934). Further references in *Schanz-Hosius* I (ed. 4, 1927), 150 ff.

SALLUST: from the struggles at the end of the Roman Republic come the "open letters to Caesar" attributed to Sallust, edited by A. Kurfess, *C. Sallustii Crispi epistulae ad Caesarem senem* (Leipzig 1955). The question of Sallust's authorship has been much studied recently, but there is still no agreement. Their authenticity ic accepted by G. Carlsson, *Eine Denkschrift an Cäsar über den Staat* (Lund 1936), W. Steidle, *Historia*, Einzelschrift 3 (1958), 95 ff., and K. Büchner, *Sallust* (1960), 40 ff.; it is denied by E. Fraenkel, *JRS* 41 (1951), 192 ff., in a review of a monograph by

M. Chouet (Paris 1950), and by R. Syme, *MH* 15 (1958), 46 ff. Probably counterfeit is the "Invective against Cicero" attributed to Sallust, as argued by F. Oertel, *RhM* 94 (1951), 46 ff.; nevertheless its authenticity is maintained by K. Büchner, *Sallust* (1960), 20 ff.

SENECA's *Apocolocyntosis Divi Claudii* has been edited with commentary by Buecheler, *Symbolae philolog. Bonnens.* (1864), 31 ff.; the commentary is reprinted in Buechler's *Kleine Schriften* I (Leipzig 1915), 439 ff. Other editions are those of O. Weinreich (Berlin 1923), with German translation (see also his *Römische Satiren* [Zurich 1949]), and C. Russo (Florence 1948).

PLINY's *Panegyricus* addressed to Trajan is an important source for kingship under the Principate; for the later Empire we have the works of the so-called Panegyricists, which have been edited by Baehrens (1911) and E. Galletier, *Panégyriques latines* (3 vols., Paris 1949–1955), and have been historically interpreted by J. Straub, *Vom Herrscher-Ideal in der Spätanike* (Stuttgart 1939).

2. HISTORIOGRAPHY

Although valuable information on individual events and persons of Antiquity is furnished by the primary material, whole periods would nevertheless remain obscure were it not for the ancient historians, who give us a continuous view of the ancient world from the Persian Wars to late Antiquity. In Herodotus we have a valuable account of the crucial struggles between Greeks and Persians; Thucydides and his continuators give us a history of the Peloponnesian War.

For the Principate we have valuable accounts in the histories of Tacitus and Cassius Dio, and in the biographies of Suetonius; they cannot outweigh the inscriptions and papyri, and in fact the latter play a continually larger part in modern historical study. On the whole, however, the ancient historians still provide the basis for every modern study, and at many points they are our only source. Therefore the study of ancient historiography must necessarily be the center of the discipline of ancient history.

Since the modern historian of Antiquity must rely so heavily on ancient historiography he should be conscious of the particular problems connected with it. Every student of history must, as Eduard Schwartz emphasized,[38] be influenced by intellectual drives. Scholarly study is connected with personal wishes and values. This

[38] "Vergangene Gegenwärtigkeiten," in *Gesammelte Schriften* I, 47.

peculiar mixture of intellectual and emotional elements makes every work of history a personal statement.

In short, historiography is not simply a part of the sources; it is a part which has been given artistic form. Whoever aims to describe the past as an organic whole, to describe it in terms of chronological or topical categories, is working within a tradition which reaches back through modern, medieval, and Byzantine writers to the beginning of Western historiography.

Historiography is—as its name indicates—a creation of Greek culture, for it was among the Greeks that men first became conscious of the importance and uniqueness of personality. In the ancient Near East there was no historiography worthy of the name. There were attempts to write history—the Hittite annals, the Hebrew histories—but never in the ancient Near East was the past described for its own sake. Even the "Chronicle" of the New Babylonian era did not give rise to a genuine historiography.

Nor is there any real connection between the annals and chronicles of the ancient Near East and the origins of Western historiography. Nevertheless, the narratives of the ancient Sumerians and Babylonians resemble the first historical works of the Greeks in that neither makes a sharp distinction between myth and history. In both traditions the human and the divine are intertwined.

Myth, saga, and historical reality are the elements which come together in Homer's *Iliad*. Here the war between Greeks and Trojans around the sacred fortress of Ilium is history elevated to the world of myth, and yet it has an undeniable basis in historical reality.

The Greek word *historein* (ἱστορεῖν) means "to explore, discover," and in fact earlier Greek historiography is simply a record of "discoveries," especially about foreign peoples and lands known to the writer through stories and accounts.

At the beginning of Greek—and therefore of all Western—historiography is the figure of Hecataeus of Miletus (c. 500 B.C.). His works concerned travels and genealogies, and thus embody two fundamental aspects of Greek historical thought; the *Journey round the World* (Περίοδος γῆς) reflects the outlook of cosmopolitan Ionia, for it touches on Europe, Asia, Libya, and even the Western Mediterranean, while the *Genealogies* (Γενεηλογίαι) cover the period from the heroic age to the beginning of colonization and so give an outline of "early Greek history" which shows a remarkable grasp of continuity already present in this pioneer historian. The latter work begins with this bold declaration: "Hecataeus of Miletus says this: 'The following is the account of Hecataeus the Milesian. What I write here is what seems true to me, for the traditions of the Greeks are contradictory and seem to me foolish.' "[39] Nevertheless Hecataeus had no conception of historical criticism, for he still had the naïve belief that he could discover the truth simply through the use of logic and common sense.

The first real historian of the West, therefore, is not Hecataeus but rather Herodotus of Halicarnassus (c. 485–c. 424 B.C.). In his work ethnography is combined with a true historical interpretation which shapes and unifies his account of the great conflict between Greeks and barbarians. Herodotus developed his interpretation under the influence of Periclean Athens, for it was political events there that spurred him on to his studies. Ionia had declined in importance after the ill-fated Ionian Revolution (500–494 B.C.), and leadership in politics and culture had passed to Athens.

At the basis of Herodotus' account was information which he gained personally or received from tradition. Although Herodotus made use of Hecataeus' works,[40] the tradition on which he relied was primarily an oral one, the memories still alive in Greece of the heroic age of the Persian Wars. Herodotus used this tradition according to his own tastes, and so drew from it much that is essentially anecdotal. There are undeniable weaknesses in his work, the result of the intellectual limitations of his age, but nevertheless one must admire Herodotus' grasp of his subject and the masterly way in which he organizes his material. He recognized the central significance of the Persian Wars and the Greek victories at Marathon, Salamis, and Plataea, and he indicates why they were turning points in world history. His conception of the struggle as a clash between Persian imperialism and Greek freedom reveals the dominant forces of the age and is the foundation for deeper understanding of the historical development.

Herodotus and Thucydides had as contempories those historians who used to be grouped under the unsatisfactory term "logographers" (which means simply "prose writers"); among them were Dionysius of Miletus, Hellanicus of Lesbos, and Charon of Lampsacus. None of their works are extant, but we do have fragments

[39] *FGrH* 1.1.
[40] H. Diehls, *Hermes* 2 (1887), 411 ff.

and these reveal much about these historians' premises and methods. They wrote genealogies and ethnographies, and also local histories (Charon) and chronicles (Hellanicus). Although concern with a general interpretation of Greek history is not entirely absent, their works lack, so far as we can judge from the fragments, the central concepts which characterize the histories of both Herodotus and Thucydides. Of the local histories we should mention one, the Atthis (Ἀτθίδες); it recounts Athenian history, and was written by a series of historians ("Atthidographers") beginning with Hellanicus (c. 500–c. 415 B.C.) and ending with Philochorus (c. 340–263/2 B.C.).

Thucydides of Athens (c. 460–c. 400 B.C.) is the historian of the Peloponnesian War and therefore the creator of the historical monograph. Compared with Herodotus his analysis is deeper and is concerned with the underlying forces in history. Thucydides lived through the war between Athens and the Peloponnesians and even had a part in it himself; he gradually came to see its various stages as parts of one great struggle. In his account of the great Greek civil war we have the first work of Western historiography in which attention is directed to the underlying forces which shape the development of peoples and states. His distinction between the immediate occasion and the fundamental causes of the war, his description of the interrelation between military and diplomatic developments, his emphasis on the role of chance in history, his refusal to rely on supernatural explanations, and his description of historical development in terms of the logical conditions—all these were new and contributed to the deepening of historical interpretation. Because he shaped his subject so completely, Thucydides achieved what he had set out to do, to leave for posterity "an everlasting possession" (κτῆμα εἰς ἀεί); it is addressed to every person desiring to understand the basic direction of historical development which lies behind individual historical events. From this point of view we are justified in regarding Thucydides as the man who raised history from a subjective study and made it a scholarly discipline.

Thucydides' "discoveries" concern military history, arranged by winters and summers; the international politics of the period are discussed only where they are essential for understanding the course of events. Nevertheless Thucydides was influenced by the intellectual developments of the age, especially the Sophistic movement. This is particularly evident in the speeches; formal analysis reveals that they are neither historical nor authentic, but are rather means by which the historian examines situations from different points of view and on the basis of different values.

Thucydides' history ended abruptly at 411 B.C., and was continued by three successors: Xenophon, Theopompus, and Cratippus. Of these Xenophon of Athens (c. 430–c. 354 B.C.) owes a somewhat unjustified fame to fortune, for only his continuation, *Hellenica* (Ἑλληνικά), has survived. It covers events down to the battle of Mantinea (362 B.C.), which marked the collapse of the brief Theban hegemony (371–362) and the end of Greek history in the eyes of Xenophon and his contemporaries. Like the *Anabasis* the *Hellenica* is a lively and vigorous account, but as an historical work it has serious faults. Xenophon's preference for Sparta and Spartan values hindered him from doing justice to the Thebans and even his fellow-countrymen, the Athenians.

Form and content were unified by Thucydides with a mastery not achieved again until Sallust and Tacitus, and military and political events are the core of his work. In both respects Greek historiography of the fourth century differed, and it turned away more and more from politics, its origin. Moreover Greek historians were confronted with a difficult situation, for as the polis system of the Greeks declined the Macedonian monarchy under Philip II and then Alexander gained great power and glory; both Philip and Alexander were Macedonians rather than Greeks, even though they adopted Greek culture and furthered its expansion. Neither Philip nor Alexander found an historian equal to the challenge of describing his deeds. Theopompus of Chios (b. c. 380 B.C.) did write a *Philippika* in which he described Philip II as the greatest man in European history,[41] but no Greek was as yet able to evaluate objectively the great king and his still greater son.

During the reign of Alexander and then the struggles of the Diadochi (which lasted more than 40 years, 323–281 B.C.) war was the dominant concern, and it was then that military history arose. It was raised to a recognized literary genre by a king, Ptolemy I (d. 238 B.C.), founder of the Ptolemaic dynasty. Military history was characterized by a plain, circumstantial style, based on the traditional "military journal," (Ὑπομνήματα); as a form of historiography it represented a reaction against both the increasingly

[41] *FGrH* 115.27.

dominant trend to rhetoric and also the legends which began to develop around Alexander's figure when he was still alive and eventually took shape as the Alexander romance.

Alexander's expedition and the Macedonian conquest of Asia opened up a new world to Greek ethnography. The works of Nearchus of Crete, Onesicritus of Astypalaea (both contemporaries of Alexander), and Megasthenes of Olynthus (who visited India under Seleucus I), are connected in form with the earlier travel literature of the Ionians. These early Hellenistic ethnographers provide the basis for the wide-ranging studies of Poseidonius of Apamea (c. 130–c. 50 B.C.); his work in turn influenced Caesar and Tacitus, and through them the historians of late Antiquity, Cassiodorus (c. A.D. 480–575), the historian of the Ostrogoths, and Procopius of Caesarea, who wrote under Justinian colorful accounts of barbarian peoples.

Most of Hellenistic historiography has been lost, including the work of Hieronymus of Cardia, friend of Eumenes, on the Diadochi. This is largely due to the great change in literary standards under the Roman Empire caused by the "Atticism" of the Second Sophistic. Apart from a large number of fragments which have been recently collected by Felix Jacoby in his *FGrH* we have only one important Hellenistic historian's work, that of Polybius of Megalopolis (c. 200–c. 120 B.C.), and indeed only a part of that. Polybius was himself an active politician, a leader of the Achaean League, and after the subjection of Greece in 167 B.C. he was deported to Italy. There he was received into the circle of Scipio Aemilianus, and in his history he set himself the task of describing Rome's rise to dominance during the years 220–168 B.C., a rise which he had himself witnessed in part.

Polybius was convinced that study of history teaches lessons about political life, and so he became the founder of "pragmatic historiography."[42] Indeed the work of Polybius is concerned with "universal history," justified by the argument that in this period the Romans had by their conquests made the entire Mediterranean world into a single *Orbis Romanus*. He begins in his introduction at the point where Timaeus of Tauromenium (c. 345–c. 250 B.C.) had ended: 264 B.C. Timaeus had already written a general history of the western Mediterranean, covering Sicily, Italy, and Carthage.

---

[42] From πραγματικός, "concerning statesmanlike action"; cf. M. Gelzer, *Festschrift für C. Weickert* (Berlin 1955), 87 ff.

This universal approach was then adopted by Polybius, with the difference that he made Rome the center of his account.

Later Polybius continued his history down to 145/44 B.C., and this in turn was continued by Poseidonius of Apamea in his *Histories*, which extended to the age of Sulla. Poseidonius' history is known to us primarily through the quotes in Diodorus, who wrote a *World History* under Augustus. This universal history was essentially a compilation.

Hellenistic universal history, to some extent foreshadowed by the *Histories* of Ephorus of Cyme who wrote under Alexander, is the expression of a new attitude towards world history. Rome's military and diplomatic successes marked the end of the Hellenistic state system, and Hellenistic culture began gradually to give way to Roman culture and morality. Yet Roman culture was itself deeply indebted to Hellenism, and this applies to Roman historiography.

The Romans aimed to impose their laws on the world, and for them historiography was not a scholarly discipline but rather a continuation and a weapon of their policies. It is therefore not a coincidence that the first Roman historians were active politicians, men such as Q. Fabius Pictor, L. Cincius Alimentus, M. Porcius Cato. Fabius' *Histories* were written c. 200 B.C.; and like those of his younger contemporary Cincius (praetor 210 B.C.) they were in Greek. Their form, based on the annalistic account of events year by year, takes us to the origin of Roman historiography, the official record of events drawn up each year. This form continued to be followed to the end of the Republic, and was followed by Livy in the great work he composed under Augustus and later by Tacitus in his last work, *Ab excessu divi Augusti libri*, which he himself also called *Annales*.

Nevertheless, despite its formal reliance on the Roman annals, Fabius Pictor's work is a genuine product of cosmopolitan Hellenism. Like the works of the Egyptian Manetho of Sebennytus (c. 300–250 B.C.) and the Babylonian priest of Bel Berossus (c. 280– B.C.), both also written in Greek, Fabius' history testifies to the dominating influence of Hellenistic culture which not even the Romans could resist.

The first historical work in Latin is the *Origines* by M. Porcius Cato (234–149 B.C.) of Tusculum, and indeed it is the beginning of Latin prose literature. It too, however, is shaped by Hellenistic traditions, unmistakable even in its title, for *origines* is the equivalent of Hellenistic "foundation stories." Cato broke with the annalistic form, and as a Latin he directed his attention not only to Rome itself but also to all of Italy. This Italian approach represented a distinct break with the Rome-centered viewpoint, which in fact—as the work of Tacitus shows—was never really overcome. *Roma caput mundi*—that is especially true of Roman historiography.

In the last century of the Republic another form besides the annalistic appeared, the historical monograph. It was introduced into Roman literature by L. Coelius Antipater with his *Bellum Punicum*, an account of the Second Punic War written sometime after 121 B.C. But the finest examples of the monograph were the works of Sallust: *Coniuratio Catilinae*, *Bellum Iugurthinum*, and, especially, *Historiae*. Sallust was influenced by the theories of Poseidonius, the Hellenistic historian and polymath; his monographs give an impressive picture of the Roman Republic in decline, a picture painted in dark colors and yet not without an element of pride and admiration. All works of this gifted artist reflect a bitter resignation, and their impact is increased by the techniques which Sallust learned from Thucydides.

Just as Sallust's works are closely connected with the declining Republic, so Livy's history is an expression of the Augustan restoration of Roman traditions. Livy of Patavium (59 B.C.–A.D. 17) was as little like a modern scholar in his research methods as Sallust or Tacitus, for he never consulted archives. His huge work, which evoked astonishment in Antiquity, was simply the compilation of a literary man trained in rhetoric who took his material wherever it was ready to hand. Thus his account of early Roman history is derived from the annalists, then beginning with book 20 he drew increasingly on the work of the Greek historian Polybius. Livy's long work (142 books!) became the "standard" Roman history, not the least reason being his fine style and his warm patriotic feeling for the uniqueness of the Roman tradition. During the following centuries it was regarded as an unsurpassed and unsurpassable model, and its reliability—which was simply that of its sources—was not questioned until modern times, when Louis de Beaufort published his *Dissertation sur l'incertitude de cinq premiers siècles de l'histoire romain* (Utrecht 1738).

Livy is part of the Augustan age, and stands at a turning point in history, for the principate of Augustus marks, among other things, the beginning of a new epoch. The period is characterized by its use of two languages and by the conflict between monarchial and republican traditions. Nevertheless the Augustan age was on the whole not favorable to historiography, for the genuine study of history cannot flourish in the shadow of a court. That had been demonstrated in the Hellenistic age, when not a single historian of note appeared in the kingdoms (Polybius came from the world of the Achaean League, and Poseidonius spent his formative years in Rhodes).

A contemporary of Livy is the Greek rhetorician Dionysius of Halicarnassus; his *Roman Archaeology* was published in 7 B.C. It describes Rome's history to 264 B.C., but of its 20 books only the first ten are extant, although we have most of book 11 and fragments of the others. For the historian the work is a disappointment, since Dionysius used unreliable Roman annalists as sources.

Two universal historians appeared in the Augustan age, an indication that men realized a new age was dawning. One is Pompeius Trogus, a Romanized Celt (Vocontian) who still put Hellenistic history at the center of his work. The other is a Hellenized Syrian, Nicholas of Damascus, friend of King Herod of Judaea. His voluminous *World History* in 144 books reached from earliest times to the death of Herod in 4 B.C. Only fragments of the work survive, and it cannot be considered an independent source except for the author's own time; even here one must be cautious, since Nicholas showed himself unreliable at times in his other writings (which included a biography of Emperor Augustus).

In general the historiography of the Principate is characterized by emphasis on the dynastic principle and by predominance of the biographic element, especially in connection with the personalities of the Roman emperors. A document of this tendency is the *Historia Romana* of the officer Velleius Paterculus, published A.D. 30; in it Caesar Augustus and above all the reigning emperor, Tiberius, figure prominently. The revival of the Alexander myth in the early Empire is indicated by the *Historiae Alexandri Magni* of the rhetorician Q. Curtius Rufus.

However, the most important achievement is the work of Cornelius Tacitus (A. D. 55–c. 120), the historian who is for us the purest embodiment of traditional Roman aristocratic values. His *Historiae* ("contemporary history") covers the years from A.D. 69 to the death of Domitian in A.D. 96; of this only the account of the first two years is extant. His *Annales*, or, to use its official title, *Ab excessu*

divi Augusti libri (from the death of Augustus to the end of the
Julio-Claudian dynasty), survives only in part: books 1–5 (beginning), 6 (end), 11 (end), 16 (end incomplete), so that we lack
the accounts of most of A.D. 29–31 and all of A.D. 37–47 and 66
(end)–68. One can appreciate these works only if one understands
them as the political credo of a man who never fully accepted the
Principate. Although he applauds Trajan, the *optimus princeps*, and
the adoptive monarchy, as is shown by the speech which he has
Galba deliver at the adoption of Piso (*Hist.* 1:15–16), he remains a
devotee of the lost *libertas* which could flourish only under the *res
publica*, not the *principatus*. Although the authorities on which Tacitus relied gave him (and Suetonius too, see below) fully formed interpretations of the individual emperors and their reigns, Tactius
himself made these interpretations more sweeping and wove them
into a single splendid tapestry. That is his great achievement, attained through his reflective and psychological style, unsurpassed
in its impressionistic power, albeit at times a detriment to historical
truth. Pessimism shaped Tacitus' world view, and because of that
his works do not do justice to the Empire and its values.

Livy displaced the annalists, and Tacitus did the same to the
imperial historians who were his predecessors. For this reason we
know hardly anything but the names of the works of Aufidius Bassus, Pliny the Elder, Cluvius Rufus, and Fabius Rusticus. Only a
few works escaped Tacitus' competition, among them the histories
written in Greek by Flavius Josephus (c. A.D. 37–100). These
works were the history of his people, doughty foes of Rome: *Jewish
Antiquities*, a history of the Jews from earliest times to the beginning
of the great revolt in A.D. 66; and an earlier work, *The Jewish War*,
about the great revolt in the reigns of Nero and Vespasian. While
Tacitus remained silent under the hated Domitian, Josephus the
renegade published his *Antiquities* in A.D. 93 and dedicated it to
an imperial freedman.

In the second century Greek culture enjoyed a great revival. Witnesses to the revival are the historical works of Arrian of Nicomedia
(c. A.D. 95–175), a Bithynian consular, especially his *Anabasis of
Alexander* as well as his *Indica*, along with the more thoughtful
work of Appian of Alexandria (born c. A.D. 160), *Roman History*,
arranged according to where Rome's wars were fought.

No work, however, indicates the superiority of the Greeks in
historiography so clearly as the *Roman History* of Cassius Dio

Cocceianus (c. A.D. 155–235), also a native of Bithynia. He chose Livy, not Tacitus, as his model, and in eighty books traced Rome's history from its beginnings to A.D. 229; the parts about his own times are a valuable primary source. For the Byzantines, Dio was a link between the new and the old Rome, and thereby performed a service in cultural history. His historical role may be compared to that of Polybius in the Hellenistic age.

Another Greek historian, although not the equal of Dio, was his younger contemporary Herodian, a Hellenized Syrian. His history of the Empire from the death of Marcus Aurelius to A.D. 238 is in eight books, and lacks any distinct point of view; nevertheless the loss of other contemporary works renders it of some importance.

Besides biography and chronography, which reached their high point in the early fourth century with the work of Eusebius of Caesarea, a new historical genre appeared after Constantine set Christianity on a par with other religions—church history. It took its place with the publication of Eusebius' *Ecclesiastical History*, which covered the subject to A.D. 324 in ten books. Eusebius ignored the classical rules of style and included in his work the original texts of documents, some complete, and so preserved valuable primary materials for posterity. His work is the classic apologia of the Universal Church, formerly persecuted and now triumphant. It has had many imitators.

Other works of church history are Lactantius' *De mortibus perse-cutorum* (published c. A.D. 318), and the world history of the Spanish presbyter Paulus Orosius called *Adversus paganos* (published shortly after A.D. 417). Orosius wrote his work at the suggestion of St. Augustine and depended heavily on Livy's history.

St. Augustine (A.D. 354–430) exercised a remarkable—one might almost say epoch-making—influence, especially through the philosophic history he wrote late in life, *De civitate Dei*. This work, composed after the shock caused by Alaric's sack of Rome (A.D. 410), established the Christian concept of two coexisting worlds, the City of God and the Earthly City, and transmitted it to the Middle Ages.

Ammianus Marcellinus (c. A.D. 332–c. 400), a pagan from Syrian Antioch, wrote a secular history at the end of the fourth century. It is one of the masterpieces of Latin historiography, and indeed the last important historical work of classical culture, by then in its decline. The use of Latin by a Greek reveals the complexity of the age. Ammianus began his work as a continuation of Tacitus' *His-*

toriae, but the first part has been lost, and we have only his description of the troubled quarter century A.D. 353–378 (books 14–31); Ammianus was, in fact, an active participant in the events of these years. At the center of his work stands the figure of the last pagan on the throne of the Caesars, Emperor Julian, for whom Ammianus had high regard.

None of the Greek histories written in the fifth and early sixth centuries can begin to compare with Ammianus'. Not until the reign of Emperor Justinian (A.D. 527–565) does a genuine historian appear, Procopius of Caesarea. He described Justinian's wars in his *History* (eight books, like Appian's arranged according to where the wars were fought). Then he wrote his *Secret History*, in which he revealed his dislike of the "tyrant" Justinian; he could do this without fear since Justinian had died by then.

With Procopius the historiography of Antiquity came to an end. The *World Chronicles* of John Malalas (sixth century) from Syrian Antioch and of another writer from that city, John Antiochenus (seventh century), lead into the Middle Ages, when this form of history became dominant.

In general, ancient historiography shows one characteristic. Whether one thinks of Herodotus or Thucydides, of the historians of the fourth century B.C. or of Xenophon, Theopompus, Ephorus, Polybius, or Livy—all wrote either about their own times or, if they attempted universal history, at greater length with more detail as soon as they came to their own times. Thus about a third of Herodotus' history describes the invasion of Xerxes in 480/79 B.C.; Ephorus, who wrote a universal history in Greek from the Dorian invasion on, used ten of his thirty books to describe the last 50 years, from the King's Peace of 387/86 to 340 B.C. The same is true of the Roman annalists and even of Livy. Ancient historiography is therefore in large part devoted to contemporary history, taken in a broad sense. "Men did not study the past in order to discover how things actually happened, but rather to learn how the existing state of affairs had come about" (F. Münzer).

Biography was sharply distinguished in both theory and practice from ancient historiography. History was concerned with πράξεις, *res gestae*, deeds; biography aimed to portray the ethos, the physical and mental characteristics of its subjects, that they might appear as heroes and models. As to the origins of ancient biography, its roots lay partly in the development of the "literary portrait" (see, for example, Xenophon's *Agesilaus* and Isocrates' *Evagoras*), partly in the study of man's psychology, cultivated especially in the Peripatetic School of Aristotle (e.g., Theophrastus' *Characters*).

Biography was fully developed by the mid-Hellenistic age, but the first extant works in the genre were written by a contemporary of Cicero, the *De viris illustribus* of Cornelius Nepos. This short work clearly derives from the Hellenistic genre of biography, "About Famous Men." The high point of ancient biography was reached in Plutarch of Chaeronea (c. A.D. 45–c. 125). In his work, *Parallel Biographies* (Βίοι παράλληλοι), he arranged his subjects in pairs, a Greek and a Roman in each, in order to compare them. The points of reference are generally superficial, and are emphasized in a concluding comparison ("synkrisis") of each pair. His collection included twenty-three pairs and four single biographies. The learned Plutarch collected a great mass of material, much of it from first-rate sources. Since we have lost so much of Hellenistic literature it is impossible for us to identify his sources. In the introduction to his Alexander (ch. 1) Plutarch tells us that he considered anecdotal information more important for his purposes than facts about deeds, however important they might be in world history. This genuine biographic emphasis in Plutarch explains why he is rather indifferent to the underlying forces of history, and in fact he touches on them only on rare occasions.

What has been said about Plutarch's *Parallel Lives* applies also to the imperial biographies of C. Suetonius Tranquillus (c. A.D. 75–c. 160), private secretary (*ab epistulis*) to Hadrian. Suetonius made the first attempt to describe the lives of the emperors (from Julius Caesar to Domitian) within the traditions of dynastic history. Nevertheless he remains on the superficial level, mixing valuable historical information with trivial court gossip, and as a result his work leaves an ambiguous general impression. Nevertheless Suetonius as biographer of the Roman emperors started a tradition, and in the age of the Severi he was followed by Marius Maximus; his work is not extant, but we can estimate its character from the citations in later historians. He is the connecting link with the *Scriptores Historiae Augustae,* a work which claims to be written by six different writers of the age of Diocletian and Constantine, but is in reality a forgery by some writer under Julian or Theodosius I. Its veiled anti-Christian attitude along with its idealization of Julian (hidden in the praise of the Syrian Severus Alexander, actually an insignificant emperor) reveals the forgery as a product of pagan propaganda in the period A.D. 350–400. The biographies cover the period from Hadrian to Carus and his sons (A.D. 117–285). The work poses many still unsolved problems, which will require the efforts of philologists, historians, numismatists, historians of religion, and others to solve. In any case, scholars rightly regard the work as a "popular work," not a product of historical thought. Jacob Burck-hardt's judgment on the authors of the *Historia Augusta* sums up the matter: "They are fools, but interesting."

In the *Caesares* of Sextus Aurelius Victor (written c. A.D. 360) the content has been abbreviated to the length of a compendium, in accordance with the taste of the time. It is in the lives of the saints that we find the link with the biographic literature of the Middle Ages. Of these an important example is the *Life of St. Severinus* by Eugippus (written c. A.D. 511); the *Life* gives a colorful picture of conditions in the Danubian provinces in the period A.D. 450–500.

In the *Vita Caroli Magni* by Einhard the spirit of Antiquity is revived in the form shaped by Suetonius. Thus it became for future ages the classic model of imperial biography.

This summary has been too brief to do more than trace the main lines of ancient historiography from its beginnings to the end of Antiquity. Distinctions and nuances have been ignored, and indeed it is here that the work of the individual student must begin. The student who wishes to grasp the essence of the ancient historians must set himself the task of understanding the individuals within the framework of the general development of which they were a part, and must then judge what they aimed to do and how far they succeeded. He who wishes to comprehend historians such as Thucydides or Sallust must be able to understand their lives as well as their books, and he must be conscious of the inner connection between life and work. Above all, however, the student must attempt to understand the principles of historical research ancient historians followed.

Finally, no study of the ancient historians can ever be fruitful unless the student uses scholarly commentaries. For this reason the following bibliography is important.

BIBLIOGRAPHY

GENERAL: No adequate survey of ancient historiography exists. A valuable summary of information in the ancient literary tradition is given by A. Schaefer and B. Nissen, *Abriss der Quellenkunde der griechischen und römischen Geschichte* I (ed. 4, 1889) and II (1881); also useful are the sections on the historians in C. Wachsmuth, *Einleitung in das Studium der Alten Geschichte* (Leipzig 1895). For orientation see first the histories of literature—of Greek by Schmid and Stählin, and of Roman by Schanz and Hosius, both in *Müller*. Admirable also is the *Griechische Literaturgeschichte* (2 vols., Heidelberg 1926–1934), unfortunately incomplete. Valuable surveys are included in the work edited by P. Hinneberg, *Kultur der Gegenwart* I.8 (ed. 3, 1912), in which U. von Wilamowitz-Moellendorff writes on Greek literature, F. Leo on Roman literature. Leo also published a *Geschichte der römischen Literatur* (Berlin 1913), regrettably not completed. The beginning student will find especially helpful the outlines of Greek literature (E. Bethe and M. Pohlenz) and Roman literature (E. Norden) in *Gercke-Norden* I.3–4 (ed. 3, 1923–1924); Norden's essay was supplemented by bibliographic essays by E. Koestermann (1933) and H. Fuchs (1952). There have been great advances in particular fields, noted in the survey of Roman studies by H. Fuchs, *MH* 4 (1947), 147–198. Valuable also are A. Lesky, *A History of Greek Literature*, tr. J. Willis and C. de Heer (London and New York 1966); G. De Sanctis, *Studi di storia della storiografia greca* (Florence 1951); F. Jacoby, *Abhandlungen zur griechischen Geschichtsschreibung* (Leiden 1956); M. Laistner, *The Greater Roman Historians* (Berkeley and Los Angeles 1947); *Histoire et historiens dans l'antiquité: Fondation Hardt Entretiens* 4 (Vandoevres-Geneva 1958), with essays on Herodotus, Thucydides, Tacitus, etc.

Briefer surveys of ancient historiography are given in the historical works of E. Meyer, *Geschichte des Altertums*; K. Beloch, *Griechische Geschichte*; G. De Sanctis, *Storia dei Romani*; and these volumes in *Müller*: H. Bengtson, *Griechische Geschichte* (ed. 3, 1965), and B. Niese and E. Hohl, *Grundriss der römischen Geschichte* (1923). For the Roman Empire see the survey by E. Kornemann in *Gercke-Norden* III.2 (ed. 2, 1933), 149 ff.

COLLECTIONS OF FRAGMENTS: The serious student of ancient historiography will consult the great collections of the extant fragments of otherwise lost works: C. and T. Müller, *Fragmenta Historicorum Graecorum*, abbreviated *FHG* (5 vols., Paris 1841–1870);

F. Jacoby, *Die Fragmente der griechischen Historiker*, abbreviated *FGrH* (Berlin and then Leiden 1923-). The latter work has an outstanding commentary; it is to take the place of Müller's old work, but is not yet completed. For the Roman historians: H. Peter, *Historicorum Romanorum reliquiae* I (ed. 2, 1914) and II (1906).

EDITIONS OF HISTORIANS: Beside the standard texts of the Teubner and Oxford series (*BT, OCT*), there are also the editions of the Loeb Classical Library (*LCL*) of most works, generally with useful texts and with English translations; similarly a few historians appear in the Collection Budé (*CB*) with French translation. See below for individual historians.

HISTORIOGRAPHY IN THE ANCIENT NEAR EAST: Survey by R. Laqueur, *NJA* 7 (1931), 489 ff.; also H. Guterbock, "Die historische Tradition und ihre literarische Gestaltung bei Babylonern und Hethitern," *ZA* N.F. 8 (1934); W. v. Soden, "Leistung und Grenze sumerischer und babylonischer Wissenschaft," *WG* 2 (1936), 411 ff., 451.

HITTITE ANNALS: A. Goetze, *Kulturgeschichte des Alten Orients, Kleinasien*, in *Müller* (ed. 2, 1957), 174–175; A. Kammenhuber, *Saeculum* 9 (1958), 136–155.

HISTORIOGRAPHY OF THE ISRAELITES: E. Meyer, *Geschichte des Altertums* II.2 (ed. 2, 1931), 198 ff.; G. Holscher, "Die Anfänge der hebräischen Geschichtsschreibung," *SHAW* 1941/42, No. 3.

CHALDAEAN CHRONICLES: D. Wiseman, *Chronicles of Chaldaean Kings (626–556 B.C.) in the British Museum* (London 1956); on this see also H. Bengtson, *Historia* 6 (1957), 499–502. For a general view see B. Landsberger and T. Bauer, *ZA* 37 (1927), 61 ff.; W. v. Soden, *WG* 2 (1936), 455. In the same category are the so-called Diadochi Chronicles, about wars in Babylonia after the death of Alexander the Great: S. Smith, *Babylonian Historical Texts* (London 1924), 140 ff., 154 ff.; see on this W. Otto, *SBAW* 1925, Schlussheft, p. 1.

HOMER'S ILIAD: For the history of the Homeric Question see M. Nilsson, *Homer and Mycenae* (London 1933). New interpretations of Homer's relation to his society were suggested by W. Schadewaldt, "Homer und sein Jahrhundert," *Das Neue Bild der Antike* (1942), 51 ff., and *Von Homers Welt und Werk* (ed. 2, Stuttgart 1951). More recent bibliography is given in H. Bengtson, *Griechische Geschichte*, (ed. 3, 1965), 61, note 2. Also important: H. Lorimer, *Homer and the Monuments* (London 1950). Survey: A. Lesky, *Die Homerforschung in der Gegenwart* (Vienna 1952). Most recent review article: A. Heubeck, *Gymnasium* 71 (1963), 43–72.

GREEK HISTORIOGRAPHY: Surveys by J. Bury, *The Ancient Greek Historians* (London 1907, repr. 1958); F. Jacoby, *Klio* 9 (1909), 80 ff.; U. v. Wilamowitz-Moellendorff, *Greek Historical Writing*, tr. G. Murray (Oxford 1908). An individual but interesting work is E. Howald, *Vom Geist antiker Geschichtsschreibung* (Munich 1944), with discussions of Herodotus, Thucydides, and Polybius.

BEGINNINGS OF GREEK HISTORIOGRAPHY: W. Schadewaldt, *Die Antike* 10 (1934), 144 ff.; L. Pearson, *Early Ionian Historians* (Oxford 1939). On the concept ἱστορεῖν see B. Snell, "Die Ausdrücke für den Begriff des Wissens in der vorplatonischen Philosophie," *Philologische Untersuchungen* 29 (1924), 59 ff., and in the *Festschrift für K. Reinhardt* (1952). Hecataeus' fragments are in *FGrH* 1; on his rationalism see A. Momigliano, *Atene e Roma*, n.s. 12 (1931), 133 ff.; G. De Sanctis, *Studi di storia della storiografia greca* (1951), 3 ff.

HERODOTUS: Edition by Hude in the *OCT* (1909), by P. Legrand (Paris 1932–1955); editions with commentary by H. Stein (first publ. 1856 ff., thereafter often repr.) and by W. How and J. Wells (ed. 2, Oxford 1928). Report on more recent editions, commentaries, and translations by G. Grosskinsky, *Gnomon* (1952), 265 ff.–Special edition with commentary: *Herodotus I–III*, by A. Sayce (London 1883: out of date); *Herodotus IV–VI, VII–IX* by R. Macan (2 vols., 1895–1908: basic); *Herodotus 2. Buch* (on Egypt) by Wiedmann (Leipzig 1890), with which see W. Spiegelberg, *Die Glaubwürdigkeit von Herodots Bericht über Ägypten im Lichte der ägyptischen Denkmäler* (*Orient und Antike* 3, Heidelberg 1926); J. Vogt, "Herodot in Ägypten," *Festschrift W. Schmid* (*Tübinger Beiträge* 5, 1929), 95 ff.; H. de Meulenaere, *Herodotus over de 26. dynastie (II.147–III.15)*, in Flemish (Louvain 1951); and an essential work: E. Powell, *A Lexicon to Herodotus* (Cambridge 1938).

Still fundamental for Herodotus' life and work is the article by F. Jacoby, *RE* Supp. II (1913), 205 ff. See also W. Aly, *Volksmärchen, Sage und Novelle bei Herodot und seinen Zeitgenossen* (Göttingen 1921); J. Wells, *Studies in Herodotus* (Oxford 1923), though in part strongly hypothetical; F. Focke, *Herodot als Historiker* (*Tübinger Beiträge* 1, 1927); K. v. Fritz, "Herodotus and the Growth of Greek Historiography," *TAPA* 67 (1936), 315 ff.; M. Pohlenz, "Herodot, der erste Geschichtsschreiber des Abendlandes," *Neue Wege zur Antike* 2 (1937), Nos. 7–8; F. Eggermann, "Das Geschichtswerk des Herodot," *NJA* (1938), 191 ff., 239 ff. (with new interpretations, especially on the conclusion of Herodotus' history); E. Powell, *The History of Herodotus* (Cambridge 1939); J. Myres, *Herodotus, Father of History* (Oxford 1953). A useful work is *Herodot: Eine Auswahl aus der neueren Forschung*, ed. W. Marg (Munich 1962).

LOGOGRAPHERS: Thucydides (1.21.1) uses the term for prose writers, Herodotus included. Modern scholars use it in the sense proposed by F. Creuzer in *Die historische Kunst der Griechen* (1803), to refer to the earlier Greek historians before Herodotus, though this is contrary to Thucydides' usage; cf. Bux, *RE* XIII, 1021 ff.—Their fragments are in *FGrH* I and III. The fragments of the Atthidographers are in *FGrH* III, 323a ff.; cf. Jacoby's fundamental work, *Atthis: The Local Chronicles of Ancient Athens* (Oxford 1949).

THUCYDIDES: Edition by C. Hude (Leipzig 1898–1908, 1908–1913); new edition based on Hude's by O. Luschnat, so far only books 1–2 (ed. 2, Leipzig 1960). Other editions by H. Jones and E. Powell in the *OCT* (1942); with commentary by J. Classen and Steupp (eds. 3–5, Berlin 1900–1922); commentary alone by A. Gomme, *A Historical Commentary on Thucydides* (3 vols., Oxford 1945–1956), going up to 5.24.—Personality and work are discussed by E. Meyer, *Forschungen zur Alten Geschichte* II (Halle 1899), 269 ff.; A. Gomme, *Essays in Greek History and Literature* (Oxford 1937), 156 ff.; H. Berve, *Thukydides* (Frankfurt/Main 1938); G. De Sanctis, *Storia dei Greci* II (1939), 409 ff.; F. Eggermann, "Die Geschichtsbetrachtung des Thukydides," *Das Neue Bild der Antike* 1 (1942), 272 ff. (with bibliography at p. 272, note 1); G. Grundy, *Thucydides and the History of His Age* (2 vols., Oxford 1948); F. Adcock, *Thucydides and His History* (London 1963). Very suggestive are the recent publications of H. Strasburger "Die Entdeckung der politischen Geschichte durch Thukydides," *Saeculum* 5 (1954), 395 ff., and "Thukydides und die politische Selbstdarstellung der Athener," *Hermes* 86 (1958), 17 ff. (especially on the speeches).

More than a century ago F. Ullrich raised the question of Thucydides' original intent; he argued that at first Thucydides planned to describe the Archidamian War alone, and only later came to see the Peloponnesian War as a unity. Followers of this hypothesis ("analysts") receive their strongest support from the co-called second preface at 5.26.1; cf. F. Ullrich, *Beiträge zur Erklärung des Thukydides* (Hamburg 1846), and E. Schwartz, *Das Geschichtswerk des Thukydides* (Bonn 1919–1929), W. Schadewaldt, *Die Geschichtsschreibung des Thukydides* (Berlin 1929), J. de Romilly, *Thucydides et l'impérialisme athénien: La pensée de l'historien et la genèse de l'oeuvre* (Paris 1947–1951), all of which support the "analysts'" view. Their opponents, the "unitarians," maintain that Thucydides from the first intended to describe the whole war, and include, besides E. Meyer: H. Patzer, *Das Problem der Geschichtsschreibung des Thukydides und die thukydidische Frage* (Berlin 1937); J. Finley, Jr., "The Unity of Thucydides' History," *Athenian Studies Presented to W.S. Ferguson* (*HSCP*, supp. 1; Cambridge, Mass. 1940), 225 ff., and his *Thucydides* (Cambridge, Mass. 1942).

On the speeches see F. Eggermann, *DLZ* (1937) 1471 ff., 1503 ff., and in *Das neue Bild der Antike* I (1942), 285 ff.; also O. Luschnat, *Die Feldherrnreden im Geschichtswerk des Thukydides* (*Philologus*, supp. 34, no. 2; Leipzig 1942); F. Adcock, "Thucydides in Book 1," *JHS* 71 (1951), 21 ff. (conservative view).–On the documents see C. Meyer, *Die Urkunden im Geschichtswerk des Thukydides* (Zetemata 10, Munich 1955).

XENOPHON: Editions by Marchant in *OCT* (1900 ff.), by C. Hude in *BT* (1930 ff.), by J. Hatzfeld, *Helleniques* (2 vols., Paris 1949, 1948), with introduction and notes.–Historical criticism: E. Schwartz, *RhM* 44 (1889), 104 ff., 169 ff.; A. Banderet, *Untersuchungen zu Xenophons Hellenika* (Diss. Berlin 1919); H. Breitenbach, *Historiographische Anschauungsformen Xenophons* (Diss. Basel, Freiburg in Switzerland 1950); E. Delebecque, *Essai sur la vie de Xénophon* (Paris 1957).–There is still much dispute regarding Xenophon's premises and purposes in the *Anabasis*, and the extent to which it is derivative.

THEOPOMPUS OF CHIOS: The fragments are in *FGrH* 115; he is discussed by H. Berve, *Das Alexanderreich auf prosopographischer Grundlage* II (1926), no. 365; R. Laqueur, *RE* VA, 2176 ff.

CRATIPPUS: *FGrH* 64. An additional *Hellenica* was discovered in the Oxyrhynchus papyri, eds. Grenfell and Hunt (1909), reprinted in *FGrH* 66; new fragments have been published in *Papiri della Società Italiana* 13 (1949), no. 1304. Edition by V. Bartoletti, *Hellenica Oxyrhynchia* (Leipzig 1959), with bibliography. See especially H. Bloch in *Athenian Studies ... Ferguson* (*HSCP*, supp. 1; Cambridge, Mass. 1940), 303 ff.

PTOLEMY: The attested fragments are given in *FGrH* 138; cf. H. Strasburger, *Ptolemaios und Alexander* (Leipzig 1934); E. Kornemann, *Die Alexandergeschichte des Königs Ptolemaios I von Ägypten* (Leipzig 1935), which however goes too far at times in its reconstruction.

ALEXANDER LEGENDS: On their origin see E. Mederer, *Die Alexanderlegenden bei den ältesten Alexanderhistorikern* (*Würzburger Studien zur Altertumswissenschaft* 8, 1936). The Alexander

Romance (attributed to pseudo-Callisthenes) has been edited by
W. Kroll, *Historia Alexandri Magni* I: *Recensio Vetusta* (Berlin
1926); cf. A. Ausfeld, *Der griechische Alexanderroman* (Leipzig
1907); F. Pfister, "Studien zum Alexanderroman," *Würzburger
Jahrbuch für Altertumswissenschaft* 1 (1946), 29 ff., and his many
other publications; R. Merkelbach, *Die Quellen des griechischen
Alexanderromans* (*Zetemata* 9, Munich 1954).

ETHNOGRAPHERS OF AGE OF ALEXANDER: Nearchus: fragments
in *FGrH* 133; cf. W. Berve and W. Capelle, *RE* XVI, 2132 ff.
Onesicritus: *FGrH* 134; cf. H. Strasburger, *RE* XVIII.1, 460 ff.,
T. Brown, *Onesicritus* (Berkeley 1949). Megasthenes: fragments
collected by Schwanbeck (1846); cf. T. Brown, *AJP* 76 (1955),
18–33, and *Phoenix* 11 (1957), 12 ff.

EPHORUS OF CYME: *FGrH* 70. His work was in thirty books,
began with the "Return of the Heraclids" (i.e., the Dorian invasion),
and continued to 340 B.C., book 30 being added by Ephorus' son
Demophilus. Basic study is E. Schwartz, *RE VI* (1907), 1 ff.; on
time of composition see B. Niese, *Hermes* 44 (1909), 170 ff., who
argues for age of Alexander vs. Schwartz; see also G. Barber, *The
Historian Ephorus* (Cambridge 1935).

TIMAEUS OF TAUROMENIUM: Fragments in *FGrH* 566. On
his work see J. Beloch, *Fleckeisens Jahrbuch für Philologie* (1881),
697 ff.; E. Schwartz, *Gesammelte Schriften* II (1956), 175 ff.; R.
Laqueur, *RE* VI A, 1076 ff.; J. Geffcken, *Timaios' Geographie des
Westens* (*Philologische Untersuchungen* 13, Berlin 1892); K. Stroheker, "Timaios und Philistos," in *Satura: Festschrift O. Weinreich*
(1952), 139 ff.; G. De Sanctis, *Ricerche sulla storiografia siceliota*
(Palermo 1958), published posthumously; T. Brown, *Timaeus of
Tauromenium* (Berkeley 1958).

POLYBIUS: Books 1–5, concerning the years 264–216 B.C.,
are extant, plus fragments of books 6–40. Edition by Th. Büttner-
Wobst (1889 ff.). An essential tool is F. W. Walbank, *A Historical
Commentary on Polybius* I (Oxford 1957), covering books 1–6.
A *Polybius-Lexikon*, ed. A. Mauersberger, is appearing; so far two
fascicles have been published, covering alpha through zeta (Berlin
1956–1961). Important monographs include R. v. Scala, *Die Studien
des Polybios* I (1890), not continued; O. Cuntz, *Polybios und sein
Werk* (Leipzig 1902); C. Wunderer, *Polybios: Lebens- und Weltanschauung aus dem 2. vorchristlichen Jahrhundert* (Leipzig 1927);
W. Siegfried, *Studien zur geschichtlichen Auffassung des Polybios*
(Leipzig 1928); K. Lorenz, *Untersuchungen zur Geschichtswerk
des Polybios* (Stuttgart 1931), concerning especially the prefaces
to books 1 and 3.—The theory of R. Laqueur, *Polybios* (Leipzig

1913), that one can find in the extant work five successive editions is hypercritical and unconvincing; for an opposite view see E. Meyer, *Kleine Schriften* II (1924), 334 ff.; K. Lorenz, *op. cit.*, 69 ff.; more recently M. Gelzer, "Die hellenistische προκατασκευή im 2. Buche des Polybios," *Hermes* 70 (1940), 27 ff.; "Die Achaica im Geschichtswerk des Polybios," *SB Berlin* 1940, no. 2; "Über die Arbeitsweise des Polybios," *SHAW* 1956, no. 3; all these works are now available in Gelzer's *Kleine Schriften* (3 vols., Wiesbaden 1962–1963). The unitarian view, as expressed in extreme fashion recently by H. Erbse, "Zur Entstehung des polybianischen Geschichtswerkes," *RhM* 94 (1951), 157 ff. (see also *Philologus* 101 [1957], 269 ff.), is as unacceptable as Laqueur's extreme analytic hypothesis. A middle way must be found.–A brief orientation is given by A. Rosenberg, *Einleitung und Quellenkunde zur römischen Geschichte* (1921), 188 ff., and by Glover, *CAH* VIII (1930), 1 ff. A valuable survey is the long article by K. Ziegler, "Polybios," *RE* XXI (1952), 1440 ff. See too K. v. Fritz, *The Theory of the Mixed Constitution in Antiquity: A Critical Analysis of Polybius' Political Ideas* (New York 1954).

POSEIDONIUS OF APAMEA: Fragments in *FGrH* 87. On his life and thought see K. Reinhardt, *Poseidonios* (Munich 1921), *Kosmos und Sympathie* (Munich 1926), and "Poseidonios," *RE* XXII (1953); E. Schwartz, *Charakterköpfe aus der Antike*, ed. J. Stroux (Leipzig 1943), 89 ff., with bibliography of recent studies on pp. 288–289.

DIODORUS SICULUS: Of the forty books of his *Universal History* only books 1–5 on the ancient Near East and the mythical age, and 11–20 on the period 480–302 B.C. are extant. Edition by Vogel and Fischer (repr. Stuttgart 1964) is incomplete. For discussions see E. Schwartz *RE* V, 663 ff.; W. Schmid, *Geschichte der griechischen Literatur* II.2 (ed. 6, 1920), 403 ff.; A. v. Mess, "Untersuchungen über die Arbeitsweise Diodors," *RhM* 61 (1906), 244 ff. On his sources see C. Volquardsen, *Untersuchungen über die Quellen der griechishchen und sizil. Geschichte bei Diodor 11–15* (Kiel 1868); G. De Sanctis, *Ricerche sulla storiografia siceliota* (Palermo 1958), 78 ff.; R. Laqueur, *Hermes* 86 (1958), 256 ff.; J. Palm, *Über Sprache und Stil des Diodoros von Sizilien* (Lund 1955).

BEGINNINGS OF ROMAN HISTORIOGRAPHY: See the literary histories of Schanz-Hosius and Leo; also the survey by F. Klingner, *Die Antike* 13 (1937), 1 ff.

ANNALISTS: Survey with indication of important problems in *Rosenberg*, 113 ff., and in J. Vogt, "Römische Geschichte," *Gercke-Norden* III.2 (ed. 3, 1933), 45 ff. A new synthesis based on formal and historical analysis is needed.—Annual lists of priests are noted by Servius, *ad Aeneid* 1.373 and by Cicero, *De oratore* 2.12.52.

Q. FABIUS PICTOR: His work is discussed in *Rosenberg*, 123, who considers it a tool of the Greek policies of T. Quinctius Flamininus; cf. M. Gelzer, "Römische Politik bei Fabius Pictor," *Hermes* 68 (1933), 129 ff. Gelzer has not proved his theory that Fabius did not write annals but rather "pragmatic" history, as argued in *Hermes* 69 (1934), 46 ff. New aspects discussed by F. Bömer, *SO* 29 (1925), 34 ff., opposed by Gelzer, *Hermes* 82 (1954), 342 ff.—MANETHO: fragments in *LCL*, ed. W. Waddell (1940) and in *FGrH* 609. See study by R. Laqueur, *RE* XIV, 1060 ff.—BEROSSUS: see study by P. Schnabel, *Berossos und die babylonisch-hellenistische Literatur* (1923), as well as C. Lehmann-Haupt, *Klio* 22 (1929), 125 ff., and in *Reallexikon der Assyriologie* I, s.v.

M. PORCIUS CATO: Fragments of *Origines* are printed in H. Peter, *Historicorum Romanorum reliquiae* I (ed. 2), 55 ff. Study: F. Klingner, "Cato Censorius und die Krisis des römischen Volkes," *Die Antike* 10 (1934), 239 ff., reprinted in *Römische Geisteswelt* (ed. 4, 1961), 36 ff.

ROMAN HISTORICAL MONOGRAPHS: Fragments of L. Coelius Antipater in H. Peter, *op. cit.*, 158 ff.; cf. *Rosenberg*, 167 ff., and W. Hoffmann, *Livius und der zweite Punische Krieg* (*Hermes*, Einzelsch. 8; Berlin 1942).

C. SALLUSTIUS CRISPUS: Editions of the short works by W. Ahlberg (Leipzig 1919); A. Kurfess (ed. 3, 1957); of the fragments of the *Histories* by B. Maurenbrecher (Leipzig 1891–1893); and of all works by A. Ernout (Paris 1947). Studies: K. Bauhofer, *Die Komposition der Historien Sallusts* (Diss. Munich 1935); the older study of E. Schwartz, "Die Berichte über die catilinarische Verschwörung," *Hermes* 32 (1897), 554 ff., now reprinted in his *Gesammelte Schriften* II (1956), 275 ff.; O. Seel, *Von den Briefen ad Caesarem zur Coniuratio Catilinae* (Diss. Erlangen 1930); F. Egermann, "Die Proömien zu den Werken des Sallust," *SAWW* 214 (1932), no. 3; W. Schur, *Sallust als Historiker* (Stuttgart 1934), with addition in *Klio* 29 (1936), 60 ff. J. Vogt, *Cicero und Sallust über die catilinarische Verschwörung* (Frankfurt/Main 1938); suggestive is E. Howald, *Vom Geist antiker Geschichtsschreibung* (Munich 1944), 140 ff. On the *Jugurthine War* we have the recent work of K. Büchner, *Der Aufbau von Sallusts Bellum Iugurthinum* (*Hermes*, Einzelschrift 9; 1953), and W. Steidle, *Sallusts historische Monographien* (*Historia*, Einzelschrift 3; 1958).—Interpretive study: K. Büchner, *Sallust* (Heidelberg 1960); R. Syme, *Sallust* (Berkeley 1964) is an important work.

LIVY: Edition with commentary by W. Weissenborn and H. Müller (repr. Berlin 1962); for the text, consult the edition of Conway and Walters in *OCT* (1914–1935); an edition in the *CB* by J. Bayet has been published since 1940.—Of Livy's work remain books 1–10 (to 293 B.C.), 21–45 (219–167 B.C.); in short, about a fourth of the enormous work is extant. The contents of the lost books can be reconstructed from the *Periochae* (summaries) and also from the collection of prodigies made by Julius Obsequens, beginning with 190 B.C. In addition, a summary of books 37–55 (189–137 B.C.) was recently discovered; cf. E. Kornemann, *Die neue Livius-Epitome* (*Klio*, Beiheft 2; 1904), and F. Münzer, *Klio* 5 (1905), 135 ff.

On Livy's sources a basic work is H. Nissen, *Kritische Untersuchungen über die Quellen der 4. und 5. Dekade des Livius* (Berlin 1863); see also A. Klotz, *Livius und seine Vorgänger* (Berlin 1940–41), with review by M. Gelzer, *Gnomon* (1942), 220 ff., and his article, "Livius," *RE* XIII (1927), 816 ff.

Livy as artist and scholar: E. Burck, *Die Erzählungskunst des T. Livius* (*Problemata* 11, Berlin 1934), and "Livius als augusteischer Historiker," *WG* 1 (1935), 446 ff.; W. Hoffmann, *Antike und Abendland* 4 (1954), 170 ff.; H. Bruckmann, *Die römischen Niederlagen im Geschichtswerk des T. Livius* (Diss. Münster 1936); W. Wiehemeyer, *Proben histor. Kritik aus Livius XXI–XLV* (Diss. Münster 1938). Very suggestive, although at times his conclusions have been disputed, is K. Petzold, *Die Eröffnung des zweiten Röm.-Makedonischen Krieges* (Berlin 1940).

DIONYSIUS OF HALICARNASSUS: Edited by C. Jacoby, (4 vols., 1885–1905); recent studies by E. Gabba, *Athenaeum*, n.s. 38 (1960), 125 ff., 39 (1961), 98 ff.; H. Hill, *JRS* (1961), 88 ff., on Dionysius and the origins of Rome.

NICHOLAS OF DAMASCUS: Fragments in *FGrH* 90.

HISTORIOGRAPHY OF PRINCIPATE: Survey with bibliography of sources in *Rosenberg*, 242 ff.; *Schanz-Hosius* II (ed. 4, 1935), 644 ff.; F. Klingner, "Tacitus . . . ," *MH* 15 (1958), 194 ff.

POMPEIUS TROGUS: Of his *Historiae Philippicae* in 44 books only the *Prologi* (tables of contents) are extant, but we do have selections from the remainder made by M. Junianus (or Junianius) Justinus (c. third century A.D.). A good edition of Justin was published by O. Seel (Leipzig 1935), who also published the fragments of Trogus (1955). The basic work on the sources is by A. v. Gutschmid, reprinted in his *Kleine Schriften* V (1894), 218 ff., but a new study is needed. More recent work is reviewed by J. Pendorf, *Bursians Jahresber.* 273 (1941), 104 ff.

VELLEIUS PATERCULUS: Edition of the *Historia Romana* by C. Stegmann von Pritzwald (Leipzig 1935). The well-known passage on Arminius (2.18.2) has been newly interpreted by E. Hohl, "Zur Lebensgeschichte des Siegers im Teutoburger Walde," *HZ* 167 (1943), 457 ff.; Hohl argues for *Armenius* as the correct form, but see W. Ensslin, *Gymnasium* (1943/44), 64 ff.—A general study is I. Lana, *Velleio Patercolo o della propaganda* (Turin 1952).

Q. CURTIUS RUFUS: Of his *Historia Alexandri Magni* in ten books we have lost books 1 and 2 entirely and 5, 6, and 10 in part. New manuscript collations enrich the edition of K. Müller and H. Schönfeld, *Q. Curtius Rufus: Geschichte Alexanders des Grossen* (Munich 1954), with German translation. Other editions are those of H. Bardon (Paris 1947–1948), and J. Rolfe (*LCL*: 1947). Still valuable is the old commentary by J. Mützell (Berlin 1841).—When the work was written is still an unsolved problem, though one can say that it was sometime between the time of Augustus (for which W. Tarn argues, *Alexander the Great* II [Cambridge, 1948], 91 ff.) and that of Vespasian (for which see J. Stroux, *Philologus* 84 [1929], 233 ff.); the latter is more probable, as indicated in an article by G. Scheda, *Historia* 18 (1969). Whether Curtius is to be identified with the Curtius Rufus mentioned by Tacitus, *Ann.* 11.21, is an unsolved problem.

AUFIDIUS BASSUS: He began his history with the death of Caesar, but the point at which he stopped is unknown; cf. F. Marx, *Klio* 29 (1936), 94 ff.

PLINY THE ELDER (A.D. 23–79): His historical work, *A fine Bassi*, continued the history of Bassus; cf. A. Momigliano, "Osservazioni sulle fonti per la storia di Caligola, Claudio, Nerone," *RAL* ser. 6, vol. 8 (1932), 293 ff. Pliny also wrote an account of the German wars, besides of course his *Historia naturalis*.

CLUVIUS RUFUS: His history covered the reign of Nero and the revolutions of A.D. 69, but as a whole it remains unknown to us. Cluvius has, however, gained a somewhat unearned prominence because Mommsen believed his work was the common source behind Tacitus' *Histories* and Plutarch's *Lives* of Galba and Otho; cf. Th. Mommsen, "Cornelius Tacitus und Cluvius Rufus," *Hermes* 4 (1870), 295 ff., reprinted in *Gesammelte Schriften* VII, 224 ff. Nevertheless the verbal parallels must be otherwise explained, for Tacitus undoubtedly consulted a number of sources, and evidently one of them was used by Plutarch, too; cf. G. Townsend, *AJP* 85 (1964), 337–377.

FABIUS RUSTICUS: See Tacitus, *Ann.* 13.20; 14.2; 15.61.

CORNELIUS TACITUS: Editions: *Historiae* and *Annales* by

Halm, Andresen, Koestermann (Leipzig 1934–1936; ed. 8, 1957–1960); *Annales* by H. Fuchs (Frauenfeld 1946–1949); *Kleine Schriften* by E. Koestermann (ed. 8, Leipzig 1957); edition with notes of *Historiae* by Wolff, Andresen (ed. 2, 1914–1926; commentary on books 1–2 by H. Heubner, (3 vols., 1963–1967); edition with notes of *Annales* by Nipperdey, Andresen, books 1–6 (ed. 11, 1915) and books 11–16 (ed. 6, 1908); commentary on *Annales* by E. Koestermann (4 vols., Heidelberg 1963–1968); *Germania* with commentary by Reeb (1930), Much (1937), Anderson (Oxford 1938), Fehrle (ed. 4, 1944). *Agricola* has been edited by H. Furneaux and J. G. Anderson (ed. 2, Oxford 1922)—Full bibliography in *Schanz-Hosius* II, 603 ff.; see also *CAH* X (1934), 963 ff., and a later review by E. Koestermann, *Bursians Jahresber.* 282 (1943), 78 ff. For a general synthesis important articles are R. Reitzenstein, "Tacitus und sein Werk," *Neue Wege zur Antike* 4 (1926); F. Klingner, "Tacitus," *Antike* 8 (1932), 151 ff., and also his "Die Geschichte des Kaisers Otho bei Tacitus," *SB Leipzig* 1940, no. 1, and "Tacitus über Augustus und Tiberius," *SBAW* 1953, no. 7 (published 1954); H. Drexler, *Tacitus, Grundzüge einer politischen Pathologie* (Frankfurt/Main 1939), but this requires critical judgment; E. Howald, *Vom Geist antiker Geschichtsschreibung* (Munich 1944), 193 ff.; E. Koestermann, *Tacitus* (Wiesbaden 1946), with good bibliography of recent studies. A study based on intensive original research, especially in prosopography, is R. Syme, *Tacitus* (2 vols., Oxford 1958).—On E. Paratore, *Tacito* (ed. 2, Rome 1962) see review of R. Güngerich, *Gnomon* (1954), 85 ff. and (1965), 422 ff. Useful studies are in *Würzburger Studien zur Altertumswissenschaft* 9 (1936) (*Festschrift Hosius*), including the important study by J. Vogt, "Tacitus und die Unparteilichkeit des Historikers," reprinted in *Orbis* (1960), 110 ff., which also contains his "Die Geschichtsschreibung des Tacitus," 128 ff.—On *Ann.* 15.44 see H. Fuchs, "Tacitus u. die Christen," *VChr* 4 (1950), 65 ff.; on Tacitus' psychology see H. Nesselhauf, "Tacitus u. Domitian," *Hermes* 80 (1952), 222 ff. Numerous studies by E. Koestermann are incorporated in his commentary on *Annales*. Also valuable is V. Pöschl, *WG* (1962), 1 ff.—Older studies worth consulting include L. v. Ranke, *Weltgeschichte* III.1, 286 ff., and R. v. Pöhlmann, "Die Weltanschauung des T.," *SBAW* 1910, 3 ff.—On the sources of *Historiae* and *Annales* see P. Fabia, *Les sources de Tacite dans les hist. et les ann.* (Paris 1893), and C. Questa, *Studi sulle fonti degli Annales di Tacito* (ed. 2, Rome 1963), and summary by S. Borzsak, *RE* Supp. XI (1968), 373–512. An important, though unfinished study is Mommsen's "Das Verhältnis des T. zu den Akten des

Senats," *SPAW* 1904, 1146 ff., reprinted in *Gesammelte Schriften* VII, 253 ff.—On the *Germania* two fundamental works are a speech by T. Mommsen, *SPAW* 1886, 39 ff., reprinted in *Reden u. Aufsätze* (Berlin 1905), 144 ff., and E. Norden, *Die germanische Urgeschichte in Tacitus' Germania* (ed. 3, Leipzig, 1923).

FLAVIUS JOSEPHUS: A complete and exemplary edition by B. Niese (8 vols., 1885–1895). Studies include B. Niese, *HZ*, n.f. 40 (1896), 193 ff.; G. Hölscher, *RE* IX (1916), 1934 ff.; R. Laqueur, *Der jüdische Historiker Flavius Josephus* (Giessen 1920), penetrating but not always convincing; M. Charlesworth, *Five Men: Character Studies from the Roman Empire* (Cambridge, Mass. 1936), 67 ff.—Useful also are W. Otto, *Herodes* (Stuttgart 1913), a reprint with minor changes of his article in *RE* Supp. II, 1 ff., and W. Weber's useful although at times very hypothetical *Josephus und Vespasian* (Stuttgart 1921).

ARRIAN OF NICOMEDIA: Edited by A. G. Roos (2 vols., 1907–1928, repr. 1967–1968 with additions by G. Wirth), exemplary. A fundamental study is E. Schwartz, *RE* II, 1230 ff.; good orientation by *Schmid-Stählin* II (ed. 6, 1924), 746 ff.; and most recently G. Wirth, *Historia* 13 (1964), 209 ff.

APPIAN OF ALEXANDRIA: Edited by L. Mendelssohn, A. Roos, and P. Viereck (2 vols., 1905–1939; vol. 1 repr. by E. Gabba in 1962). *Bella civilia* 1 edited by E. Gabba (Florence 1958; ed. 2, 1967). For his sources, begin with E. Schwartz, *RE* II, 216 ff.; more recent studies include E. Kornemann, *Klio* 17 (1920), 33 ff., and A. Klotz, *Appians Darstellungen des 2. Pun. Krieges* (Paderborn 1936); but their conclusions are not proved. See above all E. Gabba, *Appiano e la storia delle guerre civili* (Florence 1956).

CASSIUS DIO COCCEIANUS: Edited excellently by U. Boissevain (5 vols., Berlin 1895–1931; vols. 1–4 repr. 1955). Extant are books 36–60, covering 68 B.C.–A.D. 47, book 36 lacking part of its beginning, book 60 part of its conclusion. Extracts of the other books exist, those of John Xiphilinus (11th century A.D.) from books 1–21, those of Zonaras (12th century A.D.) from books 44–80, and in addition the extracts made by Constantine VII Porphyrogenitus (10th century A.D.). We still do not have a clear idea of Dio's sources for his account of Caesar and Augustus, *contra* E. Schwartz, *RE* III, 1684 ff. Nevertheless it is clear that Dio has been overrated, as in H. Andersen, *Cassius Dio und die Begründung des Prinzipats* (Berlin 1938), and P. Strack, "Zum Gottkönigtum Cäsars," a note added to his essay "Der augusteische Staat," in *Probleme der augusteischen Erneuerung* (Frankfurt/Main 1938), 21 ff. Valuable studies are: E. Gabba, *RSI* 67 (1955), 289 ff.; F. Millar, *A Study of Cassius Dio* (Oxford 1964), rev. G. Bowersock, *Gnomon* (1965), 469 ff.

HERODIAN: Edited by Stavenhagen (Leipzig 1922, repr. 1967). We still lack a critical study of Herodian which takes into account studies of the *Historia Augusta.* He is judged favorably by F. Altheim, *Literatur u. Gesellschaft im ausgehenden Altertum* I (1948), 165 ff., unfavorably by E. Hohl, "Kaiser Commodus und Herodian," *SDAW* 1954, no. 1. Later bibliography is given by E. Gabba, *RSI* 71 (1959), 381, note 95, W. Widmer, *Kaisertum, Rom und Welt in Herodians . . . historia* (Zurich 1967).

EUSEBIUS OF CAESAREA: *Historia ecclesistica* edited by E. Schwartz (3 vols., Leipzig 1903–1909); *editio minor* was published in 1914 (repr. 1952). Good introductions are: E. Schwartz's "Prolegomena" to his large edition and also *RE* VI, 1395 ff.; *Schmid-Stählin* II.2 (ed. 6, 1924), 1351 ff.; E. Kornemann, *Gercke-Norden* III.2 (ed. 3, 1933), 158.—On the dispute over authenticity (or, rather, degree of forgery) of the *Vita Constantini* (ed. Heckel, 1902) see F. Vittinghoff, *RhM* 96 (1953), 330 ff., and J. Vogt, *Historia* 2 (1954), 463 ff., both of whom argue well for authenticity against H. Grégoire and his followers in Brussels. Important evidence is a papyrus discussed by A. Jones, "Notes on the Genuineness of the Constantinian Documents in Eusebius' Life of Constantine," *JEH* 5 (1954), 196 ff.

LACTANTIUS: Edited by S. Brandt (*CSEL* 27.2, Vienna 1897), and by J. Moreau, *De la mort des persécuteurs* (2 vols., Paris 1954), with a comprehensive commentary.—The idea that God punishes his enemies is ancient: W. Nestle, *ARW* 33 (1936), 246 ff.—On L.'s sources see K. Roller, *Die Kaisergeschichte in Laktanz' De mortibus persecutorum* (Diss. Giessen 1927). An important critical study is M. Gelzer, "Der Urheber der Christenverfolgung von 303," *Kleine Schriften* III (1964), 378 ff.

OROSIUS: Edited by C. Zangemeister, *CSEL* 5, Vienna 1882, *editio minor* (Leipzig 1889). A philological study is J. Svennung, *Orosiana* (Uppsala 1922).

ST. AUGUSTINE: *De civitate Dei* has been edited by B. Dombart (Leipzig 1928–1929). A fundamental study is H. Fuchs, *Augustin und der antike Friedensgedanke* (Berlin 1926), as is H. Marrou, *Augustin et la fin de la culture antique* (Paris 1938). See also Marrou's *Retractatio* (1949), and F. G. Maier, *Augustin u. das antike Rom* (Stuttgart 1955).

AMMIANUS MARCELLINUS: Edited by C. U. Clark (Berlin 1910–1915), and by J. C. Rolfe, with English translation (3 vols., *LCL*: repr. 1950–1952).—Good bibliography given by Kornemann,

Gercke-Norden III.2 (ed. 3, 1933), 161. More recent works are:
J. Straub, *Vom Herrscherideal in der Spätantike* (Stuttgart 1939);
E. A. Thompson, *The Historical Work of A. M.* (Cambridge 1947);
J. Vogt, "A. M. als erzählender Geschichtsschreiber der Spätzeit,"
Abh. Akad. Mainz 1963, no. 8. A critical study is W. Ensslin, *Zur
Geschichtsschreibung und Weltanschauung des A. M.* (*Klio*, Bei-
heft 16; 1923). More recent contributions include W. Hartke,
Gnomon (1939), 261 ff.; A. Demandt, *Zeitkritik und Geschichts-
kritik im Werk Ammians* (Bonn 1965); H. T. Rowell, "A. M.,
Soldier Historian of the Later Roman Empire," *Lectures in Mem-
ory of L. Taft Semple* (Princeton 1967), 261–313.—A comprehensive commentary is needed.

PROCOPIUS OF CAESAREA: Edited by Haury (3 vols., repr.
Leipzig 1962–1963 by G. Wirth). A general study is F. Dahn,
Procopius von Caesarea (Berlin 1865); later studies include E.
Schwartz, "Zu Cassiodor u. Prokop," *SBAW* 1939, no. 2; O. Veh,
*Zur Geschichtsschreibung und Weltanschauung des Prokop von
Cäsarea* (Bayreuth 1950–1951). Every student must now consult
the article "Prokopios" by B. Rubin, *RE* XXIII (1957), 273–599.

CASSIODORUS: Of the twelve books of his *Historia Gothorum*
only an extract remains, in Jordanes' *Getica*, published A.D. 551, ed.
T. Mommsen (*MGH, AA* 5.1: 1882). C. was minister under Theod-
erich, king of the Ostrogoths, and we have the collection he made
from his official correspondence, *Variae*, ed. T. Mommsen (*MGH,
AA* 12: Berlin 1904).—A valuable study is A. Momigliano, "C. and
Italian Culture of His Time," in his *Secondo contributo alla storia
degli studi classici* (Rome 1960), 191 ff.

JOHN MALALAS: edition in the *Bonn Corpus of Byzantine
Historians*. For his imperial history see A. Schenk v. Stauffenberg,
Die römische Kaisergeschichte bei Malalas (Stuttgart 1931).

JOHN OF ANTIOCH: Fragments in Müller, *FHG* IV, 535 and
V, 27.

BIOGRAPHY: F. Leo, *Die griech.-röm. Biographie* (Leipzig
1901); M. Pohlenz in *Gercke-Norden* I.3 (ed. 3, 1924), 171 ff.;
D. E. Stuart, *Epochs of Greek and Roman Biography* (Berkeley
1928). See also W. Steidle, *Sueton u. die antike Biographie* (Zetemata 1, Munich 1950); A. Dihle, *Studien zur griech. Biographie*
(*Abh. Akad. Göttingen*, phil.–hist. Kl., no. 37; 1956).

CORNELIUS NEPOS: *De viris illustribus* ed. Halm (Leipzig
1871); edition with commentary by K. Nipperdey and K. Witte
(ed. 11, Berlin 1913); edition with German translation by H. Fär-
ber, *Cornelius Nepos: Kurzbiographien und Fragmente* (Munich
1952).

PLUTARCH OF CHAERONEA: eds. Lindskog and Ziegler (Leipzig 1914–1939; vols. 1.1, 1.2 and 2.1, repr. 1957–1964).—On his methods see F. Leo, *Die griech.-röm. Biographie* (Leipzig 1901), 146 ff.; on his publication see J. Mewaldt, *Hermes* 42 (1907), 564 ff. Other studies include: U. v. Wilamowitz, "Pl. als Biograph," in *Reden und Vorträge* II (ed. 4, 1926), 247 ff.; C. Theander, "Pl. und die Geschichte," *Jahresberichte Lund* (1950/51), 1; R. Barrow, *Plutarch and His Times* (London 1967), which I have not seen.— Little was established by scholars' efforts, especially in the 19th century, to identify Plutarch's sources, and recent studies in that vein have also been unsatisfactory; cf. the authoritative study of E. Meyer, *Forsch. z. Alten Geschichte* II (1899), 1 ff., on the Cimon biography. But a valuable and methodologically interesting study is B. Niese, *Hermes* 31 (1896), 481 ff., on the Pyrrhus biography; likewise E. Gabba's study of the biographies of Agis and Kleomenes, *Athenaeum*, n.s. 35 (1957), 3 ff. and 193 ff.—Dutch scholars have published a series of editions of individual biographies with excellent commentaries: *Pyrrhus*, ed. A. B. Nederlof (Amsterdam 1940); *Aratos*, ed. W. P. Theunissen (Nimwegen 1935) and later by A. L. Koster (Leiden 1937); *Aemilius Paulus*, ed. C. Liedmeier (Utrecht 1935), etc.

SUETONIUS: Edited by Ihm, *editio minor* 1908, *ed. maior* 1922, now being reprinted; good edition also by J. C. Rolfe (*LCL*: 1914). There is no general commentary. For bibliography on the individual biographies see *Schanz-Hosius* VIII (ed. 3, 1922), 48 ff.; *CAH* XI, 866. Studies include: G. Funaiola, "C. Suetonius Tranquillus," *RE* IV A, 593 ff.; F. della Corte, *Suetonio eques Romano* (ed. 2, Florence 1967); F. Grosso, *RAL* (1959), 263–296. On date of composition of the *Lives* see G. Townsend, *CQ* 9 (1959), 285–293. An important work is W. Steidle, *Sueton und die antike Biographie* (*Zetemata* 1, Munich 1950); Steidle rehabilitates Suetonius as an historian, and his work replaces Leo's as fundamental.

MARIUS MAXIMUS: General study: M. Rostovtzeff, "Das Militärarchiv von Dura," *Münchner Beiträge z. Papyrusforschung* 19 (1934), 373 ff. Maximus was popular in the fourth century A.D., as attested by Ammianus 28.4.14; cf. E. Kornemann, *Die römische Kaiserzeit* (1933), 154; F. Miltner, *RE* XIV, 1830 f.

SCRIPTORES HISTORIAE AUGUSTAE: Edited by E. Hohl (2 vols., Leipzig 1927; ed. 2, 1965). A general commentary, considered necessary by Mommsen, is still lacking, but a great many monographs have been produced, including: J. Schwendemann, *Der histor. Wert der Vita Marci bei den Script. hist. Aug.* (Heidelberg 1923); J. Heer, *Der histor. Wert der Vita Commodi: Untersuch.*

z. *Geschichte des Kaisers Septimius Severus* (Heidelberg 1921); W. Reusch, *Der historische Wert der Caracalla-Vita in den S.h.A.* (*Klio*, Beiheft 24; 1931); E. Hohl, "Vopiscus und die Biographie des Kaisers Tacitus," *Klio* 11 (1911), 178 ff. Further bibliography is given in E. Hohl, *Bursians Jahresberichte* 171 (1915), 15 ff.; *ibid.* 200 (1924), 167 ff.; *ibid.* 256 (1937), 127 ff., as well as his article in *Klio* 27 (1934), 149 ff., and "Über die Glaubwürdigkeit der Historia Augusta," *SDAW* 1953, no. 2.

Study of the *SHA* really began with the fundamental article of H. Dessau, *Hermes* 24 (1889), 337 ff., also *ibid.* 27 (1892), 561 ff., in which he argued that the work was written by a single person under Theodosius II and revealed its six supposed authors as "swindlers"; cf. *Rosenberg*, 231 ff. N. Baynes, *The Historia Augusta* (Oxford 1926), argued persuasively for a date of composition under Emperor Julian. He was opposed in a clever but unconvincing study by W. Hartke, "Geschichtsschreibung und Politik im spätantiken Rom," *Klio*, Beiheft 45 (1940), arguing for the authorship of the younger Nicomachus; see also his learned book *Römische Kinderkaiser* (Berlin 1951). Nevertheless, the alternative, "Julian" or "Theodosian," has not been decided yet, though the evidence inclines to the latter and it has been accepted by A. Alföldi, *Kontorniaten* (Budapest 1943); J. Straub, *Studien zur Historia Augusta* (*Diss. Bern.* 1.4, 1952), and *Heidnische Geschichtsapologetik in der christl. Spätantike* (Bonn 1963), with new arguments for a date of composition in the early fifth century. An important summary of the problem is A. Momigliano, "An Unsolved Problem of Historical Forgery: the Scriptores Historiae Augustae," in *Secondo Contributo* (Rome 1960), 144 ff., reprinted in *Studies in Historiography* (New York 1966), 143–180. Valuable studies have been published in: *Atti del Colloquio Patavino sulla Historia Augusta* (Rome 1963); *Historia-Augusta Colloquium, Bonn 1963*, eds. J. Straub and A. Alföldi (Bonn 1964); *idem* 1964/65 (Bonn 1966). New approches are suggested by R. Syme, *Ammianus and the Historia Augusta* (Oxford 1968).

SEXTUS AURELIUS VICTOR: Edited by F. Pichlmayr (Leipzig 1911, repr. 1961); see the essay by R. Laqueur, "Die Geistige Bildung im Urteil des A. V.," in *Probleme der Spätantike* (Stuttgart 1930), 25 ff.—Similar compendiums are those of Eutropius, *Breviarium ab urbe condita*, ed. F. Rühl (1887), and Rufius Festus, *Breviarium rerum gestarum populi Romani*, eds. C. Wagener (Leipzig and Prague 1886) and J. W. Eadie with commentary (London 1967). Festus wrote his work in A.D. 369 or 371. Both histories give a very brief sketch of Roman history up to the author's time, the imperial period being treated as simply a succession of biographies of rulers. A similar work is *Epitome de Caesaribus*, ed. F. Pichlmayr and printed with his *Aurelius Victor*; it was published in A.D. 395. On all these works see W. Hartke, *De saeculi IV exeuntis histori-arum quaestiones* (Diss. Berlin 1932).

LIFE OF ST. SEVERINUS (d. A.D. 482): Ed. T. Mommsen (*MGH, AA* 1.2, ed. 2, 1898), M. Schuster (Vienna 1946), and R. Noll (Linz 1947).—This biography attracted special attention from the great cultural historian Jakob Burckhardt (1818–1897); cf. *J. Burckhardt: Briefe z. Erkenntnis seiner geistigen Gestalt*, ed. F. Kaphahn (Leipzig 1935), 58 and 117 of the Introduction, and see also F. Kaphahn, *Zwischen Antike und Mittelalter: Das Donaual-penland im Zeitalter St. Severins* (Munich 1947). For more recent studies see H. Diesner, *Wiss. Zeitschr. d. Martin-Luther-Univ. Halle-Wittenberg (Gesellschaftswiss. u. sprachwiss. Abt. 7.6, 1958)*, 1165 ff.

3. MYTH, SAGA, FOLKTALES

A third branch of tradition is the mythic and folk forms. In An-tiquity as in later periods they contributed to shape the record left by individuals and events. Scholars have judged this branch very differently, depending on their individual theoretical premises. In general earlier scholars were sceptical, but myth and folktales have been given more respect since the studies of U. v. Wilamowitz and Eduard Meyer.

Recent research has in particular directed much interest toward myth. W. Otto, R. Pettazoni, and G. van der Leeuw have concerned themselves with the relation between myth and history, though from different points of view. Of course the tendency to equate myth and history has dangers; hence the opposite point of view represented by Rudolph Bultmann's insistence on "de-mythologizing." His work is important, not only for New Testament studies.

Myth, saga, and legends are found in the traditions of all peoples, beginning with ancient Egyptians and Babylonians down to the end of Antiquity, not to mention other epochs and areas. Everyone knows the stories in *Genesis* (ch. 11 ff.) about the "patriarchs" Abraham, Isaac, and Jacob. Formerly these stories were treated sceptically under the influence of Julius Wellhausen and his school, but now a middle view prevails. Scholars tend to view the stories not as fiction, but rather as works written under the influence of genuine historical traditions, which are in many respects accurate. Thus, for example, the appearance of Hittites in *Genesis* (23.3 ff.; 26.34; 27.46) corresponds well with the historical situation, for the presence of Hittite groups in Syria c. 1600–1200 B.C. has been confirmed, *e.g.*, by the Amarna Tablets of the 14th century; cf. A. Jirku, *Geschichte d. Volkes Israels* (1931), 54 ff. Modern scholars do not, however, agree in their evaluation of the story of the Exodus of the Children of Israel from Egypt to the Promised Land. J. V. Bekkerath, *Tanis und Theben* (*Ägyptologische Forsuchungen* 16, 1951), argues that the saga is based on a Canaanite tradition from the Hyksos period, and that this was adopted by the Israelites. On the other hand M. Noth, *Geschichte Israels* (ed. 4, Göttingen 1959), believes that in fact some tribes did leave Egypt for Palestine, and that they later contributed to the formation of the nation of Israel; he identifies the oppressive Pharaoh as Rameses II (1290–1223 B.C.). Positive views are also maintained by H. H. Rowley, *From Joseph to Joshua: Schweich Lectures 1948* (London 1950), 116 ff., and also in *Festschrift H. Nyberg* (Uppsala 1954), 195 ff.

Mythic tradition is especially important for the study of early Hellenic history. The Greeks themselves thought that their earliest history was reflected in their myths about the gods and heroes, and it was because of this that in the fifth century B.C. the "logographers" collected the myths and evaluated them as historical resources. Today no one would still deny that the *Iliad* or the saga of the Seven against Thebes has an historical core. The latter records an expedition against Thebes by an Argive king. The *Iliad* is based on the wars of the Greeks in the Troad in the age of Hellenic expansion in western Asia Minor. Historical elements include the predominance of Aeolian and Thessalian groups, exemplified in the heroic figure of Achilles, and also the hegemony of Argive Mycenae, as evidenced in the position of Agamemnon. Schliemann's excavations in Troy and Mycenae provided the proof that the heroic saga, taken as a whole, preserves a record of historical events and conditions, though of course not all details are accurate.

In general there is a close connection between the centers of Mycenaean culture and the centers of the heroic sagas of the Greeks, as was established by the researches of M. P. Nilsson. Today no one doubts that Greek saga is based on an historical tradition, although this cannot be demonstrated in all instances. However, one must beware of uncritically accepting myth and saga in reconstructing historical events, a fault in the work of some archeologists.

Ever since the discovery of the Hittite epic of *Cumarbi*, and the recognition that its mythology parallels in some respects that of Hesiod's *Theogony*, links between Greek and Oriental mythology have been discussed.[43] This is not only a literary problem; it is of great historical importance, for it concerns the extent to which Hellas and the Orient were in contact.

In early Greek historiography and in Ephorus as well much space is taken up with elaborate geneaologies. They are not based on genuine tradition, but were rather the product of ancient scholarly conjecture; however, they are still of interest, for they tell us how the Greeks pictured their own past. These genealogies do not represent real history, but a form of myth, often of markedly subjective character.

Another peculiarity of Greek mythography deserves note here: just as the myths often reveal historical connections between different peoples and states, as for instance the saga of Theseus indicates an early connection between Athens and Crete,[44] so myth and saga were used continually by the Greeks to support political claims, and were even shaped for such purpose. Examples are found from earliest times to the end of Hellenic independence, and even under Roman domination. The letter of Speusippus to Philip II of Macedonia shows that the political propaganda of that time tended to use myths to support territorial claims.[45]

In general one may say that the critical evaluation of myth and saga is a difficult but valuable study which has illuminated important aspects of political and cultural history. Thus the immigration of the Elymi from Asia Minor to Sicily in the period after the great Aegean migrations (1200–1100 B.C.) has been confirmed by the Aeneas saga,[46] and similarly the *Odyssey* seems to give the historical background of the historical journeys of the Chalcidians c. 750 B.C.

[43] H. Güterbock, "Kumarbi: Mythos vom Churritischen Kronos," *Istanbuler Schriften* 16 (1946); *idem, AJA* (1948), 123 ff.; A. Lesky, "Griechischer Mythos u. Vorderer Orient," *Saeculum* 6 (1955), 35 ff.

[44] H. Herter, "Theseus der Ionier," *RhM* 85 (1936), 177 ff., 193 ff.; *idem*, "Griechische Gesch. im Spiegel der Theseussage," *Antike* 17 (1941), 209 ff.

[45] E. Bickermann and J. Sykutris, "Speusipps Brief an König Philipp," *Ber. Sächsische Akad. d. Wiss.* 80, no. 3 (1928), 20 and 44.

[46] L. Malten, *ARW* 29 (1931), 33 ff.

to the western Mediterranean—those journeys which marked the
beginning of the second great epoch of Greek colonization.[47]

The heroic sagas of the Greeks are known to us only from literary
sources—the Homeric epics, the dramas, lyric poetry, and the stories
reported by historians. But besides saga, there existed in Greece as
well as in Rome and the ancient Near East "popular stories" which
are part of tradition, although not the historical tradition in its
narrower sense. Popular stories preserve for us historical facts, characteristics of leading personalities, information about historical situations and events—all enlivened and mixed with anecdotal and
fabulous elements. This is especially true in Greek history for the
famous tyrants and "aristocratic lords" of the seventh and sixth
centuries B.C. Men forgot their political significance, but memory
preserved a record of their characteristics in anecdotal form. Sometimes the stories are transferred from one person to another, so that
historical figures such as Cypselus, Periander, Polycrates, even
Peisistratus, and foreigners like Gyges and Croesus, all appear to us
in a historical twilight in which history and saga are so intermixed
that often they cannot be separated. Popular tradition supplied
many stories to Herodotus and his contemporaries.

As a result, the historian must strive to avoid rejecting popular
tradition as worthless or, conversely, to use it as the basis for an
historical account; either course would be mistaken. It is useful for
the scholar to know what people said about Pausanias, the victor at
Plataea, or about Miltiades and Themistocles. These tales reveal, as
it were, the impression which these great men left in the memories of
their fellow countrymen. Similarly the caricature of Socrates which
Aristophanes gives in his *Clouds* is not only funny but also revealing,
for it shows how a contemporary poet regarded Socrates, and the
historian must set this beside the idealized portrait left us by Plato
and Xenophon.

Since the invention of the printing press modern man has not
relied much on his memory, and we tend in general to trust written
rather than oral tradition. It was different in Antiquity. For that
reason the traditions concerning early Roman history are not to be
suspected simply because they are "only" oral, as was argued hyper-
critically by E. Pais, E. Kornemann, and others. Examples from the
world of the Scandinavian peasantry have been cited by Martin

[47] W. Schadewaldt, "Homer und sein Jahrhundert," *Das neue Bild der
Antike* 1 (1942), 41 ff.

Nilsson to show an extraordinary tenacity in preserving memory of historical events. Furthermore, many stories have been passed on from grandfather to grandson, so that often a generation is skipped and the chain of transmission is shorter than might at first appear. In particular the traditions of the great Roman families preserved a great number of facts, although of course they were not studied as historical records until after they had been rejected for a long time as "mere" anecdotes.

That is true, for example, of the story about the strict Roman dictator, A. Postumius Tubertus, who supposedly sentenced his own son to be executed because he had disregarded an order and engaged in single combat. This story, told by Diodorus (12.64) and Livy (4.29), has often been referred to as a legendary example of traditional Roman *severitas*, and its core is in fact a kind of saga. Its background is the fundamental change in Roman military institutions which resulted from the introduction of hoplite tactics: in place of the reckless warrior fighting in single combat came the strictly disciplined phalanx in which every member had his appointed place. Thus the story about Postumius Tubertus and his son gives valuable historical information about the transition period when hoplite tactics had been introduced but were still on occasion ignored.

As a final example we may cite an illuminating "family legend" from archaic Rome. Tradition recounts that after the Romans suffered a defeat at the Cremera River (c. 477 B.C.) the *gens Fabia* assumed the burden of the war on its own, and then lost all its able-bodied men, 306 in all, in a battle with the Etruscans. Many have labeled this as nothing more than a saga, but it has been rightly argued that this story is nothing *less* than a saga! The battle of Cremera River took place a time when the Roman army was recruited from the great clans and their clients. The story of the Fabii illuminates Roman military institutions as they were before the introduction of centuria organization and hoplite tactics.

This example indicates how advisable it is to study the tradition of earlier Roman history with an open mind, even those stories which rest only on oral tradition. Our knowledge of the earlier periods of Greek and Roman history rests in large part on the archeological monuments, and only in rare cases does this allow us to control the literary tradition. Because of this situation it is better to approach the tradition with a positive attitude rather than with scepticism and destructive criticism.

BIBLIOGRAPHY

For Egypt see, among recent works, S. Schott, "Mythe und Geschichte," *Jahrb. d. Akad. Mainz* (1954), 243–266; for Mesopotamia see F. de Liagre Böhl, "Mythos u. Geschichte in der altbabylonischen Dichtung," *Opera Minora* (Groningen 1953), 217 ff.

Historical study of Greek mythology began with C. O. Müller, *Orchomenos und die Minyer* (1820), *Die Dorier* (1824), and *Prolegomena zu einer wissenschaftlichen Mythologie* (1825). Roman myths were first evaluated by B. G. Niebuhr, *Römische Geschichte* (2 vols., 1811–1812). Müller's works served a valuable function in their time, but they are in many respects vitiated by a subjective approach. More recently research methods in the field have been furthered by the work of admirable scholars like H. Usener, U. v. Wilamowitz, Carl Robert, Ed. Meyer, and M. P. Nilsson. Today two schools prevail: the ethnological, most eminently represented by Nilsson; and the theological, represented by W. Otto and K. Kerényi. See, for example, Otto's *Die Götter Griechenlands* (1929), *Dionysos* (1933); also R. Pettazoni, *Miti e leggende* (Turin 1948), and *Mythe, Mensch und Umwelt* (Bamberg 1950); G. van der Leeuw, "Die Bedeutung der Mythen," in *Festschrift . . . Bertholet* (Tübingen 1950), 289 ff. For R. Bultmann's theories see his *Neues Testament und Mythologie* (ed. 2, Tübingen 1958).—An historical survey of the older research is given by O. Gruppe, "Gesch. d. Klass. Mythologie während des Mittelalters in Abendland und während der Neuzeit," *Roschers Mytholog.-Lexikon*, Erg.-Band (Leipzig 1921). All study of Greek mythology requires use of the relevant articles in Roscher and *RE* and also the indispensable handbook of L. Preller, *Griechische Mythologie* I (ed. 4 by C. Robert, 1894) and II, rewritten by Carl Robert and published under the title *Die griechische Heldensage* (Berlin 1920–1926: the index still is lacking). A useful work is the brief survey by H. J. Rose, *Handbook of Greek Mythology* (London 1928); also valuable, especially for use of modern folklore material, is L. Radermacher, *Mythos und Sage bei den Griechen* (ed. 2, Vienna 1943). See also J. Bayet, "L'étude des légendes dans la methodologie de l'histoire ancienne" in his *Mélanges de la littérature latine* (Rome 1967), 339–350.

OTHER GUIDES: F. Pfister, "Die Religion der Griechen und Römer," *JAW* 229 (1930), especially pp. 146 ff., includes an introduction on comparative religion and a bibliography of studies during 1918–1930.

The *Archiv für Religionswissenschaft* (1898 ff.) is an important journal. Also suggestive for the historian is the series *Religionsgeschichtliche Versuche und Vorarbeiten*, founded by A. Dieterich and R. Wünsch (Giessen 1903 ff.).

MYTH, SAGA, AND HISTORY: Of older studies *Sagwissenschaftliche Studien* by v. Hahn (Jena 1876) should be mentioned and, above all, U. v. Wilamowitz's works: *Euripides' Herakles* (ed. 2, 1909); "Die griechische Heldensage," *SPAW* 1925, 41 ff., 214 ff.; *Der Glaube der Hellenen* (Berlin 1931–1932). Valuable too are the works of Martin Nilsson: *The Mycenaean Origins of Greek Mythology* (Berkeley 1932); *Homer and Mycenae* (London 1933); and his discussions in *Geschichte der griechischen Religion* I (ed. 3, Munich 1967), 24 ff., and in *Cults, Myths, Oracles, and Politics in Ancient Greece* (Lund 1951); also works by his students: S. Solders, *Die ausserstädtischen Kulte und die Einigung Attikas* (Lund 1931); K. Hanell, *Megarische Studien* (Lund 1934). Interesting but very hypothetical is A. W. Persson, "Legende und Mythos in ihrem Verhältnis zu Bild und Gleichnis im vorgeschichtlichen Griechenland," *Festschrift . . . Nilsson* (Lund 1939), 379 ff. Italian scholars persistently follow the strongly negative attitude of K. J. Beloch toward the historical element in Greek myth, as in A. Gitti, *Mythos: La tradizione prestoriografica della Grecia* (*Studi Baresi* 1, Bari 1949).

Still fundamental for all matters relating to ancient religion and mythology is O. Gruppe, *Griech. Mythologie u. Religionsgeschichte* (in *Müller* [Munich 1906]); it has been replaced only in part by the new standard work of M. Nilsson, *Geschichte d. gr. Religion* (2 vols., in *Müller*).

Compared with Greek myth and saga that of the Romans is much less developed and also less studied. From the first it was influenced by Greek tradition and therefore was much infiltrated by foreign elements. Niebuhr's negative verdict on the tradition of early Roman history was long dominant, until at last historical criticism of Roman saga was developed. The way was opened by A. Schwegler, *Römische Geschichte* (3 vols., 1853–1858). Recently outstanding work among German scholars has been done by F. Altheim, *Römische Religionsgeschichte* (3 vols. in *Sammlung Göschen*, 1931–1933), and *Italien und Rom* (2 vols., Amsterdam 1941). For late Antiquity see N. Lukman, "Der historische Wolfdietrich (Theodorich d. Grosse)," *Classica et Mediaevalia* 3 (1940) 253 ff.; 4 (1941), 1 ff.

POPULAR TRADITION: See M. Nilsson, "Über die Glaubwürdigkeit der Volksüberlieferung, mit besonderem Bezug auf die Alte

Geschichte," *Opuscula selecta* II (1952), 816 ff. On ancient stories see B. Erdmannsdörfer, "Das Zeitalter der Novelle in Griechenland," *Preussische Jahrbücher* 25 (1870), 121 ff., 283 ff., published separately (Berlin 1870) and repr. in *Kleinere histor. Schriften* II, ed. H. Lilienfein; W. Aly, *Volksmärchen, Sage und Novelle bei Herodot und seinen Zeitgenossen* (Göttingen 1921); E. Bethe, *Märchen, Sage, Mythos* (Leipzig 1922), reviewed by W. Otto, *DLZ* (1924), 325 ff.

V

The Monuments

By "monuments" we mean all the material remains of Antiquity, all that is not part of the written tradition. Today that includes an enormous mass of information, even though the careful study of ancient sites has been pursued for less than a century. Individual buildings and the sites of entire cities, works of art, originals as well as copies, and objects used in daily life—they can all tell the historian something, depending on the questions he has in mind when studying them. However, not even archeologists can master all the remains of Antiquity or keep up with the additions to knowledge constantly being made. For this reason it is the more important for historians to realize the extent of the material available and to know the important aids for their study.

Most noteworthy of the monuments are those created to glorify historical events or personalities. Examples are the reliefs of the temples in Der-el-Bahari and Karnak from the age of the XVIIIth dynasty, the account of the expedition of Queen Hatshepsut to the Land of Punt with pictures of foreign animals and plants in Der-el-Bahari,[1] and the pictures in Karnak of the booty won by Thutmose III, the great conqueror, in his Syrian campaigns. Historical monuments in the narrower sense are the battle reliefs of Seti I and Rameses II; there are five representations of the battle of Kadesh between Egyptians and Hittites, c. 1294 B.C.[2] The struggles connected with the migration of the Sea Peoples reached the coasts of Egypt, and are reflected in the picture of a sea battle between Egyptians and Philistines on the temple walls of Medinet Habu,

[1] *Handbuch der Archäologie* I, Tafelband, figure 88, 3.
[2] W. Wreszinski, *Atlas z. altägyptische Kulturgesch* II (Leipzig 1935), plates 16–25, 96–106.

a picture which no written description, however colorful, could equal.[3]

Valuable insights into the culture and life of ancient Mesopotamia may be drawn from its monuments. The victory monument of Naramsin of Akkad (c. 2300 B.C.)[4] is an impressive picture of a triumphant king at the head of his forces pursuing the defeated foe, despite the incomplete state of the monument—or, perhaps, because of it. Assyria has left no representations more impressive than its pictures of battles and hunts; there is nothing comparable in ancient art, except in Sassanian. Everyone who studies these pictures will understand the frightful dread which the Assyrians inspired in the peoples of the Near East. The relief of the Assyrian king Sanherib, showing the expulsion of the inhabitants of Lachis in Judaea,[5] shows more clearly than could words the misery of innocent people (cf. 2 *Kings* 18.14) on whom war has burst in all its fury; compare the impressive description in *Isaiah* 1.7 ff.

An example of historical pictures from the Greek world is the famous Alexander Mosaic, found in the House of the Faun in Pompeii and now in the National Museum of Naples. It is based on an original by Philoxenus, an artist from Eretria of the age of the Diadochi, and it portrays—almost certainly—a turning point in world history, the confrontation of Darius III and Alexander at the battle of Issus (333 B.C.); the Persian king gazes with terror at Alexander charging at him with lance in hand. Karl Justi compared this picture with Velasquez's *Surrender of Breda*; in both, he says, an historical event is humanized by focusing on its central emotion. Goethe saw a picture of the mosaic after its discovery in 1831 at Pompeii and admired it greatly, and it is in fact an outstanding example of Hellenistic historical art.

Nothing similar to this wonderful mosaic is known to us from Roman art, even though great deeds were often glorified in Rome in metal or stone. Aemilius Paulus erected a monument to commemorate his defeat of Perseus at Pydna (168 B.C.), and fragments of it are preserved at Delphi with scenes of the battle, but they would mean nothing to us were it not for literary sources. The same is true for the columns of Trajan and Marcus Aurelius in Rome, though

[3] Nelson, *Medinet Habu* (Chicago 1930), plates 37 ff.
[4] *Handbuch der Archäologie* I, Tafelband, plate 142.
[5] A. Jirku, *Die Welt der Bibel* (1957), plate 91.

they are valuable archeological commentaries on the Dacian and Marcomanni wars and give us much information on the weapons, tactics, and siegecraft of the Romans in the Antonine age. Similarly the many Roman triumphal arches erected in Italy and the provinces[6] with their historical figures are important sources. The great struggle between the Roman and Sassanid empires is represented for us in the relief of Naqsh-i-Rustam which Sapor I set up to mark his victory over Valerian in A.D. 260.[7]

These notes must suffice as a suggestion of the importance of monuments. It is regrettable that we do not yet have an illustrated atlas for historians which would give a survey of the most important monuments.

However, the monuments provide more than illustrations. Adolf Schulten's excavations in Numantia in northern Spain, for example, have greatly increased our knowledge of Roman military institutions during the Republic. Twelve Roman legionary camps were uncovered, seven of them from the campaign of Scipio Aemilianus' siege of Numantia in 134–133 B.C. He surrounded the city with a rampart eight kilometers long which connected the camps and isolated the city. The other five camps were found on a hill east of Numantia, and one of them is the two-legion camp layed out by Fulvius Nobilior in 153 B.C. and described by Polybius as a typical example.

Study of the Roman Empire's border policies is primarily based on analysis of the *limites* (plural of *limes*, "frontier"). The *limes* between the Rhine and Danube has been the subject of a most thorough examination, the results of which are given in a monumental work edited by E. Fabricius, *Der Obergermanisch-rätische Limes des Römerreiches*. This work is fundamental for our knowledge of colonization and cultural relations between Romans and Germans.

In general the monuments are most important as historical sources for those epochs for which a coherent literary tradition is not extant, and this is true above all for the early history of the Mediterranean area. Since Cretan and Cypriote cannot yet be read, we are primarily dependent on the monuments. Of the works which use specialized studies to form an historical picture of the epoch, one in particular deserves mention: Diedrich Fimmen, *Die cretisch-mykenische Kul-*

[6] H. Kähler, *RE* VII A, 373 ff.
[7] F. Sarre, *Die Kunst der alten Persien* (Berlin 1922), figures 74–75.

tur, ed. 2 by G. Karo (Leipzig, 1924). It shows the ways in which archeology uses datable foreign objects, especially Egyptian, to fix the chronology of the levels of native cultures in Crete and Hellas. The history of these areas is still subject to debate, and the early history of Italy is even more unsettled at this time. It is therefore important that the student of Antiquity form a general picture of these periods as a basis for evaluating the conclusions of current research.

One can also regard ancient cities as historical monuments, and many sites have been brought to light by modern excavations.[8] For a long time the Campanian town of Pompeii was a unique example of an early imperial city, and even today it has a special importance because its ruins give us a view of 600 years of life in ancient Italy. However, since 1875 systematic excavations have revealed a series of cities: Ostia in Latium, Thugga and Timgad in Africa, Leptis Magna in Tripolitania, Cyrene in Cyrenaica, and Ephesus, Miletus, Pergamum, Priene, Cnidos, and many others in Asia Minor. Since 1950 French excavations under Louis Robert in the sacred area of Clarus near Colophon have greatly enlarged our knowledge about the famous oracle. Also of great interest are the excavations at the great necropolis of Spina in the Po valley; the numerous discoveries, of which only a part could be published, have revealed the interrelation of Greek and Etruscan cultures. On the Euphrates excavations were undertaken jointly by the Académie des Inscriptions et Belles Lettres of Paris and Yale University at Dura-Europus, a Hellenistic city founded in the age of the Diadochi, which reached its greatest prosperity under the Roman and Parthian empires.

These few examples, chosen from hundreds, indicate that archeology is just beginning to uncover hidden treasures. Moreover there are still only a few definitive publications of a particular site. Rarely is the extent of a city so fortunately limited as in the case of Assur, the history of which can be traced to the third century A.D.

At one time archeologists thought it beneath their dignity to concern themselves with simple objects of the so-called "material culture." They conceived their mission as rather excavation of temples and shrines like the Mausoleum of Halicarnassus or the Didymaion of Miletus, of royal palaces, baths, gymnasia, theaters, and palaestrae. This attitude, however, has long been discarded. Every

[8] A. v. Gerkan, *Griechische Städteanlagen* (Berlin 1924).

student of ancient economic history, for example, must concern himself with the remains of ancient harbors, villas, and farms, and must be able to evaluate gravestones, works of applied art, earthenware (*terra sigillata*), clay lamps, the wall paintings in Crimean graves, the floor mosaics of North African cities, and many other objects of similar historical significance. Michael Rostovtzeff made use of a massive amount of such archeological material in his studies of Hellenistic and Roman civilizations, and as a result his works give us the fullest and most immediate picture of Antiquity ever achieved by scholarship.

In Heinrich Schliemann's time archeologists hastily plowed through the upper strata as "worthless" in order to reach the oldest, but this has long ceased. Now archeologists methodically study each stratum and give each epoch the attention it deserves; the leading German representatives of this approach are W. Dörpfeld and Th. Wiegand. Thus while the 19th-century excavations in Mesopotamia were primarily concerned with the older strata, the recent excavations in Hatra, Ctesiphon, Seleucia on the Tigris, and the Caliph's residence of Samara, north of Babylon, have been pursued to illuminate more recent periods, from Hellenistic to Arabian times.

In general, no other study has contributed as much as archeology to expand the horizon of ancient historians. Excavations and research are being pursued from one end of the oecumene to the other, from Spain and Britain to Chorasmien (Toprak Kale), Turkestan, and India (Begram, Taxila, Arikamedu near Pondicherry). Methodology has been refined through careful attention to stratigraphy, and for more than twenty years air photography has been used to aid research, as for example in the study of the Syrian *limes* and the *Fossatum Africae*.[9] Another new field has been opened up by underwater archeology, pursued with success especially off the coasts of southern France and Italy. It is therefore not surprising that systematic study and historical interpretation cannot keep pace with the rapidly increasing mass of material.

Nevertheless, no student of Antiquity will content himself with study of the written sources; no poet or historian can tell of the greatness of the Roman Empire as eloquently or impressively as the amphitheaters, baths, aqueducts, highways, and frontier walls.

[9] R. Chevallier, in *Études archéologiques* (École pratique des Hautes Études: Paris 1963), 33 ff., with good illustrations.

Similarly the Acropolis of Athens and the sacred precincts of Delphi and Olympia bear witness to the essence of classical Greece, as do the pyramids and temples for the ancient Near East. "Whatever else may be changed there will always remain certain memorials, the foundations and fragments of the immortal cities and their monuments." (B. G. Niebuhr, letter of July 18, 1797.)

BIBLIOGRAPHY

GENERAL: There is no guide to ancient monuments for the historian. W. Otto started a "Handbook of Archeology" within the series *Handbuch der Altertumswissenschaft*. Before his death in 1941 only the first volume (1939) had appeared, giving a good introduction to the monuments of ancient Egypt and the Near East; its authors include A. Scharff, W. Andrae, and C. Watzinger. Publication of this handbook is to be continued. In accordance with the format of the *Handbuch* the material is all discussed, covering architecture, fine arts, and decorative arts; the objective is to give a complete picture of each culture, and this is achieved particularly well by W. Andrae for Mesopotamia on the basis of a new system of classifying the material. At present a new edition is in press, edited by U. Hausmann.

Also valuable is G. Contenau, *Manuel d'archéologie orientale* (4 vols., Paris 1921–1947), and the review of research by K. Schefold, *Orient, Hellas u. Rom in der archäol. Forschung seit 1939* (Bern 1949). Much material is available in J. Pritchard, *The Ancient Near East in Pictures Relating to the Old Testament* (Princeton 1954); and, with recent bibliography, *Enciclopedia dell' arte antica, classica e orientale*, ed. F. Bäum (Rome 1958–1966).—On methodology see, e.g., Sir Mortimer Wheeler, *Moderne Archäologie: Methoden, Technik der Ausgrabung* (Hamburg 1960).

MONOGRAPHS ON ANCIENT MONUMENTS: (1) Egypt: Historians will find useful and accessible the collection of illustrations added as a supplement to J. Breasted, *Gesch. Ägyptens*, tr. H. Ranke (Vienna 1936). Other excellent works are: W. Wolf, *Die Kunst Ägyptens: Gestalt u. Geschichte* (Stuttgart 1957); K. Lange and M. Hirmer, *Ägypten: Architektur, Plastik, Malerei in drei Jahrtausenden* (Munich 1967); J. Vandier, *Manuel d'archéologie égyptienne*, not yet completed (Paris 1952–).

(2) Mesopotamia: Especially informative are the works of André Parrot, *Sumer* (Munich 1960) and *Assur* (Munich 1961) in the series *Universum der Kunst*; also the work of Eva Strommenger and

M. Hirmer, *5 Jahrtausende Mesopotamien* (Munich 1962), with many fine illustrations.

(3) Asia Minor: T. Bossert, *Anatolien: Kunst u. Handwerk in Kleinasien von den Anfängen bis zum völligen aufgehen in die griech. Kultur* (Berlin 1942); E. Akurgal, *Die Kunst Anatoliens von Homer bis Alexander* (Berlin 1961).

(4) Iran: H. v. d. Osten, *Die Welt der Perser* (Stuttgart 1957); E. F. Schmidt, *Persepolis I: Structures, Reliefs, Inscriptions* (Chicago 1953); II (Chicago 1957) deals with monumental constructions; K. Erdmann, *Die Kunst Irans zur Zeit der Sasaniden* (Mainz 1943).

(5) Crete: Sir Arthur Evans, *The Palace of Minos at Knossos* (4 vols. and index, London 1921–1936); T. Bossert, *Altkreta: Kunst u. Handwerk in Griechenland, Kreta u. in der Aegäis von den Anfängen bis zur Eisenzeit* (ed. 3, Berlin 1937), with references to written sources; F. Matz, *Kreta, Mykene, Troja* (ed. 2, Stuttgart 1956).

(6) Greece and Rome: A. v. Salis, *Die Kunst der Griechen* (ed. 2, Leipzig 1922); A. Springer, *Die Kunst des Altertums*, ed. P. Wolters (ed. 12, Leipzig 1923); G. Rodenwaldt, *Die Kunst des Altertums*, in *Propyläen-Kunstgeschichte* III (ed. 4, 1927); E. Strong, *Art in Ancient Rome* (2 vols., ed. 2, London 1930); A. Rumpf, "Griechische u. röm. Kunst," in *Gercke-Norden* II.3 (ed. 3, Leipzig 1931); W. Schuchhardt and W. Technau, *Geschichte der Kunst: Altertum* (Berlin 1940); G. Lippold, *Die griech. Plastik*, in *Hdb. der Archäologie*, fasc. 5 (1950); A. Rumpf, *Malerei u. Zeichnung*, in *ibid.*, fasc. 6 (1953); H. Berve, G. Gruben, and M. Hirmer, *Griechische Tempel u. Heiligtümer* (Munich 1961); H. Kähler, *Rom u. seine Welt* (2 vols., Munich 1958–1960), with many illustrations and comments thereon, but without references to studies.

(7) Etruscans: P. Ducati, *Storia dell' arte etrusca* (2 vols., Florence 1927); B. Nogara, *Gli Etrusci e loro civiltà* (Milan 1933); G. Q. Giglioli, *L'arte etrusca* (Milan 1935); K. Pfister, *Die Etrusker* (Munich 1940), with admirable illustrations, but the text is out of date; P. J. Riis, *An Introduction to Etruscan Art* (Copenhagen 1953).

(8) Eastern Frontier Regions: A. v. Le Coq, *Auf Hellas Spuren in Ostturkestan* (1923), and *Bilderatlas zur Kunst u. Kulturgeschichte Mittelasiens* (1925); A. Ippel, "Werkungen griechischer Kunst in Asien," *Alte Orient* 39, nos. 1–2 (Leipzig 1940).

REVIEW OF ARCHEOLOGICAL DISCOVERIES: A. Michaelis, *Die archäologischen Entdeckungen des 19. Jahrhunderts* (ed. 2, Leipzig 1908); F. v. Oppeln-Bronikowski, *Archäolog. Entdeckungen im 20. Jahrhundert* (Berlin 1931); *Neue deutsche Ausgrabungen im Mittelmeergebiet und im Vorderen Orient*, ed. E. Boehringer (Berlin 1959–), continuing. Of monographs on individual areas the following deserve note: R. G. Collingwood, *The Archaeology of Ro-man Britain* (London 1930), and *Roman Britain* (ed. 3, Oxford 1934); A. Grenier, *Manuel d'archéologie gallo-romaine* (3 vols., Paris 1931–1958); F. Stählin, *Die Schweiz in der röm. Zeit* (ed. 3, Basel 1948); A. Schober, *Die Römerzeit in Österreich* (ed. 2, Baden [Austria] 1953); A. W. Byvanck, *Nederland in den romeinschen tijd* (2 vols., Leiden 1943); A. Garcia y Bellido, *Hispania Graeca* (3 vols., Barcelona 1950); C. Watzinger, *Denkmäler Palästinas* (2 vols., 1933–1935); A. Jirku, *Die Ausgrabungen in Palästina u. Syrien* (Halle 1956). Among the many excavation reports the follow-ing are especially useful for the historian: E. Unger, *Babylon: Die heilige Stadt* (Berlin 1931); M. Schede, *Die Ruinen von Priene* (Ber-lin and Leipzig 1934); K. Bittel, *Die Ruinen von Bogazköy, der Hauptstadt des Hethiterreiches* (Berlin and Leipzig 1937); L. Vin-cent and M. Steve, *Jerusalem de l'Ancien Testament* (4 vols., Paris 1954–1956).

ARCHEOLOGY AND HISTORY: G. Körte, *Archäologie u. Ge-schichtswissenschaft* (Göttingen 1911); G. Rodenwaldt, "Das Erleb-nis der Geschichte in der griechischen Kunst," *Forschungen u. Fortschritte* (1943), 90 ff.

MONOGRAPHS: EGYPT: E. Naville, *The Temple of Deir-el-Bahari* (vols. 3–4, London 1898–1901); Jéquier, *L'architecture et la décoration dans l'ancien Égypte: Les temples memphites et the-baines* I (Paris 1920), plate 47 (Karnak).

ALEXANDER MOSAIC: F. Winter, *Das Alexandermosaik aus Pompeji* (Strasburg 1909); L. Curtius, *Die Wandmalerei Pompejis* (1929): p. 323: "the most royal picture in the world." See also H. Fuhrmann, *Philoxenos von Eretria* (Göttingen 1931), reviewed by A. Ippel, *Gnomon* (1934), 79 ff.

COLUMN OF TRAJAN: C. Cichorius, *Die Reliefs der Trajans-säule* (Berlin 1896–1900); E. Petersen, *Trajans dakischer Krieg* (Leipzig 1899–1904); A. v. Domaszewski, "Die Dakerkriege Tra-jans auf den Reliefs der Säule," *Philologus* 65 (1906), 321 ff.; K. Lehmann-Hartleben, *Die Trajanssäule* (Berlin 1926).

COLUMN OF MARCUS AURELIUS: E. Petersen, A. v. Domaszew-ski and G. Calderini, *Die Markussäule auf Piazza Colonna in Rom* (Munich 1896); W. Zwikker, *Studien z. Markussäule* I (Amster-dam 1941); C. Caprino, M. Colini, *et al., La colonna di Marco Au-relio* (Rome 1955).

NUMANTIA: Fundamental work: Adolf Schulten, *Numantia* (4 vols., Munich 1914–1929), and his brief synthesis, *Geschichte v. Numantia* (Munich 1933).

LIMES STUDIES: The outstanding German work is *Der ober-*

germanisch-rätische Limes des Römerreiches, noted in the text; its last fascicle (No. 56.2) appeared in 1938; the work was edited by F. Hettner, O. v. Sarwey, and then E. Fabricius alone, and includes fourteen volumes (1894–1938). For surveys of the field see E. Fabricius, *Die Entstehung der römischen Limes-anlagen* (Trier 1902); his comprehensive article "Limes," *RE* XIII (1926), 572 ff., which discusses other frontiers; and W. Schleiermacher, "Der obergermanische Limes u. spätrömische Wehranlagen am Rhein," *33. Bericht d. Röm.-Germ. Kommission 1943–1950* (1951), 133–184.— *Syria and Mesopotamia*: A. Poidebard, *La trace de Rome dans le désert de Syrie: Le limes de Trajan à la conquête arabe: Recherches aériennes (1925–1932)* (Paris 1934); with this see W. Ensslin, *SBAW* 1942, no. 1, 66 ff., on Diocletian's Eastern policies. *Africa*: J. Baradez, *Fossatum Africae: Recherches aériennes sur l'organisation des confins sahariens à l'époque romaine* (Paris 1949).—On study of Roman frontiers, see: *Congress of Roman Studies 1949* (Durham 1952), ed. E. Birley; *Carnuntina (Röm. Forschungen in Niederösterreich* 3, ed. E. Swoboda (Graz 1956).

EARLY HISTORY OF THE MEDITERRANEAN AREA: A new comprehensive account is given by fascicle 4 of the *Hdb. der Archäologie* (1950), with articles by O. Menghin, F. Matz, and G. v. Kaschnitz-Weinberg. A useful introduction is J. Wiesner, *Vor- u. Frühzeit der Mittelmeerländer (Sammlung Göschen* 1149–1150, Berlin 1943). For European implications a fundamental although one-sided work is C. Schuchhardt, *Alteuropa* (ed. 3, Berlin and Leipzig 1935). Admirable too are F. Matz, "Griechische Vorgeschichte," *Neue Bild. d. Antike* 1 (1942), 13 ff., and *Kreta, Mykene, Troja* (ed. 2, Stuttgart 1956), with excellent illustrations.

EASTERN MEDITERRANEAN: Works useful to the historian include: G. Karo, *Die Schachtgräber von Mykenai* (Munich 1930–1933), and "Mykenische Kultur," *RE*, Supp. VI (1935), 584 ff. Karo's article "Kreta," *RE* XI (1922), 1743 ff., has been rendered partly out of date by subsequent research. J. Pendlebury, *The Archaelogy of Crete* (London 1939), gives a useful synthesis of archeological discoveries on the island. See also F. Schachermeyr, *Die ältesten Kulturen Griechenlands* (Stuttgart 1955); and "Prähistorische Kulturen Griechenlands," *RE* XXII (1954), 1350–1548, with full references to the sources.—For Troy the reference work is now the large new excavation report of the Americans under C. W. Blegen, *Troy* (4 vols., Princeton and Oxford 1950–1959).—French excavations since 1929 at Ras Shamra, the ancient Ugarit, of cuneiform texts, 12 km. north of Laodicea in northern Syria, have revealed a new center of culture and commerce in the eastern Mediterranean which was in close contact with Crete and Greece. For this see especially C. F. Schaeffer, "Die Stellung Ras-Schamra-Ugarits zur kretischen u. mykenischen Kultur," *JDAI* 52 (1937), 139 ff., and *Ugaritica* (3 vols., Paris 1939–1956); C. Gordon, *Ugaritic Manual*, (3 vols., *Analecta Orientalia* 35; Rome 1955). Excavation reports have been published in the journal *Syria* (Paris) since 1929. Cf. O. Eissfeldt, "Die Bedeutung der Funde von Ras Schamra für die Gesch. des Altertums," *HZ* 168 (1943), 457 ff.–On Asia Minor see the excellent work of K. Bittel, *Grundzüge der Vor- u. Frühgeschichte Kleinasiens* (ed. 2, Tübingen 1950).

WESTERN MEDITERRANEAN: Italy's early history, much discussed recently, is surveyed by F. Matz, *NJA* (1938), 367 ff., 385 ff., and (1939), 32 ff. Italian scholars have sought to minimize the significance of "Nordic" migrations; cf. G. Patroni, *La Preistoria* (Milan 1937; ed. 2, 1951). The fundamental work in this theory-ridden field was F. v. Duhn, *Italische Gräberkunde*, 2 vols., vol. 2 edited by F. Messerschmidt (Heidelberg 1924–1939). See now F. Messerschmidt, *Bronzezeit u. frühe Eisenzeit in Italien* (Berlin 1935); G. Säflund, *Le terremare delle provincie di Modena, Reggio Emilia, Parma, Piacenza* (Lund and Leipzig 1939). Further bibliography is given by A. Piganiol, *Hist. de Rome* (ed. 5, 1962), 15 ff., 528 ff.– Recent excavations of the Forum Romanum are reported on by E. Gjerstad, *Early Rome* (4 vols. and continuing, Lund 1953–1966). Gjerstad follows Hanell in dating the regal period c. 575–450 B.C., but the last date is too late.

Pompeii: A. Mau, *Pompeji in Leben u. Kunst* (ed. 2, Leipzig 1908), and with a supplement by F. Drexel (1913); A. Mau and A. Ippel, *Führer durch Pompeji* (ed. 6, Leipzig 1928). Additions to our knowledge have been realized through the recent excavations directed by A. Maiuri, for which see his *Pompeii*, tr. V. Priestley (ed. 7, Rome 1954), and *Raccolta di studi per il secondo centenario degli scavi di Pompei* (Naples 1955). Useful too is R. Etienne, *La vie quotidienne à Pompéi* (Paris 1966).

Spina: So far the best work is N. Alfieri, P. Arias, and M. Hirmer, *Spina* (Munich 1958). See also *Spina e l'Etruria padana* (*Studi etruschi* 25, supplement 1959); and S. Aurigemma, *Scavi di Spina* I.1 and I.2: *La necropoli di Spina in Valle Trebbia* (Rome 1960–1965).

EXCAVATION REPORTS: A bibliography of classical archeology cannot be given here. The student should consult the survey of excavations in the *Hdb. d. Archäologie* I (1939), 851 ff. Some outstanding works follow. On Dura-Europus: F. Cumont, *Fouilles de Dura-Europos 1922–1923* (Paris 1926), supplemented by *The Exca-*

vations at Dura-Europos: Preliminary Reports (9 vols. to date, New Haven 1929–1946). On North Africa: A. Lantier, Les grandes champs de fouilles de l'Afrique du Nord 1915–1930 (Paris 1931). A valuable tool is the generous bibliography in the two great works of M. Rostovtzeff, The Social and Economic History of the Roman Empire (Oxford 1926; ed. 2, revised by P. M. Fraser, 1957), and The Social and Economic History of the Hellenistic World (3 vols., Oxford 1941). Much of the literature is cited by Andrae, Fabricius, and Lehmann-Hartleben, "Städtebau," RE III A (1929), 1947 ff., and by A. Piganiol, Histoire de Rome (ed. 5, Paris 1962), 354 ff., 381 ff.—But the student who wishes to inform himself regarding current archeological research in a particular city or area will peruse, after first consulting the relevant articles in RÉ, the reports in AA, which has been published as a supplement to the JDAI since 1889; and the student will also profit from the German Archeological Institute's annual Bibliographie zum Archäologischen Jahrbuch (1923/24 ff.). Excavations in the Near East are reported in the Archiv für Orientforschung, ed. E. F. Weidner (1926 ff.). For the Romano-German field the essential tool is the Jahresberichte der römisch-germanischen Kommission.

SELECTED ARCHEOLOGICAL JOURNALS: (1) Germany: Jahrbuch des Deutschen Archäologischen Instituts (1886 ff.); Mitteilungen des Deutschen Archäologischen Instituts: Athenische Abteilung (1876 ff.); Mitteilungen . . . Römische Abteilung (1886 ff.); Germania: Korrespondenzblatt der Röm.-Germ. Kommission d. Deutschen Archäologischen Instituts (1917 ff.)

(2) France: Bulletin de Correspondance hellénique (1877 ff.); Revue archéologique (1844 ff.).

(3) Greece: Ἐφημερὶς αρχαιολογική (1837 ff.)

(4) Britain: Annual of the British School at Athens (1895 ff.); Journal of Roman Studies (1911 ff.).

(5) Italy: Notizie degli scavi di antichità (Rome 1876 ff.); Monumenti antichi a cura dell' Accademia dei Lincei (Milan 1892 ff.); Fasti archeologici (Florence 1946 ff.). The latter is an important source for bibliography.

(6) Austria: Archäologisch-epigraphische Mitteilungen aus Österreich (1878–1898); Jahreshefte des Österreichischen Archäologischen Instituts (1898 ff.).

(7) USA: American Journal of Archaeology (1885 ff.; series 2, 1897 ff.); Hesperia (1932 ff.).

VI

Basic Disciplines:
Epigraphy, Papyrology,
Numismatics

———

Within the great mass of primary materials some categories deserve special attention, namely inscriptions, papyri, and coins. During the 19th century special disciplines developed around the intensive study of these sources, and these disciplines have a particular importance for ancient historians because they deal with the kinds of material still being discovered. Once these disciplines were called "auxiliary," but that term gives an erroneous impression and should be dropped from the vocabulary of scholars.

The immense variety and dispersion of inscriptions, papyri, and coins make it difficult for the historian to integrate and synthesize the evidence they provide. As a result they are often not regarded seriously as sources, a fact which is a discredit to scholarship in Germany. For it was after all a group of German scholars, including August Böckh, Theodor Mommsen, and Ulrich von Wilamowitz-Moellendorff, who organized the great collections of inscriptions and so made them available to scholars.

On the other hand those scholars who devote themselves to editing and interpreting ancient inscriptions, papyri, and coins should never forget that their objective is to illuminate and deepen our knowledge of Antiquity.

Beginning students of epigraphy forget easily that every document on stone is a reflection of ancient life. Therefore it is necessary to use a photographic facsimile to form an idea of the original. Arrangement, form, and position of inscriptions, especially those connected with a monument, are often as important as the content of the inscription itself. Thus, no other monument illustrates so well the collapse of the Macedonian monarchy and the great victory of Rome at Pydna (168 B.C.) as the arrow-shaped monument, 26 feet high, which honors L. Aemilius Paulus at Delphi. Originally the monument had been erected for King Perseus of Macedon; now it bears the equestrian statue of the Roman victor with this inscription: *L. Aemilius L. f. imperator de rege Perse Macedonibusque cepet.*[1] It is regrettable that publications of inscriptions, including recent ones, include few illustrations. This failing should be corrected.

Many ancient inscriptions survive only in fragments, but epigraphers have discovered methods of remedying this, and even what seem hopelessly tiny remains have often been expanded to give a message. Nevertheless, "restorations"—that is, those words reconstructed by the epigrapher and printed in brackets [ ]—are in many cases necessarily no more than guesses. Therefore, whenever one uses inscriptions with restorations one should use brackets where appropriate, a precaution which is often neglected. Restoration of inscriptions requires an exact knowledge of relevant formulas, such as those used for laws, honorary inscriptions, and treaties; it also requires thorough knowledge of the diction and style of the period. Thus, only the student conversant with Polybius, Diodorus, and Josephus can feel equipped to restore Hellenistic inscriptions.

Geographic distribution deserves attention. Much the largest portion of Greek inscriptions has been found in Attica; the wealth of epigraphic material from this area, especially that dating from the Hellenistic and Roman periods, is overwhelming. All other areas are far behind Attica: the Peloponnesus, central and northern Greece, Macedonia. The only competitors are the small communities of Asia Minor which flourished in Hellenistic and, to some extent, in Roman times, including Miletus, Ephesus, Pergamum, Priene, Magnesia on the Meander, and Sardis. The same applies to the great religious centers of Greece: Delphi, Delos, and Olympia. Little has been found in inland Anatolia, though this may be due to the want of exploration in that area; on the other hand Syria, Egypt, and Cyrenaica have yielded a number of inscriptions important for the history of the Hellenistic and Roman periods.

Latin inscriptions are distributed otherwise. They are not con-

[1] For an illustration of the monument, see M. Rostovtzeff, *Social and Economic History of the Hellenistic World* II (Oxford 1941), 740, plate 82. See also *Fouilles de Delphes* III.4, 30, figure 4. The inscription itself is printed in *CIL* I (ed. 2), no. 622.

centrated in any single locality, but rather are found scattered from Britain to the Euphrates, from the Rhine and Danube to the Sudan. However, the western provinces have yielded far more than has the Greek East, for there Latin was the language of the army and administration only. It is because of the great mass of Latin inscriptions that scholars have been able to free themselves from the Rome-centered viewpoint of the ancient historians and, instead, describe the Imperium Romanum as a great organism within which the various regions developed their individuality.

As for the time span involved, the Greek inscriptions begin with a text on an Athenian jug in the so-called Dipylon style dated 800–750 B.C. (*IG* I, ed. 2, no. 919), and continue on to the Byzantine period, with the largest part falling in the Hellenistic and Roman periods. The distribution of Latin inscriptions is different, for they do not begin to appear in numbers until the Sullan epoch; what we have from earlier years is in the nature of precursors, like the earliest inscription, *Manios med fhefhaked Numasioi* (*Manius me fecit Numerio*; *CIL* I, ed. 2, no. 3) on a fibula from Praeneste dating from c. 600 B.C. The golden age of Latin epigraphy is the Roman Empire, especially the first two centuries A.D. The decrease of inscriptions in the third century reflects the political, economic, and intellectual crisis of the Empire. Under Diocletian and Constantine a temporary revival in the use of inscriptions occurred, but by the sixth century they gradually disappeared as ancient civilization declined and gave way to a new spirit and a new age.

A few examples must suffice to indicate the importance of epigraphy for ancient history. All we know about the organization of the Delian League, founded in 478/477 B.C., we owe to inscriptions, not to historians, in particular to the so-called Athenian Tribute Lists (they should be called "tribute quota lists"), in which is given a part (1/60) of the total amount each ally was required to pay Athena as protector of the League.[2] From variations in the number of allies and in the amounts of tribute levied one can form a reasonably accurate picture of this great Hellenic organization which furthered Athenian power and so decisively affected the political history of the fifth century.

Sometimes inscriptions reveal important events. For example, the founding of the Second Corinthian League in 302 B.C. by the

[2] B. Meritt, H. Wade-Gery, and M. McGregor, *The Athenian Tribute Lists* (4 vols., Cambridge, Mass. 1939–1953).

Diadochi Antigonus I and Demetrius Poliorketes is known to us through an inscription from the Asclepion in Epidaurus (*IG* IV.1, ed. 2, no. 68; cf. U. Wilcken, *SPAW* 1922, p. 122 ff., and 1927, p. 277 ff.). This document, in fact, first made it possible to understand a passage (ch. 25) in Plutarch's *Life of Demetrius*.

An important historical source are the royal letters sent by Hellenistic kings to cities and governors. They date from Alexander to Mithridates VI Eupator, and provide a valuable addition to the sources for this still obscure period; *cf.* C. B. Welles, *Royal Correspondence in the Hellenistic Period* (New Haven 1934). Another important document is the inscriptions found at the marketplace of Cyrene, which give us much information on the relation of Augustus to the senatorial provinces and also on the position of Greek culture in Cyrenaica (*SEG* IX, no. 8).[3]

Our knowledge of Greek civic and federal constitutions similarly rests primarily on the evidence of inscriptions. It is almost entirely to epigraphic documents that we owe our knowledge of officials and of how the councils and assemblies functioned, how votes were taken, and what honors were given to citizens and foreigners. Furthermore the inscriptions tell us about temple rules, sacrificial procedures, and the character, regulations, and membership of clubs, about private and public foundations, and so in this way give us a glimpse into areas of ancient life otherwise hidden from us. A good example of this is the documents of manumission, which give us important data on social conditions especially in the Hellenistic period.

Among the Latin inscriptions which concern political life three groups are particularly important: resolutions of the Senate (*senatus consulta*), laws passed by the popular assemblies (*leges rogatae*), and edicts of magistrates (*leges datae, edicta, decreta*). These together with imperial decrees (*constitutiones*) afford a mass of evidence for the study of Roman government during the Republic and Principate.

An outstanding example of such extant documents is the *senatus consultum de Bacchanalibus* of 186 B.C. (*CIL* I, ed. 2, no. 581), which concerns the measures voted to check the spread of the orgiastic cult of Dionysus lately imported from the Hellenistic East.

---

[3] Great interest has been aroused by an inscription discovered in Troezen, published by M. H. Jameson, *Hesperia* 29 (1960), 198 ff. Its authenticity is disputed; C. Habicht, *Hermes* 89 (1961), 1 ff., argues against it, H. Berve, *SBAW* 1961, no. 3, for it.

Of the *leges rogatae* extant we can cite the so-called Enabling Act passed for Emperor Vespasian (*lex de imperio Vespasiani*; CIL VI.1, no. 930); this gave the new princeps a number of political powers and so assimilated his position to the model created by Augustus, Tiberius, and Claudius; in general it is of fundamental importance for understanding the emperors' constitutional position.

Important inscriptions have been discovered recently, among them the Germanicus inscription found in the South Etrurian town of Heba (today Magliano). This is a bronze plaque on which is inscribed a *rogatio*, that is, a law submitted to and passed by the popular assembly in Rome (*comitia*).[4] It concerns the honors paid the memory of Germanicus, who died in A.D. 19, and it gives valuable information on the *destinatio* of consuls and praetors and in general on election procedure under Tiberius.

Two categories of Latin inscriptions are peculiarly Roman: military diplomas and milestones. The first consist normally of two bronze tablets punched and fitted so as to fold together; they are documents to record that their possessors, veterans who had completed their service, had been granted citizenship (*civitas Romana*) or else the right to marry a foreigner (*ius conubii*). By now more than 150 military diplomas have been found, dating from Claudius to Diocletian, a period of 250 years. They give valuable information on the national recruitment of the Roman Empire's army and on the history of individual units.

Roman milestones, similarly, have no counterpart in Greek epigraphy. They document the building activities of the Republican magistrates, the emperors, and the cities; sometimes they even give information about the planning and preparations made for military campaigns, as has been shown with regard to the Raetian roads built by Septimius Severus; see H. Instinsky, *Klio* 31 (1938), 33 ff.

However, the primary value of the great mass of Latin inscriptions is that they help us to understand the life of the average man— the artisan, the freedman, the slave; that is, they take us into the kind of social groups which hardly ever appear in the literary tradition, the only exceptions being the *Cena Trimalchionis* of Petronius and the poems of Martial and Juvenal. It is only through the inscriptions that we can form a picture of the social and economic condi-

[4] Text given by H. Nesselhauf, *Historia* 1 (1950), 105 ff., cf. *PP* 14 (1950), which gives the text and also scholarly studies, mostly by Italians; also *AJP* 75 (1954), 225 ff.

tions which caused the internal development of the Roman Empire, the fateful transition from a welfare-state system to that of a garrison state, a development in which eventually the individual was degraded to the role of slave to an omnipotent state.

Price statistics are provided by Greek inscriptions of the Hellenistic period, though the evidence is still fragmentary.[5] For the economy of the Roman Empire we have valuable evidence in the material collected in *Inscriptiones instrumenti domestici* (see below), mostly short inscriptions on articles of daily use such as earthenware dishes (*terra sigillata*), wine jugs, and bricks.

Finally, through the inscriptions (and coins as well) we get information on the geographic extension of Hellenic culture in the East, and similarly learn of the spread of Oriental religions and missions in the Greek world and in the western provinces of the Roman Empire. And where the doctrine of a religion remains unknown to us, as is the case with the Mithra cult from Persia, then through epigraphic documents we learn much at least about its ceremonial forms. This applies especially to the ceremonies connected with the ancient ruler cult, which modern scholars have come to stress as an important factor in ancient political life. Likewise our historical understanding of early Christianity has been placed on a new basis partly through epigraphic studies. Thanks to the researches of Sir William Ramsay and others in Central Anatolia we know now the environment in which the mission of St. Paul developed during the first century A.D., and through study of the formulas used in gravestone inscriptions we can trace the advance of Christianity and the decline of paganism. In studying religious history the inscriptions are incorruptible witnesses; thus the internal weakening of paganism in the Roman Empire becomes evident from the decline of dedications during the third century A.D.

Still another aspect of the ancient inscriptions is their importance for the study of family relationships, called prosopography. Only the study of inscriptions has made possible such works as the *Prosopographia Attica* of Johannes Kirchner and the *Prosographia Imperii Romani* published by the Prussian Academy of Sciences.

Compared with epigraphy and numismatics, papyrology is a very young discipline. Just as the plan and publication of the *Corpus Inscriptionum Latinarum* is connected with Theodor Mommsen, so

[5] As an example see F. Heichelheim, *Wirtschaftliche Schwankungen der Zeit von Alexander bis Augustus* (Jena 1930).

the publication and historical criticism of papyri are associated with Ulrich Wilcken (1862–1944). He enjoyed the help of many colleagues from Germany and other countries, among them the "Oxford Dioscuri" B. P. Grenfell and A. S. Hunt, along with Sir Frederic Kenyon and H. I. Bell, the Italians G. Vitelli and Medea Norsa, the Frenchmen J. Lesquier and P. Jouguet, and the German W. Schubart.

Egypt's dry sand has preserved a mass of papyri from a period of more than a thousand years, from the conquest of Alexander the Great (332 B.C.) to the Arab period, which began in A.D. 641. The last Greek-Arabic bilingual text is dated A.D. 996 by Wilcken. Most of the papyri are in Greek, but some are in Demotic, Aramaic, Coptic, Latin, and Middle Persian. Besides the papyri there are also the inscriptions on sherds (*ostraca*) and on wax and wooden tablets to be studied by the papyrologist. Recently papyri have also been discovered outside Egypt, in Palestine, and before that parchment documents from the Parthian period had been found in far-off Kurdistan (Media Atropatene) and in the Hellenistic City of Dura-Europus on the Euphrates.[6]

Using content as the criterion, papyri fall into two groups: literary papyri and documents. The literary papyri have preserved for us many fragments of ancient authors and are therefore important for textual criticism. Most important are papyri with hitherto unknown texts, some of poets such as Archilochus, Alcaeus, Sappho, Bacchylides, Menander (whose plays *Dyskolos* and *Sicyonios* were discovered on papyri a few years ago), and others; but papyri have also preserved fragments of historical works. Among these by far the most important is Aristotle's work *The Constitution of the Athenians* (᾿Αθηναίων πολιτεία). It came to light in 1881 on a papyrus in the British Museum Collection, and was recognized as one of the 158 constitutions collected by Aristotle.

A somewhat less important work is the *Oxyrhynchos Hellenika*, a history of the years 409–407 and 396–395 B.C. Another is the Latin papyrus with an epitome of books 37–55 of Livy's history. There is also a commentary on four orations of Demosthenes by the Alexandrine polymath Didymus, who lived under Augustus, but this is of interest to the student of literature, not history.

[6] From Dura-Europus came the so-called *Feriale Duranum*, a papyrus with the official ceremonial calendar of the Roman garrison; it dates from the reign of Emperor Severus Alexander (A.D. 222–235).

But the majority of papyri are documents, and they are more important for the historian. They have a peculiar value in that their writers did not expect them to be preserved, indeed in many cases they probably did not want them to be preserved. Therefore these papyri surpass even the inscriptions as direct and uncensored witnesses to their age, for often inscriptions were set up for reasons of propaganda or pride.

In using papyri for historical purposes the local origin of each individual document must be remembered. The damp earth of the Nile delta and also the site of ancient Alexandria have not preserved any documents, but occasionally documents of Alexandrine origin are found in the hinterland, as for examples the well-known *Dicaimata*. But by far the largest portion of papyri have been discovered in Middle Egypt, in particular in the Fayum with its villages of Medinet-el-Fayum, Absusir-el-Meleq, Harit (ancient Theadelpheia), and—above all—Tebtunis. Outside the Fayum the most important findspots are Memphis and Oxyrhynchos. Discoveries in Upper Egypt have been relatively fewer; findspots here include Siut, Hermopolis Magna, and Thebes. Only a few papyri have come to light in the southern frontier area, the so-called Dodekaschoinos, which includes Ombos, Syene, and Elephantine.

Most of the documents date from the Roman Empire, especially from the first and second centuries A.D. Many documents also come from the Ptolemaic period, much fewer from the Byzantine (beginning with Constantine I).

Of the many documents preserved the most important for the historian are the official regulations issued by various bureaucratic agencies. From these one can form an accurate idea of the strengths and weaknesses of the bureaucracy fashioned by the Ptolemies and maintained by the Romans. It is difficult to select a few examples to discuss, but certainly among the most important for every student of Antiquity are the law of Ptolemy II on the oil monopoly,[7] the *Gnomon of the Idios Logos* (a section of the regulations governing the operations of the chief financial officer of Roman Egypt), and the extant fragments of the *Constitutio Antoniniana* of A.D. 212 (preserved on a papyrus in the Giessen collection). However,

[7] B. P. Grenfell, *The Revenue Laws of Ptolemy Philadelphus* (1896); U. Wilcken, *Chrestomathie der Papyruskunde* (1912), nos. 258 and 299. A new edition of the text is given by J. Bingen, *Sammelbuch griech. Urkunden*, Beiheft 1 (Göttingen 1952).

expectations of revelations about foreign policy are doomed to disappointment; the report of Ptolemy III on his Syrian campaign of 246 B.C., a semiliterary document, is unique.[8] Something similar exists from the Roman Empire in the edicts of Germanicus in Egypt, a valuable supplement to Tacitus, *Annals* 2.59.[9] And during recent years a number of Hebrew and Greek documents found in South Palestine have cast light on the period of the Bar Kochba insurrection under Hadrian, an event of great significance in cultural history. However, the most important additions to our knowledge have not been in the field of political history, but rather in that of administrative history. For example, Ptolemaic Egypt greatly influenced the organization of taxation in the Roman Empire, for it was the Egyptian institution of the liturgy which was eventually extended to all Roman provinces and so laid the foundation for creation of the authoritarian state of late Antiquity.

Above all, the papyri provide a great mass of information for the economic historian, information which is only now beginning to be exploited. For example, Egypt was the major grain-producing land of Antiquity, and so the papyri tell us about ancient agriculture, about transportation of the grain from the farms to the granaries of Alexandria, and about the grain monopoly of the Ptolemies, which provided the foundation of their state economy, a system comparable to the mercantilism of early modern Europe.

During the Hellenistic period Egypt was part of the Macedonian political system in the East; after the fall of Alexandria and the death of Cleopatra in 30 B.C. it became the private domain of the Roman emperor. Therefore although the papyri came mainly from Egypt they tell us much about the history and culture of Hellenism and the Roman Empire. This concerns, of course, only a part of the picture, and therefore the historian must look beyond to the larger contexts, to the general history of Hellenism and the Roman Empire.

Numismatics, the study of coins, is the third basic discipline. Our knowledge of Antiquity's political institutions depends greatly on the coins because their inscriptions, forms of dating, language used, and the pictures and attributes of the gods and rulers pictured reflect only those institutions recognized and sanctioned by the state.[10] For the same reason much can be learned about political and religious

---

[8] U. Wilcken, *Chrestomathie* . . . , no. 1.

[9] U. v. Wilamowitz and F. Zucker, *SPAW* 1911, 794 ff.

[10] B. Pick, *Aufsätze zur Numismatik u. Archäologie* (Jena 1931), 144.

history; and of course much also about ancient money and economy in general, for "just as a doctor measures the general health of a patient by listening to his heartbeat, so we can estimate the health of a state by checking the purity and weight of its coins."[11]

Antiquity's coinage begins with Lydian coins minted c. 700 B.C. out of electrum, an alloy of gold and silver; it ends with the solidus of Constantine I in late Antiquity. Under the Roman Empire the coinage provides what is almost a running commentary on the history of emperors and the Empire; in earlier periods it is not so rich, but still the coinage of the fifth century B.C. and of the Hellenistic period illustrates the history of those times.

In general the historian will find the coinage informative on five general topics: on who had the right to mint coins; on the representation of historical events on coins and medals; on questions of religious history, especially the existence of state-sanctioned cults; on the character of ancient propaganda; and on ancient chronology, based on rulers and eras.

In Antiquity the exercise of minting power was equivalent to political independence or at least to a degree of autonomy, whether this was possessed by custom or allowed by a ruler's decree. In this connection the use of a ruler's portrait on ancient coins has a special importance, for it expresses symbolically the possession of sovereignty. Thus the appearance of Hellenistic monarchs on their coins marks a decisive change in the position of the ruler, who now is raised into the sphere of "divine right."

Historical events are represented on coins in the design, in the legend, and in special issues. There have also been genuine "historical coins" issued on occasion, such as the coin minted by Demetrius Poliorketes which shows a Nike standing on the prow of a ship, a design which commemorates Demetrius' naval victory over Ptolemy I at Cyprian Salamis in 306 B.C.[12] Many similar coins were issued by the Roman emperors, for example, the Flavian issue inscribed IUDAEA CAPTA.

Religious history in particular is illuminated by coins, especially in the period of the Roman Empire. In the designs and legends of Roman coins we see the protective deities of the Greek city states, and also Dea Roma and the many typical Roman personifications such as Spes, Concordia, and Fides. From the evidence of the coins

[11] L. Schwabe, *Kunst u. Geschichte aus antiken Münzen* (Tübingen 1905), 9.
[12] K. Regling, *Die antiken Münzen* (ed. 3, Berlin and Leipzig 1929), 50.

we can judge the extent of worship accorded individual gods, especially those of the Orient, by the emperors and their court. Thus it is no coincidence that the temple of Isis first appears on the coins of Vespasian, and the temples of Sarapis and Cybele first on those of Domitian. Coins record the bizarre devotion of Commodus to Hercules, the leanings of Septimius Severus toward Africa and its gods, and those of the Syrian Elegabalus toward the sun god of Emessa. Aurelian announces the primacy of *Sol invictus* on his coins, and Constantine records his changes of religious allegiance, first to Hercules, then to Sol-Apollo, finally to the monogram of Christ (which his soldiers had on their shields before the battle at Mulvian Bridge in A.D. 312).

Use of coins for propaganda in the narrower sense is illustrated by the "Contorniates," whose significance was first revealed in a masterly work by Andreas Alföldi. They were tokens distributed in Rome at the New Year's games. Their pagan symbols and designs from Roman history indicate that they were an important means of propaganda used by the pagan aristocracy of Rome during the latter fourth and early fifth centuries A.D.

Dating by regnal years and eras on coins is an important topic which can only be noted briefly here. The chronology of the Roman Empire benefits greatly from the evidence of the coinage issued by the second mint of the Empire, Alexandria; there regnal years were not indicated, as elsewhere, by the number of *tribunicia potestas* held by the emperor, but rather in accord with the civil calendar of Egypt, in which the regnal year was figured (as in Ptolemaic times) as the time from accession to the next first of Thoth, the Egyptian New Year (which in Augustus' time was August 29). The Alexandrine coinage is a source of the first importance for the third century, marked by frequent usurpations and coups.

As in modern times so in Antiquity coins were above all a part of the economic system. Therefore coin discoveries provide evidence which, used cautiously, allows conclusions as to the intensity and extension of trade. Thus the appearance of Athenian παρθένοι (also called γλαῦκες) in lands such as Arabia and India during the fifth and fourth centuries B.C. indicates the wide range of Attic commerce. Statistics based on ancient coin hoards are therefore valuable for economic history.

British numismatists (H. Mattingly, E. S. Robinson) have reached radical conclusions as to the older Roman coinage, revising the date of the Romano-Campanian silver issue from 340 to 269 B.C., and of the first denarius from 269 B.C. to 187 B.C. Many scholars have accepted their arguments, but others have not (G. De Sanctis, Laura Breglia), and the controversy is not yet ended. The dispute is not simply a matter of numismatics but rather of general history, for it concerns our evaluation of Roman economic life in the later fourth century B.C., and our determination of when Rome sought and found entry into the Hellenistic economic system.

In Greece during the sixth and fifth centuries B.C. a number of competing money systems existed, which would have led to accounting difficulties had there not been agreement on a single standard as a common point of reference. This seems to have been found in a weight measure borrowed from the Near East, the Babylonian pound of about 436 grams, the *mana*, called in Greek μνᾶ. This unit seems to be the basis of most Greek money systems, and in particular the most important ones. Thus the Athenian drachma was 1/100, the heavier Aeginetan drachma 1/70 of a μνᾶ. The coins of that period evidently did not possess one quality we take for granted in our own coins: an exact weight. As a result all the relationships between monetary systems must be regarded as only approximate, but this approximation was evidently sufficient for practical purposes.

BIBLIOGRAPHY

EPIGRAPHY

HISTORY OF EPIGRAPHY: S. Chabert, *Histoire sommaire des études d'épigraphie grecque* (Paris 1906); W. Larfeld, *Griech. Epigraphik* in *Müller* I.5 (ed. 3, 1914), 7–105; H. Dessau, "Lat. Epigraphik," *Gercke-Norden* I.10 (1925), 1–7; L. Robert, *L'épigraphie grecque au Collège de France* (Limoges 1939).

INTRODUCTIONS TO TECHNIQUE: F. Hiller v. Gaertringen, "Griechische Epigraphik," *Gercke-Norden* I.9 (1924), 3 ff.; A. Rehm, in *Hdbk. d. Archäologie* I (1939), 185 ff.; L. Robert, "Epigraphie," *Encyclopédie de la Pléiade* (Paris 1961), giving a modern view with attention to new aspects.

HANDBOOKS: For Greek epigraphy see S. Reinach, *Traité d'épigraphie grecque* (Paris 1885); W. Larfeld, see above; but both works are now much out of date. Briefer, but giving all essentials, is G. Klaffenbach, *Griechische Epigraphik* (ed. 2, Göttingen 1966); also M. Guarducci, *Epigrafia greca* I (Rome 1967); for Latin epigraphy see R. Cagnat, *Cours d'épigraphie latine* (ed. 4, Paris 1914); J. E. Sandys, *Latin Epigraphy*, ed. 2 by S. Campbell (Cambridge 1927). For Christian epigraphy see C. M. Kaufmann, *Hdbk. der altchristlichen Epigraphik* (Freiburg i. Br. 1917); for Semitic see M. Lidzbarski, *Hdbk. der nordsemit. Epigraphik* (1898); for Etruscan, G. Buonamici, *Epigrafia etrusca* (Florence 1932).

ILLUSTRATIONS OF INSCRIPTIONS: J. Kirchner, *Imagines Inscriptionum Atticarum: Ein Bilderatlas epigr. Denkmäler Attikas*, ed. 2 by G. Klaffenbach (Berlin 1948). Latin inscriptions: Bruns-Gradenwitz, *Simulacra* (1912: a supplement to Bruns, *Fontes iuris Romani*).

DISTRIBUTION OF GREEK INSCRIPTIONS: best survey in J. J. Hondius, *Saxa loquuntur* (Leiden 1938), 65 ff.; good, though brief, is A. Rehm, *Hdbk. d. Archäologie* I (1939), 183.

COLLECTIONS OF GREEK INSCRIPTIONS: A. Böckh and colleagues published under the auspices of the Prussian Academy of Sciences the *Corpus Inscriptionum Graecarum* (*CIG*); it appeared during 1825–1859 (but the indices were not published until 1877!), and by now is largely out of date. Its place has been taken by the *Inscriptiones Graecae* (*IG*), also sponsored by the Prussian Academy, and in process of publication since 1873.

Following is a summary of the published and planned volumes of the *IG*; some are themselves superseded by a second edition ("editio minor").

IG I (ed. 2): *Inscriptiones Atticae Euclidis anno anteriores*,[13] ed. F. Hiller v. Gaertringen (1924).

IG II, III (ed. 2): *Inscriptiones Atticae Euclidis anno posteriores*, ed. J. Kirchner (1913–1940): only part of the indices has appeared.

IG IV: *Inscriptiones Argolidis*, ed. M. Frankel. A part of this has been published separately as a second edition: IV.1 (ed. 2): *Inscriptiones Epidauri*, ed. F. Hiller v. Gaertringen (1929).

IG V.1: *Inscriptiones Laconiae et Messeniae*, ed. W. Kolbe (1913).

IG V.2: Inscriptiones Arcadiae, ed. F. Hiller v. Gaertringen (1913).

IG VI: *Inscriptiones Elidis et Achaiae*: not published.

IG VII: *Inscriptiones Megaridis et Boeotiae*, ed. W. Dittenberger (1892).

---

[13] The year in which Eucleides was archon (403/2 BC) is a dividing point in Attic epigraphy, since thereafter the Ionian alphabet was used in inscriptions instead of the Old Athenian alphabet previously used.

IG VIII: *Inscriptiones Delphorum*: not published; see below for comments.

IG IX.1: *Inscriptiones Phocidis, Locridis, Aetoliae, Acarnaniae, insularum maris Ionii*, ed. W. Dittenberger (1897). A part has been reedited as *IG IX*.1 (ed. 2).1: *Inscriptiones Aetoliae* (1932) and *IG* IX.1 (ed. 2).2: *Inscriptiones Acarnaniae* (1957), and *IG* IX.1 (ed. 2).3: *Inscriptiones Locridis* (1968), all ed. G. Klaffenbach.

IG IX.2: *Inscriptiones Thessaliae*, ed. O. Kern (1908).

IG X: *Inscriptiones Epiri, Macedoniae, Thraciae, Scythiae*: not published.

IG XI: *Inscriptiones Deli*: only two parts have been published: *IG* XI.2 and XI.4, *Inscriptiones Deli liberae* (nos. 105–289 and 510–1349), eds. F. Durrbach (1912) and P. Roussel (1914), respectively. See comments below.

IG XII: *Inscriptiones insularum maris Aegaei praeter Delum*:
   XII.1: *Inscriptiones Rhodi, Chalces, Carpathi cum Saro Casi*, ed. F. Hiller v. Gaertringen (1895).
   XII.2: *Inscriptiones Lesbi, Nesi, Tenedi*, ed. G. R. Paton (1899).
   XII.3: *Inscriptiones Symes, Teutlussae, Teli, Nisyri, Astypalaeae, Anaphes, Therae et Therasiae, Pholegandri, Meli, Cimoli*, ed. F. Hiller v. Gaertringen (1898), with Supplement (1904).
   XII.4: *Inscriptiones Coi et Calymni*: not published.
   XII.5: *Inscriptiones Cycladum*, ed. F. Hiller v. Gaertringen (1903 and 1909).
   XII.6: *Inscriptiones Chii et Sami*: not published.
   XII.7: *Inscriptiones Amorgi et insularum vicinarum*, ed. J. Delamarre (1908).
   XII.8: *Inscriptiones insularum maris Thracici*, ed. C. Fredrich (1909).
   XII.9: *Inscriptiones Euboeae insulae*, ed. E. Ziebarth (1915).
IG XII: *Supplementum*, ed. F. Hiller v. Gaertringen (1939).
IG XIII: *Inscriptiones Cretae*: not published, but see comments below.
IG XIV: *Inscriptiones Siciliae et Italiae additis Graecis Galliae, Hispaniae, Brittaniae, Germaniae inscriptionibus*, eds. G. Kaibel and A. Lebègue (1890).
IG XV: *Inscriptiones Cypri*: not published, but see below.

Special publications must be used for those areas not yet published in the *IG*. These include the following: *Die Inschriften von*

Olympia, eds. W. Dittenberger and K. Purgold (Berlin 1896), in place of *IG* VI; *Fouilles de Delphes* III: *Épigraphie*, eds. Bourget, Colin, Daux, Salač, Valmin, Flacelière (6 fascicles, 1909–1954), in place of *IG* VIII; South Russia's inscriptions in *Inscriptiones antiquae orae septentrionalis Ponti Euxini Graecae et Latinae* (abbreviated *IPE*; 3 vols., St. Petersburg, 1885–1901; vol. 1 in ed. 2, 1916); now in publication are the inscriptions of Bulgaria, *Inscriptiones Graecae in Bulgaria repertae*, ed. G. Mihailov (4 vols., Sofia 1956–1966), in place of *IG* X; the main part of Delos' inscriptions has been published by the Académie des Inscriptions et Belles Lettres in Paris, as *Inscriptions de Délos* (nos. 1–88, 290–509, 1400–2879), eds. Plassart, Durrbach, Roussel, Launey (6 fascicles, 1926–1950), in place of the missing sections of *IG* XI.—Important new inscriptions from Rhodes (*IG* XII.1) have been reported by the Italian Journal *Clara Rhodos* (10 vols., Rhodes 1928 ff.), also by Blinkenberg, *Lindos: Fouilles de l'Acropole 1902–1914*: vol. 2, *Les inscriptions* (2 vols., 1941).—For Cos (*IG* XII.4) see R. Herzog and G. Klaffenbach, *Asylieurkunden aus Kos*, *ADAW* 1952, no. 1.—Cretan inscriptions have been published as an independent collection by Margherita Guarducci, *Inscriptiones Creticae* (4 volumes so far, Rome 1939–1950), in place of *IG* XIII.—A collection of Cypriot inscriptions is planned by T. B. Mitford of St. Andrew's University.

No collections exist of the Greek inscriptions of Asia Minor, Syria, and Egypt, except for these: *Inscriptions grecques et latines de la Syrie*, eds. L. Jalabert and R. Mouterde (6 vols., 1929–1967); *La Carie* II (so far the only volume), eds. L. and J. Robert (1954).

Many special publications exist; for a survey see Hondius, *Saxa loquuntur* (Leiden 1938), 82 ff., or (better) G. Pfohl, *Griechische Inschriften* (Munich, n.d. [1965]), 185 ff.—A few of the most important are: *Tituli Asiae Minoris* I–III.1 (abbreviated *TAM*, published by the Vienna Academy of Sciences, 1901–1944); *Monumenta Asiae Minoris Antiqua* I–VIII (abbreviated *MAMA*, Manchester 1928–1962).—The most important inscriptions found up to his time were collected and excellently commented upon by W. Dittenberger, *Orientis Graecae Inscriptiones Selectae* (abbreviated *OGI*, 2 vols., Leipzig 1903–1905); see also C. B. Welles, *Royal Correspondence in the Hellenistic Period* (New Haven 1934).

SELECTIONS OF GREEK INSCRIPTIONS: W. Dittenberger, *Sylloge Inscriptionum Graecarum* (4 vols., ed. 3, Leipzig 1915–1924), abbreviated *Syll.³*; this has a thorough commentary in Latin, and is essential for every student of Greek history. See also Ch. Michel, *Receuil des inscriptions grecques* (Brussels 1900) with Supplements (1912, 1927); R. Cagnat *et al.*, *Inscriptiones Graecae ad res Ro-*

manas pertinentes (4 vols., Paris 1911–1927: abbreviated *IGR*); these last two collections do not have commentary.—Almost 6,000 Greek inscriptions are included in the *Sammlung der griechischen Dialektinschriften*, eds. H. Collitz and F. Bechtel (Göttingen 1884–1915: abbreviated *GDI*). A briefer but excellent selection is given by E. Schwyzer, *Dialectorum Graecarum exempla epigraphica potiora* (Leipzig 1923).

Historians will find useful the work of M. N. Tod, *A Selection of Greek Historical Inscriptions* I: *To the End of the Vth Century B.C.* (ed. 2, Oxford 1946); II: *From 403 to 323 B.C.* (Oxford 1948).

Newly discovered inscriptions are published in the *Supplementum Epigraphicum Graecum* (Leiden 1923 ff.: abbreviated *SEG*), of which 23 volumes have appeared so far. Also important is the journal published by the American School in Athens, *Hesperia* (1923 ff.). Regular reports on new publications appear in the *Revue des Études grecques* (by Jeanne and Louis Robert), in the *Journal of Hellenic Studies* (by M. N. Tod, the last having appeared in 1955), and in the Italian journal *Epigraphica* (Milan 1939 ff.).

STUDIES: Among the many studies those of Adolf Wilhelm (Vienna) and Louis Robert (Paris) are outstanding. Wilhelm (1864–1950) wrote, among many other studies, *Urkunden dramatischer Aufführungen in Athen* (*Sonderschrift* 6 of the Österr. Arch. Institut, Vienna 1906); *Beiträge zur griechischen Inschriftenkunde* (*ibid.* 7, Vienna 1909); *Neue Beiträge zur griechischen Inschriftenkunde*, 6 vols. in *SAWW* 1911–1932; *Attische Urkunden*, 5 vols. in *SAWW* 1911–1942.—Louis Robert has published many works, among them *Villes d'Asie Mineure* (ed. 2, Paris 1962), *Études anatoliennes* (Paris 1937), *Études épigraphiques et philologiques* (Paris 1938), and *Hellenica* (13 vols., 1940–1965), the latter a document of extraordinary industry and unsurpassed knowledge.

LATIN INSCRIPTIONS: Their geographic distribution is illustrated by the work which Theodor Mommsen planned and the Prussian Academy of Sciences published, the *Corpus Inscriptionum Latinarum* (*CIL*).[14] It is now almost completed, and thanks to this great collection the Latin inscriptions are much less scattered than the Greek. The individual volumes of the *CIL* divide the various areas as follows:

CIL I (ed. 2): Fasti and inscriptions of the Republic up to Caesar's death, eds. Th. Mommsen, W. Henzen, Chr. Hülsen, E. Lommatzsch, 4 fascicles (1893–1943).

CIL II: Spain, ed. E. Hübner (1896), with Supplement (1892).

CIL III: Danube Provinces and Eastern Provinces of the Roman

[14] Cf. O. Hirschfeld, *SPAW* 1917, 45 ff.

Empire, including Egypt and Cyrenaica, eds. Th. Mommsen, O. Hirschfeld, A. v. Domaszewski (1873), with Supplements (1889–1902).

CIL IV: Grafitti from Pompeii and Herculaneum, eds. C. Langemeister, R. Schöne, A. Mau (1871), with five Supplements (1898–1955).

CIL V: Gallia Cisalpina, ed. Th. Mommsen (1872–1877).

CIL VI: Rome, eds. W. Henzen, I. B. De Rossi, E. Bormann, Chr. Hülsen, M. Bang (1876–1933).

CIL VII: Britain, ed. E. Hübner (1873).

CIL VIII: Roman Africa, eds. G. Wilmans, Th. Mommsen, R. Cagnat, J. Schmidt, H. Dessau (1881), with five Supplements (1891–1942).

CIL IX and X: Southern Italy, ed. Th. Mommsen (1883).

CIL XI: Central Italy, ed. E. Bormann (1888–1926).

CIL XII: Gallia Narbonesis, ed. O. Hirschfeld (1888).

CIL XIII: Tres Galliae and Germany, eds. O. Hirschfeld, C. Zangemeister, A. v. Domaszewski, O. Bohn, E. Stein (1899–1943).

CIL XIV: Latium, ed. H. Dessau (1887), with the *Supplementum Ostiense*, ed. L. Wickert (1930–1933).

CIL XV: *Inscriptiones instrumenti domestici* of the city of Rome, ed. H. Dressel (1891–1899).

CIL XVI: Military Diplomas, ed. H. Nesselhauf, with Supplement (1955).

The ambitious plans for a new edition of the Latin inscriptions of Italy (*Inscriptiones Italiae*) by Italian scholars have as yet not progressed beyond a beginning.—As supplement to *CIL* III see *The Inscriptions of Roman Tripolitania*, eds. J. M. Reynolds and J. Ward Perkins (Rome and London n.d. [1952]).—As supplement to *CIL* VIII see *Inscriptions latines d'Afrique*, eds. R. Cagnat, A. Merlin, L. Chatelain (Paris 1923), and *Inscriptions latines de la Tunisie*, ed. A. Merlin (Paris 1944), and *Insc. lat. de Algérie* I: *Inscriptions de la Proconsulaire*, ed. S. Gsell (Paris, 1932); II.1: (Rusicade, Cirta, and Surroundings) ed. H. G. Pflaum (Paris 1957); *Insc. Lat. du Maroc* I, ed. L. Chatelain (Paris 1942).—As supplement to *CIL* XII see *Inscr. lat. de Gaule*, ed. E. Espérandieu (2 vols., Paris 1928–1929). —As supplement to *CIL* III, *IG* X, and *IG* XIV see *Antiken Inschriften in Jugoslavien*, eds. V. Hofiller and B. Saria (Zagreb 1938).

New material was published and problems discussed in the journal *Ephemeris Epigraphica* (9 vols., 1872–1913). Reports on publication of new Latin inscriptions are given by the *Revue archéologique* (Paris) in a special section called *L'année épigraphique*.

For the historian one work besides the *CIL* itself is of basic importance: H. Dessau, *Inscriptiones Latinae selectae* (3 vols., Berlin 1892–1916: abbreviated *ILS*). This "Latin Dittenberger" includes almost ten thousand inscriptions with a thorough commentary. A selection from Christian inscriptions is given by E. Diehl, *Inscriptiones Latinae veteres Christianae* (3 vols., Berlin 1925–1931).

ITALIC DIALECT INSCRIPTIONS: R. S. Conway, *The Italic Dialects* (2 vols., Cambridge 1897); R. S. Conway, J. Whatmough, S. E. Johnson, *The Pre-Italic Dialects of Italy* (3 vols., London 1933); E. Vetter, *Hdb. der italischen Dialekte* (Heidelberg 1953). An excellent selection with commentary is given by V. Pisani, *Le lingue dell' Italia antica oltre il Latino* (ed. 2, Turin 1964).—Valuable review articles were published by E. Vetter in the journal *Glotta*.

SEMITIC INSCRIPTIONS: Most important collection is *Corpus Inscriptionum Semiticarum* (Paris 1881 ff.: abbreviated *CIS*). It is supplemented by *Répertoire d'épigraphie sémitique* (6 vols., Paris 1900–1935), ed. J. B. Chabot.

MONOGRAPHS: (1) On the Athenian tribute lists two basic studies are H. Nesselhauf, *Untersuchungen z. Geschichte der delisch-attischen Symmachie* (*Klio*, Beiheft 30; 1933), and also vol. 3 (1950) of the cited work *The Athenian Tribute Lists*.

(2) Greek Constitutions: W. Schönfelder, *Die städtischen u. Bundesbeamten des griech. Festlandes vom 4. Jarh. v. Chr. Geb. bis in die römische Kaiserzeit* (Diss. Leipzig 1917); F. Bleckmann, *Griech. Inschriften zur griechischen Staatenkunde* (*Kl. Texte f. Vorlesungen u. Übungen* 115, Bonn 1913). Many monographs are cited by Hondius, *Saxa loquuntur* (Leiden 1938), 139 ff., 144 ff.

(3) Roman Law: The most important Roman historical documents are discussed, with careful attention to genres by *Rosenberg* 6 ff., 25 ff., 29 ff. Also essential, as a collection of texts, is *Fontes Iuris Romani Anteiustiniani, Pars I: Leges*, ed. S. Riccobono (ed. 2, Florence 1941).

(4) Roman Military Diplomas: *CIL* XVI (1936) with Supplement; see also Riccobono, *op. cit.*, I, 223 ff.—In recent years the fact that diplomas ceased to be issued has been much discussed, especially in connection with the Tablet of Brigetio; of the many studies two are noteworthy: K. Kraft, *Germania* 28 (1944–1950), 242 ff.; D. van Berchem, *L'armée de Dioclétian et la réforme constantinienne* (Paris 1952), 75 ff.

(5) Roman Milestones: O. Hirschfeld, *Kleine Schriften* (1913), 703 ff.; K. Schneider, "Miliarium," *RE* Supp. VI (1935), 395 ff. A new and thorough study of the subject is now being planned, under

the leadership of Gerold Walser; see his work *Die römischen Strassen in der Schweiz* (Bern 1967).

(6) Inscriptiones instrumenti domestici: *CIL* XIII.3 (Rhineland); *CIL* XV (Rom). A selection is given in *ILS* II, nos. 8561 ff.

(7) Early Christianity: W. M. Ramsay, *The Cities and Bishoprics of Phrygia* (Oxford 1895–1897); and *A Historical Commentary on St. Paul's Epistle to the Galatians* (ed. 2, London 1900); and many other works.—Epigraphic collections relating to Christianity are noted by Hondius, *Saxa loquuntur* (Leiden 1938), 109 ff.

PAPYROLOGY

HISTORY: K. Preisendanz, *Papyruskunde und Papyrusforschung* (Leipzig 1933), and his article in *Hdb. der Bibliothekswissenschaft* I, ed. Milkau (ed. 2, Stuttgart 1950), 163–248.

INTRODUCTIONS: L. Mitteis and U. Wilcken, *Grundzüge und Chrestomathie der Papyruskunde* (4 vols., Leipzig and Berlin 1912): part 1, by Wilcken, contains the historical texts; part 2, by Mitteis, the juristic. Also valuable are: W. Schubart, *Einführung in die Papyruskunde* (Berlin 1918), and "Papyruskunde," *Gercke-Norden* I.10 (Leipzig 1924), which is very brief; W. Peremans and J. Vergote, *Papyrologisch Handboek* (Louvain 1942) in Flemish; P. M. Meyer, *Juristische Papyri* (Berlin 1920); E. G. Turner, *Greek Papyri: An Introduction* (Oxford 1968).

AIDS: F. Preisigke, *Wörterbuch der griechischen Papyrusurkunden usw. aus Ägypten* I–IV.2, ed. E. Kiessling (Berlin 1925–1958), and *Fachwörter des öffentlichen Verwaltungsdienstes Ägyptens* (Göttingen 1915); F. Preisigke, F. Bilabel, E. Kiessling, *Sammelbuch griech. Urkunden aus Ägypten* I–VIII.2 (1915–1967: abbreviated *SB*), with 10,208 items. The latter work gives inscriptions and papyri discovered in Egypt which have not been published separately; like all collections it should be used with caution, since the texts have been mostly printed without reference to the originals. See also F. Preisigke *et al.*, *Berichtigungsliste der griech. Papyrus-Urkunden aus Ägypten* I–III.2 (1913–1958: abbreviated *BL*), and also Preisigke's *Namenbuch* (Heidelberg 1922), a list of the proper names found in papyri.

SPECIAL JOURNALS: Important is *Archiv für Papyrusforschung*, ed. U. Wilcken, and then from vol. 15 by F. Zucker (Leipzig 1901 ff.); it gives excellent "Urkundenreferate" by the editor which are essential for research. Also noteworthy are: *Aegyptus: Rivista italiana di egittologia e di papirologia* (Milan 1920 ff.), ed. A. Calderini, which includes a "Bibliografia metodica"; *Journal of Juristic Papyrology* (New York, later Warsaw 1945 ff.), ed. R.

Taubenschlag. Papyrological reports are also given by *Journal of Egyptian Archaeology* (London 1914 ff.), and *Chronique d'Égypte* (Brussels). In 1967 a new journal appeared, *Zeitschrift für Papyrologie und Epigraphik*, eds. L. Koenen and R. Merkelbach.

SERIES: *Münchener Beiträge zür Papyrusforschung und antiken Rechtsgeschichte*, 53 vols. so far, founded by L. Wenger; also publications of the Papyrus Institute of Heidelberg and the Scuola di Papirologia of Milan; *Études de Papyrologie* (Cairo) and *Recherches de papyrologie* (Paris).

PARTHIAN DOCUMENTS: E. H. Minns, *JHS* 35 (1915), 22 ff.; M. Rostovtzeff and C. B. Welles, *WCeS* 2 (1931) 1 ff.; C. B. Welles in *Münchner Beiträge* 19 (1934), 379 ff.

LITERARY PAPYRI: most recent catalog is R. A. Pack, *The Greek and Latin Literary Texts from Graeco-Roman Egypt* (Ann Arbor 1952).

HISTORICAL PAPYRI: Aristotle's *Constitution of the Athenians*: editio princeps by F. G. Kenyon (London 1891); more recent edition by H. Oppermann (Leipzig 1928), with bibliography. A useful work is J. E. Sandys, *Aristotle's Constitution of Athens* (ed. 2, London 1912), with commentary. A fundamental work for its time was U. v. Wilamowitz, *Aristoteles und Athen* (2 vols., Berlin 1893). Keen but controversial is C. Hignett, *A History of the Athenian Constitution to the End of the 5th Century* (ed. 2, Oxford 1958).—Other texts are printed in F. Bilabel, *Kleineren Historikerfragmente auf Papyrus (Kleine Texte für Vorlesungen und Übungen* 149, Bonn 1922).

DOCUMENTS: A good survey of the historical documents on papyri is P. Jouguet. "L'histoire politique et la papyrologie," *Papyri u. Altertumswissenschaft (Münchener Beiträge* 19, 1934), 62 ff. Very useful is E. Kornemann, "Die röm. Kaiserzeit," *Gercke-Norden* III.2 (ed. 3, 1933), 170. Monographic publications are surveyed by H. I. Bell, *Egypt from Alexander the Great to the Arab Conquest* (Oxford 1948), 153 ff.

It is unfortunate that publication of a "Corpus papyrorum" is not possible, for the papyri have been published in a scattered manner according to origin, owner, and collection, and usually documents and literary texts of all eras have been printed together. It is almost impossible to master the field. What is essential for the cause of research is at least a general guide to the documents.

A unique product of careful scholarship is U. Wilcken, *Urkunden der Ptolemäerzeit (Ältere Funde)* I–II.3 (Berlin 1922–1957: abbreviated *UPZ*). Outstanding publications outside Germany include: *The Tebtunis Papyri*, eds. Grenfell, Hunt, Smyly, *et al.* (3 vols., 1902–1938); *The Oxyrhynchus Papyri*. eds. Grenfell, Hunt, Bell, *et al.* (33 vols., 1898–1968: abbreviated *P. Oxy.*), which includes many literary texts: *Pubblicazioni della Società italiana per la ricerca dei Papiri greci e latini in Egitto*, eds. G. Vitelli, M. Norsa, *et al.* (14 vols. so far, Florence 1912–1957: abbreviated *PSI*).

Great importance both for political and for cultural history is inherent in the Zeno Papyri, a group of documents scattered in museums throughout the world; they date from early Ptolemaic times, and come from the archive of one Zeno, who was estate manager for Apollonius, finance minister under Ptolemy II (285–246 B.C.). The most important have been published by C. C. Edgar *et al.*, *Zenon Papyri*, 4 vols. in the *Catalogue Générale des Antiquités égypt. du Musée du Caire* (1925–1940: abbreviated *P. Cairo Zen.*).

OFFICIAL REGULATIONS: U. Wilcken, "Über antike Urkundenlehre," *Papyri und Altertumswissenschaft* (*Münchener Beiträge* 19, 1934), 42 ff.

GNOMON OF THE IDIOS LOGOS: edited by W. Schubart, *Ägyptische Urkunden aus den Staatlichen Museen zu Berlin* V.1 (1919: abbreviated *BGU*), with German translation. A commentary was written by W. Uxkull-Gyllenband, *BGU* V.2 (1934); cf. review by M. Rostovtzeff, *Gnomon* (1935), 522 ff.; see also S. Riccobono, Jr., *Il Gnomon dell'Idios Logos* (Palermo 1950).

FRAGMENT OF CONSTITUTIO ANTONINIANA: E. Kornemann and P. M. Meyer, *Griech. Papyri im Museum des Oberhess. Geschichtsverein zu Giessen* (abbreviated *P. Giss.*) I, no. 40 (Leipzig 1910–1912); for more recent studies see Chr. Sasse, *Die Constitutio Antoniniana* (Wiesbaden 1958), 129 ff.

LITURGIA: F. Oertel, *Die Liturgie: Studien zur Ptolemäischen und kaiserlichen Verwaltung Ägyptens* (Leipzig 1917).

AGRICULTURE: M. Schnebel, *Die Landwirtschaft im hellenistichen Ägypten* I (*Münchener Beiträge* 7, (1925), uncompleted).

PTOLEMAIC MONOPOLIES: F. Heichelheim, "Monopole," *RE* XVI (1932), 147 ff.; Cl. Préaux, *L'économie royale des Lagides* (Brussels 1939); M. Rostovtzeff, *Social and Economic History of the Hellenistic World* (Oxford 1941).

NUMISMATICS

THE DISCIPLINE: Modern numismatic studies begin with the work of a learned Jesuit, J. Eckhel, *Doctrina nummorum veterum* (8 vols., Vienna 1792–1798); a ninth volume appeared posthumously in 1826. Still useful is E. Babelon, *Traité des monnaies grecques et romaines* (4 vols. and 4 vols. of plates, Paris 1901–1932), which discusses Greek coinage to the fourth century B.C. For Roman numismatics there is the great work, fundamental in its time, of Th. Mommsen, *Geschichte des römischen Münzwesens* (Berlin 1860); a French translation was published in four volumes (Paris 1865–1875).

SURVEYS OF GREEK COINAGE: B. V. Head, *Historia nummorum: A Manual of Greek Numismatics* (ed. 2, Oxford 1911). This work gives illustrations and descriptions of the historically important coins of Antiquity; it is a fundamental work which should be consulted first in connection with every research project, although of course other numismatic studies will be used as well.–Excellent illustrations are given in P. R. Franke and M. Hirmer, *Die griechische Münze* (Munich 1964).

GENERAL SURVEYS: K. Regling, *Die antike Münze als Kunstwerk* (Berlin 1924), and "Die antiken Münzen," in *Handbücher der Staatlichen Museen zu Berlin* (ed. 3, Berlin and Leipzig 1929), and "Das antike Münzwesen," *Gercke-Norden* II.2 (ed. 4, 1930), and "Münzwesen," *RE* XVI (1932), 457 ff. A thoughtful work is the lecture of B. Pick, *Die Münzkunde in der Altertumswissenschaft* (Stuttgart and Gotha 1922). See also R. Gobl, *Einführung in die Münzkunde der römischen Kaiserzeit* (ed. 2, Vienna 1960), and the superb survey by K. Christ, *Antike Numismatik: Einführung und Bibliographie* (Darmstadt 1967).

SOURCE PUBLICATIONS: Material is published in articles scattered among many journals. The most important journals include these: *Numismatic Chronicle* (London 1837 ff.); *Revue belge de la numismatique* (Brussels 1842 ff.); *Numismatische Zeitschrift* (Vienna 1869 ff., 1949 ff.); *Zeitschrift für Numismatik* (Berlin 1874–1935); *Revue numismatique français* (Paris 1936 ff.); *Rivista italiana di numismatica* (Milan 1888 ff.); *Jahrbuch für Numismatik und Geldgeschichte* (Munich 1949 ff.).

An essential tool is *Numismatic Literature*, published by the American Numismatic Society (New York 1947 ff.), which gives regular bibliographic reports. Bibliography is also a concern of *Schweizer Münzblätter* (Basel 1949 ff.).

Theodor Mommsen planned a *Corpus nummorum*, and a few volumes were published by the Prussian Academy, but it then ceased. Published volumes include: *Antiken Münzen Nord-Griechenlands*, eds. B. Pick, K. Regling, F. Münzer, M. Strack, and H. Gaebler (3 vols., 1898–1935); *Antike Münzen Mysiens*, ed. H. v. Fritze (1913).

An important group is formed by the publications of the collections of great museums, e.g., *The British Museum: Catalogue of the*

Greek Coins (29 vols. so far, London 1873 ff.); *Cat. des monnaies grecques de la Bibliothèque Nationale* (2 vols., Paris 1890–1893), ed. E. Babelon; and also from the *Bibliothèque*, *Les Perses achéménides*, etc. and *Les rois de Syrie*, etc. Smaller collections in Britain publish their holdings in *Sylloge Nummorum*. Other publications are those of the Danish National Museum in Copenhagen and the collection of H. v. Aulock, a German, in course of publication since 1957.

GREEK COINS: A survey is given by the cited work of B. V. Head; also see G. F. Hill, *Historical Greek Coins* (London 1906); P. Gardner, *A History of Ancient Coinage 700–300 BC* (Oxford 1918); B. V. Head, *A Guide to the Principal Coins of the Greeks from ca. 700 B.C. to A.D. 270* (London 1932); Ch. Seltman, *Greek Coins: A History of Metallic Currency and Coinage down to the Fall of the Hellenistic Kingdoms* (ed. 2, London 1955).

Following is a selection of important monographs: Ch. Seltman, *Athens: Its History and its Coinage Before the Persian Invasion* (Cambridge 1924); E. Boehringer, *Die Münzen von Syrakus* (Berlin 1929); also the older and in some respects historically unsatisfactory work of J. N. Svoronos, Τὰ νομίσματα τοῦ κράτους τῶν Πτολεμαίων (4 vols., Athens 1904–1908). The monographs of the American scholar E. T. Newell are fundamental, among them: *The Coinage of Demetrius Poliorcetes* (1927), *The Coinage of the Eastern Seleucid Mints* (New York 1938), *The Coinage of the Western Seleucid Mints* (1941). A bibliography of Newell's works was published in *AJPh* (1947), 427 ff. Historians will find useful the bibliographies of Greek numismatics published regularly in *Jahrbuch für Numismatik und Geldgeschichte*.

ROMAN COINS: For the Republic the standard work is E. A. Sydenham, *The Coinage of the Roman Republic* (London 1952), for the Empire the material is given in H. Mattingly and E. A. Sydenham, *The Roman Imperial Coinage*, 7 vols. (London 1923–1967: abbreviated *RIC*), which cover coinage from Augustus to Constantine, and vol. 9 (1951), which covers from Valentinian I to Theodosius I. See also H. Mattingly, *Roman Coins from the Earliest Times to the Fall of the Western Empire* (3 vols., ed. 3, London 1967). Still useful is G. F. Hill, *Historical Roman Coins from the Earliest Times to the Reign of Augustus* (London 1909). —An important work of historical study is P. Strack, *Untersuchungen zur römischen Reichsprägung des 2. Jahrh.* (3 vols., Stuttgart 1931–1937). Important results should come from the Numismatische Kommission der Länder in der Bundesrepublik Deutschland, which is planning a "critical reevaluation of Roman coins found in Germany." A survey of its work is given by K. Christ, *Antike Numismatik* (1967), 95.

For late Antiquity see: J. Sabatier, *Description générale des monnaies byzantines* (3 vols., Paris 1867; repr. 1930); J. Maurice, *Numismatique constantinienne* (2 vols., Paris 1906–1913); W. Wroth, *British Museum Catlogue: Imperial Byzantine Coins* (2 vols., London 1908); *idem, Catalogue of the Coins of the Vandals* ... (London 1911).

RULERS ON ANCIENT COINS: K. Regling "Münzkunde," *Gercke-Norden* II.2 (ed. 4, 1930), 98. On coins as iconographic sources see F. Imhoof-Blumer, *Porträtköpfe auf antiken Münzen hellenischer u. hellenisierter Völker* (Leipzig 1885), and *Porträtköpfe auf röm. Münzen* (ed. 2, Leipzig 1892); R. Delbrück, *Die Münzbildnisse von Maximinus bis Carinus (A.D. 235–285)* (Berlin 1940); P. R. Franke, *Röm. Kaiserporträts im Münzbild* (Munich 1961).

HISTORICAL EVENTS ON ANCIENT COINS: Th. Reinach, *L'histoire par les monnaies* (Paris 1902), is a collection of studies on Pontus, Paphlygonia, Bithynia, Commagene, and other topics, and it discusses the problems of using the coins as historical sources. See also H. Mattingly, *CAH* XII (1939), 713 ff., and, above all, the works of Andreas Alföldi, some of which are noted in the bibliography of *CAH* XII (1939), 746 ff.; more recent works by him include his studies on the origins of the Principate, entitled "Die Geburt der kaiserlichen Bildsymbolik," *MH* 7 (1950), 1 ff., *MH* 8 (1951), 190 ff., *MH* 9 (1952), 204 ff., *MH* 10 (1953), 103 ff., and his *Studien über Caesars Monarchie* (Lund 1953), and an essay in *Schweizer Münzblatter* 18 (1968), 57 ff. K. Kraft has also published a series of important studies in Roman history which depend on numismatic sources, most of them in *JNG*.

Also valuable are: H. Sutherland, *Coinage and Roman Imperial Policy (31 B.C.–68 A.D.)* (London 1951); M. Grant, *From Imperium to Auctoritas: A Historical Study of Aes Coinage in the Roman Empire 49 B.C.–A.D. 14* (Cambridge 1946, now being reprinted), an important study for the municipal policies of Caesar and August; see review by F. Vittinghoff, *Gnomon* (1950), 250 ff. A good survey of Roman coinage and history is K. Christ, "Antike Siegesprägungen," *Gymnasium* 64 (1957), 504 ff.; also suggestive on another topic is his "Die antiken Münzen als Quelle der westfälischen Geschichte," *Westfalen* 35 (1957), 1 ff.

Coins are especially important as sources for study of the otherwise document-poor Hellenistic states in Bactria and India, for which see: P. Gardner, *The Coins of the Greek and Scythic Kings of Bactria and India* (London 1886), now much out of date; W. Tarn, *The Greeks in Bactria and India* (ed. 2, Cambridge 1951); the note of N. Debevoise, *A Political History of Parthia* (Chicago 1938), 63; and, most recent, K. Christ, *Antike Numismatik* (1967), 41. For the history of Epirus see P. Franke, *Die antiken Münzen von Epirus* I (Wiesbaden 1961).

Important for methodology is Louis Robert, *Études de numismatique grecque* (Paris 1951), a collection of outstanding studies on numismatic, epigraphic, and geographic subjects.

RELIGIOUS HISTORY AND COINS: Outstanding examples of historical use of coins in the study of religious history are A. D. Nock, *CAH* XII (1939), 412 ff., and the lecture of W. Weber, "Die Vereinheitlichung der religiösen Welt," *Probleme der Spätantike* (Stuttgart 1930), 67 ff.

PROPAGANDA AND COINS: A Alföldi, "The Main Aspects of Political Propaganda on the Coinage of the Roman Republic," *Essays . . . Harold Mattingly* (1956), 63–95; and *A Festival of Isis in Rome under the Christian Emperors of the IVth Century* (*Diss. Pann.* 2.7, Budapest 1937), and *Die Kontorniaten: Ein verkanntes Propagandamittel der heidnischen stadtrömischen Aristokratie* (Budapest 1943); see also O. Th. Schulz, *Die Rechtstitel u. Regierungsprogramme auf. röm. Kaisermünzen (von Cäsar bis Severus)* (*Studien z. Geschichte u. Kultur des Altertums* 13.4, Paderborn, 1925), to be used, however, with caution.

DATING: J. Vogt, *Die alexandrinischen Münzen: Grundlegung einer alexandrinischen Kaisergeschichte* (2 vols., Stuttgart 1924); supplementary material in J. Milne, *Catalogue of Alexandrian Coins in the Ashmolean Museum* (Oxford 1932).

ECONOMIC HISTORY AND COINS: Statistics on coin hoards are of fundamental importance. For the evidence and methods used see S. P. Noe, *A Bibliography of Greek Coin Hoards* (ed. 2, New York 1937), and his "Hoard Evidence and Its Importance," *Hesperia*, Supplement 8 (1949), 235 ff. See also F. Heichelheim, "Die Ausbreitung der Münzgeldwirtschaft u. der Wirtschaftsstil im archäischen Griechenland," *Schmollers Jahrbuch* 55 (1931), 229 ff., and his "Wirtschaftshistorische Beiträge z. klassisch-griechisch u. hellenistischen Münzhortstatistik," *Transactions of International Numismatic Congress* 1938.

Especially valuable, in view of the connections between pre-Roman Britain and the Mediterranean world, is J. G. Milne, *Finds of Greek Coins in the British Isles* (London 1948), showing coins present there from Greek cities reaching from Aradus in Phoenicia to Gades in Spain; see also M. Wheeler, *Rome beyond the Imperial*

Frontiers (1954), based on Roman coin hoards found as far as the Mekong delta.

On Greek money see the synthesis of K. Christ, "Die Griechen u. das Geld," *Saeculum* 15 (1964), 214 ff. Instructive is the essay of M. Rostovtzeff, "Some Remarks on the Monetary and Commercial Policy of the Seleucids and Attalids," *Anatolian Studies ... W. H. Buckler* (Manchester 1939), 277 ff. See also on this topic G. K. Jenkins, "The Monetary Systems in the Early Hellenistic Time, with Special Regard to the Economic Policy of the Ptolemaic Kings," *Proceedings of the International Numismatic Convention at Jerusalem 1963* (Tel Aviv and Jerusalem 1967), 53 ff.

The question of when the Roman denarius was first minted is examined by H. Mattingly, "The First Age of the Roman Coinage," *JRS* 19 (1929), 19 ff., and, with E. S. Robinson, "The Date of the Roman Denarius [which he places at 187 B.C.] and Other Landmarks in Early Roman Coinage," *PBA* 18 (1932), 211 ff., and "The Romano-Campanian Coinage: An Old Problem from a New Angle," *JWI* 1 (1938), 197 ff. Also valuable are R. Thomsen, *Early Roman Coinage* (3 vols., Copenhagen 1957–1961), and, most recently, K. Christ, *Antike Numismatik* (1967), 57, and R. E. Mitchell, *NC* (1966), 66 ff.

VII

Allied Disciplines

The close connection of late Antiquity with the early Middle Ages has been repeatedly stressed by scholars in recent years, as in Henri Pirenne's *Mohammed and Charlemagne*, Ernst Kornemann's account of the Roman Empire in *Gercke-Norden* and in his *Weltgeschichte des Mittelmeerraumes*, and—above all—in the socioeconomic studies of Alfons Dopsch and H. Aubin on the transition from Antiquity to the Middle Ages. In particular these scholars have refuted the traditional "catastrophe theory," and instead have demonstrated that medieval society took form in an evolutionary manner, and that its origins reached far back into Antiquity. For these reasons no one can insist any longer on a sharp division between ancient and medieval history. On this see H. Aubin, *HZ* 168 (1942), 229 ff.

Classical philology is naturally allied to ancient history because an important part of the sources is used by both disciplines and these two disciplines have for centuries been pursued together by individual scholars. Nevertheless, the separation of ancient historical and philological studies which is now usual in universities is justified, particularly because the historian and the philologist have different objectives. The fragmentary state of the ancient tradition compels the historian, in addition to studying the ancient historians, to analyze the poets and even the technical writers to see what information they can give. The student of the Augustan age, for example, cannot confine himself to the primary sources and the historians; he must pay attention to the contemporary poets (Horace, Vergil, Ovid, Propertius, and others), scholars (Verrius Flaccus, Hyginus), and scientists (the architect Vitruvius, the geographer Strabo, the astronomer Manilius). The historian must have learned not only to read the ancient sources, but also to interpret them, and to do that he must have a thorough training in the methods of classical philology.

Generally the historian will leave the editing of texts to philologists, despite exceptions such as Mommsen's editions, B. Niese's *Josephus*, and E. Hohl's *Historia Augusta*. In matters of interpretation, however, the historian will have to depend on his own judgment. In this way the two disciplines will continue in the future to aid each other. Hence there is no real reason for the opposition stressed by Karl Beloch with his phrase "philology or history," which he used to justify attacks on philologists because he thought they were "invading" the sphere of history.

Students of Antiquity also depend on classical archeology. Literally "archeology" means "science of prehistory," but in fact the term has been extended to include the excavation and interpretation of ancient monuments. For the historian of Antiquity the important thing will not be a formal analysis of the monuments, but rather the question of how far the monuments reflect the historical experience of peoples and cultures.

Ancient Near Eastern history must concern every student who takes seriously the concept of a general history of Antiquity, as formulated by Eduard Meyer. The advanced civilizations of Egypt, Mesopotamia, Asia Minor, and Persia all provide the background against which the achievements of the Greeks and Romans must be placed to be fully appreciated. Furthermore, it is only through study of the languages that the student can grasp the essence of Near Eastern history, because language is the key that unlocks a culture's secrets. Research in the history of the ancient Near East requires Egyptology, cuneiform, and Iranian studies. Even mastery of a single language will lead to a significant expansion of a scholar's viewpoint, which will then in turn enrich his understanding of other historical periods. It would be a mistake however, to think that study of the Near Eastern languages will lead immediately to important historical conclusions; that comes only after long and patient work. This is the place to warn the student against using translations of Near Eastern texts or interpreting them philologically as if they were original texts.

Just as the ancient Near East marks the beginning of Antiquity, so Byzantium is its finale. The so-called early Byzantine period, usually defined by the names of Constantine I and Heraclius (A.D. 324–641), is studied by both Romanists and Byzantinists, though the Romanist is interested more in the period's link with the past, the Byzantinist in its connections with the Middle Ages. The central organ of Byzantine studies is the German journal *Byzantinische Zeitschrift*, founded in 1892 by K. Krumbacher (1856–1909), later edited by F. Dölger and, at present by H. G. Beck. Its thorough and critical bibliographies provide the historian with a tool to keep up with current research and so select what he can use for his own work.

Comparative linguistics and Etruscology are essential to every student interested in Helladic and Italic history, just as is archeology. The methods of linguistics can be studied in Wilhelm Schulze's *Zur Geschichte lateinischer Eigennamen* (Berlin 1904) and Eduard Schwyzer's *Griechische Grammatik* (2 vols., 1939–1950), as well as in Ferdinand Sommer's works.

Study of nonliterate cultures must depend on the discipline concerned with primitive peoples, cultural anthropology, which deals with the history of humanity from Paleolithic times to the beginnings of written history. The distinction between prehistory and ancient history is vague, hence the use of a new term, "early history," discussed above. Ancient history and anthropology are necessarily connected, for it would be absurd if the student of ancient history ignored the Helladic and Italic periods simply because they have either left no written records or have left records which, as is true of Minoan, are as yet undeciphered.

Finally, the student of ancient history will be interested in the efforts of scholars to create a conceptual framework for the analysis of ancient legal systems. In particular the question whether reciprocal influence or independent discovery lies behind the development of law is of great interest to the historian. This is especially true for the evaluation of Roman law, which Fritz Schulz has called "the purest expression of Roman civilization and the most authoritative witness to Roman greatness."

BIBLIOGRAPHY

HISTORY AND PHILOLOGY: H. Usener, "Philologie u. Geschichtswissenschaft," *Vorträge und Aufsätze* (1882), 1 ff.; Ed. Meyer, *Kleine Schriften* I (1910), 65 ff; for a different view see Werner Jaeger, *NJA* 37 (1916), 81 ff., reprinted in *Humanistische Reden und Aufsätze* (1937), 1 ff.

CLASSICAL ARCHEOLOGY: For its importance see ch. 5, which also lists the more important journals in the field.

ANCIENT NEAR EAST: Research in its languages and cultures is covered in these journals: *Archiv für Orientforschung* (Berlin, later Graz, 1926 ff.); *Mitteilungen der Deutschen Orientgesellschaft* (Berlin 1899 ff.); *Wiener Zeitschrift für die Kunde des Morgenlandes* (Vienna 1887 ff.); *Zeitschrift der Deutschen Morgenländischen Gesellschaft* (Leipzig 1846 ff.); *Zeitschrift des deutschen Palästinavereins* (Leipzig 1878 ff.); *Orientalische Literaturzeitung* (1898 ff.).

Non-German journals include: *Annual of the American School of Oriental Research* (New Haven 1920 ff.); *Bulletin of the American Schools of Oriental Research* (South Hadley, later New Haven, 1920 ff.); *Journal of the American Oriental Society* (New Haven 1851 ff.); *American Journal of Semitic Languages and Literatures*, from 1942 *The Journal of Near Eastern Studies* (Chicago 1898 ff.); *Archiv Orientalni* (Prague 1929 ff.); *Le Monde Oriental* (Uppsala 1906 ff.); *Orientalia*: new series (Rome 1932 ff.); *Bibliotheca Orientalis* (Leiden 1944 ff.).

Two series useful to the historian are: *Der Alte Orient* (Leipzig 1903–1945), which includes many brief monographs, and the series *Das Morgenland*.

EGYPTOLOGY: Introductions to language and writing: A. Erman, *Ägyptische Grammatik mit Schrifttafel, Paradigmen*, etc. (ed. 4, Leipzig 1928); H. Brunner, *Abriss d. mittelägyptischen Grammatik* (ed. 2, Graz 1967); with which use the *Wörterbuch der ägyptischen Sprache* published by the Prussian Academy (6 vols., Leipzig and Berlin 1926–1950), also the *Belegstellen*. On this venture see A. Erman and H. Grapow, *Das Wörterbuch der ägyptischen Sprache: Zur Geschichte eines grossen wissenschaftlichen Unternehmens der Akademie* (Berlin 1953). Special journals include: *Zeitschrift für Ägyptische Sprache* (Leipzig 1863 ff.); *Journal of Egyptian Archaeology* (London 1914 ff.). An important series is *Ägyptologische Forschungen* (Glückstadt 1936 ff.), founded by A. Scharff, now edited by H. W. Müller.

ASSYRIOLOGY: Introduction: A. Ungnad, *Babylonisch-assyrische Grammatik*, with cuneiform reader (Munich 1927; ed. 4 by A. Matous, 1964); R. Borger, *Babylonisch-assyrische Lesebücher* (3 vols., Rome 1963). Basic work: W. v. Soden, *Grundriss der akkadischen Grammatik* (Rome 1952). Since 1956 a large dictionary has been appearing in parts, *The Assyrian Dictionary of the Oriental Institute of the University of Chicago*. For the history of Assyrian lexicography see R. Borger, *BO* (1957), 114 ff. Also in process of publication is W. v. Soden, *Akkadisches Handwörterbuch* (Wiesbaden 1959-present; eight fascicles published by 1967). Special journals include: *Zeitschrift für Assyriologie* (Leipzig 1886 ff.);

Revue d'Assyriologie et d'Archéologie Orientale (Paris 1884 ff.); *Journal of Cuneiform Studies* (New Haven 1947 ff.).

HITTITE STUDIES: Pioneer work toward decipherment of the Hittite documents was done by B. Hrozný; see his preliminary report, "Die Lösung des hethitischen Problems," *MDOG* 56 (December 1915), and *Die Sprache der Hethither: Ihr Bau und ihre Zugehörigkeit zum indogermanischen Sprachstamm* (Leipzig 1917). Thereafter the outstanding contributions were the works of Ferdinand Sommer: "Die Aḫḫijava-Urkunden," *ABAW* n.f. 6 (1932); "Aḫḫijavafrage und Sprachwissenschaft," *ABAW* n.f. 9 (1934); "Die akkadisch-hethitische Bilingue des Ḫatušiliš I. (Labarna II.)," *ABAW* n.f. 16 (1938), written with A. Falkenstein; *Hethiter u. Hethitisch* (Stuttgart 1947). See also Johann Friedrich, *Hethitisches Elementarbuch* (2 vols., ed. 2, Heidelberg 1960–1967), and his *Wörterbuch* (Heidelberg 1952–1954) with supplements (1957, 1961). For information on journals and monographs in the field see A. Goetze, *Kulturgeschichte des Alten Orients: Kleinasien*, in *Müller* (ed. 2, 1957), 83. For recent research see G. Walser, *Neuere Hethiterforschung* (*Historia, Einzelschrift* 7, Wiesbaden 1964).

IRANIAN STUDIES: W. Brandenstein and M. Mayrhofer, *Hdb. des Altpersischen* (Wiesbaden 1964). Also useful: W. Hinz, *Altpersischer Wortschatz* (*Abh. für die Kunde des Morgenlandes* 27.1, Leipzig 1942).—An older guide to Achaemenid documents is F. H. Weissbach, *Die Keilinschriften der Achämeniden* (*Vorderasiatische Bibliothek* 3, Leipzig 1911); documents discovered thereafter are printed by E. Herzfeld, *Altpersische Inschriften* (Berlin 1938). See also R. G. Kent, *Old Persian: Grammar, Texts, Lexicon* (New Haven 1950; ed. 2, 1953). Journals: *Zeitschrift für Indologie und Iranistik* (Leipzig 1922–1936); *Archäologische Mitteilungen aus Iran*, ed. E. Herzfeld (Berlin 1929/30 ff., 1968 ff.).

BYZANTINE STUDIES: History of the discipline: E. Gerland, *Das Studium der byzantinischen Geschichte vom Humanismus bis zur Jetztzeit* (Athens 1934); G. Ostrogorsky, *History of the Byzantine State*, tr. J. Hussey (Oxford 1956, and Rutgers, N. J. 1957). Recent researches of scholars in all countries are reviewed thoroughly by F. Dölger and A. M. Schneider, *Byzanz* (Bern 1952). A thoughtful contribution is F. Dölger, "Aufgaben der byzantinischen Philologie von heute," *Altertum* 1 (1955), 44 ff. Journals: *Byzantinische Zeitschrift* (Leipzig 1892 ff.); *Byzantion*, ed. H. Grégoire (Brussels 1924 ff.).

COMPARATIVE LINGUISTICS: For an introduction see H. Krahe, *Indogermanische Sprachwissenschaft* (*Sammlung Göschen* 59 and 64, ed. 3, Berlin 1958–1959); also these older works: A. Meillet,

Introduction à l'étude comparative des langues indo-européennes (ed. 8, Paris 1937; repr. 1953); J. Schrijnen, *Einführung in das Studium der indogermanischen Sprachwissenschaft* (Heidelberg 1921), and *Stand und Aufgaben der Sprachwissenschaft: Festschrift für W. Streitberg* (Heidelberg 1924). Historians will find useful the excellent book of W. Porzig, *Das Wunder der Sprache* (*Sammlung Dalp* 71, Bern 1950), with a full bibliography, pp. 395–397. Journals: *Kuhns Zeitschrift für Vergleichende Sprachwissenschaft* (Berlin, later Göttingen, 1852 ff.); *Indogermanische Forschungen* (Strasbourg, later Berlin and Leipzig 1892 ff.); *Glotta* (Göttingen 1909 ff.). An excellent survey of the entire field with allied disciplines is given by *Indogermanische Jahrbuch* (1914 ff.).

ETRUSCOLOGY: Introduction to its problems is given by Eva Fiesel, *Geschichte der indogermanischen Sprachwissenschaft* V. 4 (1931); but now the best guide is M. Pallottino, *Etruscologia* (ed. 5, Milan 1963; in English: *The Etruscans*, tr. J. Cremona, Harmondsworth, England 1956).–Current research is indicated by the contributions of various scholars to the special Etruscan issue of *Historia* 6 (1957). See also M. Pallottino, "Nuovi studi sul problema delle origini etrusche (Bilancio critico)," *SE* 29 (1961), 3 ff.–The Etruscan inscriptions were collected in the *Corpus Inscriptionum Etruscarum* (Leipzig 1893 ff.); and a selection is printed in M. Pallottino, *Testimonia linguae Etruscae* (Florence 1954). The outstanding journal is *Studi Etruschi* (Florence 1927 ff.).

PREHISTORY: Still indispensable, though in part outdated, is *Reallexikon der Vorgeschichte*, ed. Max Ebert (15 vols., Berlin 1924–1932); there is no brief survey for the beginner. A useful substitute is the text of the *Grosser Historischer Weltatlas des Bayerischen Schulbuchverlages* I: *Vorgeschichte und Altertum* (ed. 3, 1958); the section on prehistory is by V. Milojčič, who also prepared the maps. Presently in course of publication is *Hdb. der Vorgeschichte*, ed. H. Müller-Karpe; so far published is vol. 1 (Munich 1966), covering paleolithic times.

LEGAL HISTORY: Survey of the field: L. Wenger, *Der heutige Stand der römischen Rechtswissenschaft: Erreichtes und Erstrebtes* (*Münchener Beiträge* 11, Munich 1927); see also the same scholar's bibliographic reviews of legal studies in the *Archiv für Papyrusforschung* VII ff., and his essay, "Wesen und Ziele der antiken Rechtsgeschichte," *Studi . . . P. Bonfante* II (1929), 465 ff.–The leading journal in the field is *Zeitschrift der Savignystiftung für Rechtsgeschichte: Romanistische Abteilung* (Weimar 1880 ff.); the institute's other journals on canonical and Germanic law are less useful to the student of ancient history.

VIII

Reference Works
and Journals

Scholars of ancient history, like their colleagues in classical philology, archeology, and other allied disciplines, depend on many works of reference. They may be divided among these categories: dictionaries, encyclopedias, manuals, and bibliographies.

Interpretation of ancient texts depends on dictionaries. For Latin there is the *Grosser Georges* (2 vols., ed. 8, 1913–1918, often reprinted); for research on Roman political and sacral law there is the work begun by E. Wölfflin, *Thesaurus Linguae Latinae* (1900 ff.), a splendid tool but not yet completed; so far the volumes on A–I (to *iugum*), M (to *myzon*), and its onomasticon to D have been published. The best Greek dictionary is the *Greek-English Lexicon*, ed. Liddell-Scott-Jones (ed. 9, Oxford 1940), with *Supplement*, ed. E. A. Barber (Oxford 1968). A modern thesaurus of ancient Greek is lacking; the old one by Stephanus is long out of date, but as yet there is no replacement.

The major reference work on the ancient world is the *Real-Encyclopädie der classischen Altertumswissenschaft*. It was begun in 1839 by A. Pauly, then in 1893 Georg Wissowa began publishing an entirely new edition, and his work was continued by W. Kroll, K. Mittelhaus, and (the present editor) K. Ziegler. The monumental work (abbreviated *RE*) is now almost completed, volumes having been issued for A–Q and R–Z (Z is incomplete); in addition there are 11 supplements, which deal with subjects overlooked or requiring revision. Its 60-odd thick volumes make the *RE* a mine of information on absolutely all aspects of Antiquity.

Dictionaries of biography are called prosopographies; they collect, evaluate, and render accessible the basic information on individuals of a particular period or in a particular activity. Two of these are especially important: the *Prosopographia Attica* of Johannes Kirchner, and the *Prosopographia Imperii Romani*, sponsored by the Prussian Academy, of which four volumes have been published so far.

Among the manuals the most important is the *Handbuch der klassischen Altertumswissenschaft*, begun in 1886 by the philologist Ivan von Müller. Its sphere was enlarged and its title changed to *Handbuch der Altertumswissenschaft* by the historian Walter Otto (1878–1941), and it now covers the culture, literature, and history of not only the classical Mediterranean world but also its neighboring areas—the ancient Near East and northern Europe. The core of the series are the volumes devoted to historical, constitutional, and literary syntheses, of which two are unequaled in their fields: W. Schmid and O. Stählin, *Geschichte der griechischen Literatur*, and M. Schanz and C. Hosius, *Geschichte der römischen Literatur*.

Less ambitious in scope is the *Einleitung in die Altertumswissenschaft*, eds. A. Gercke and E. Norden. The complete work is no longer in print, but individual volumes are.

More important as a guide to the current development of ancient historical studies are the journals, for they make possible the publication of shorter works. The number of journals important for research in the field is large, and the most important in all countries are surveyed here:

German journals which are particularly important are: *Historische Zeitschrift*, founded in 1859 by H. v. Sybel, and devoted primarily to studies in medieval and modern history, but nevertheless important to the student of ancient history because of its catholic viewpoint and bibliographic reports; *Klio*, containing articles on ancient history, and once again being published since 1959; and *Historia* (1950 ff.), the international journal of historians of Antiquity. Of philological journals the most noteworthy is *Hermes*, a journal of classical philology which was founded in 1866 by Theodor Mommsen. Also important is *Gnomon* (1925 ff.), which is devoted exclusively to critical evaluation of new publications in all fields of classical studies.

Valuable work in the ancient studies is published by the various learned academies. In Germany these include the German Academy (formerly the Prussian Academy) in Berlin, the Bavarian Academy in Munich, and the Academies of Göttingen, Heidelberg, Leipzig, and Mainz. Important non-German organizations include the British

Academy of London, Académie des Inscriptions et Belles Lettres of Paris, Accademia dei Lincei of Rome, Accademia di Torino of Turin, and the Akademie der Wissenschaften of Vienna. Great scholars published by the Berlin Academy include Theodor Mommsen, U. v. Wilamowitz-Moellendorff, Eduard Meyer, O. Hirschfeld, E. Norden, U. Wilcken, W. Jaeger, M. Gelzer, and E. Hohl; the Bavarian Academy published among others works by R. v. Pöhlmann, E. Schwartz, W. Otto, A. v. Premerstein, W. Ensslin, and H. Berve.

Attention should also be given to series, that is, those collections of monographs which are published separately and without any necessary connection. Some are published as *Beihefte* by journals, among them *Historische Zeitschrift, Klio, Hermes, Philologus*. Other noteworthy series include in Germany *Münchener Beiträge zur Papyrusforschung und antiken Rechtsgeschichte* (1915 ff.), and in the United States *Harvard Studies in Classical Philology* (Cambridge, Mass. 1890 ff.) and *Yale Classical Studies* (New Haven 1928 ff., so far 20 volumes).

Equally valuable are the books which contain the collected articles of important scholars. Often the individual studies are scattered and difficult to find, and their collection renders them accessible to scholars. The most important example of this is the *Gesammelte Schriften* of Theodor Mommsen (8 vols., Berlin 1905–1913). With his *Reden und Aufsätze* (Berlin 1905) these volumes constitute the great scholar's most precious bequest to future generations. Also worth noting are the following: *Kleine Schriften* of the critic and historian Alfred von Gutschmid (5 vols., ed. Fr. Rühl, 1889–1894); *Forschungen zur Alten Geschichte* of Eduard Meyer (2 vols., 1892– 1899), also his *Kleine Schriften* (2 vols., Halle 1910–1924); *Gesammelte Schriften* of U. v. Wilamowitz-Moellendorff (so far volumes 1, 2, 5, Berlin 1933 ff.). It would be a great aid to scholarship to have thus collected the scattered works of such scholars as Ulrich Wilcken, Adolf Wilhelm, and Anton von Premerstein. Outside Germany there are excellent examples of such publications, among them the works of the distinguished French scholar Maurice Holleaux, *Études d'épigraphie et d'histoire grecques*, ed. L. Robert (5 vols. so far, Paris 1938 ff.), and the articles of the Swedish scholar Martin P. Nilsson, *Opuscula selecta* (3 vols., Lund 1951–1960).

Bibliographies and review articles are indispensable for the student to keep abreast of the wealth of research published in books and articles throughout the world. Philologists and historians will profit equally from study of *Bursians Jahresberichte über die Fortschritte der klass. Altertumswissenschaft*, which published critical review articles on all fields—history, literature, language, and religion. In practice this resulted in review articles on a great variety of topics, e.g., Herodotus, Caesar and the Caesarian Corpus, the Scriptores Historiae Augustae, Greek history, Greek constitutional law, the history of the Roman Empire, etc. The later volumes of *Bursian* each have a summary of previous issues, allowing one to find the last report on any topic, and from this in turn one can learn the earlier ones. In 1944 *Bursian* ceased publication, and its place has been taken by *Lustrum* (Göttingen 1956 ff.); its editors include scholars from Germany and other countries.—Valuable bibliographies of Greek and Roman history are published in the *Revue historique*. Recently it published a review by A. Piganiol of work on Roman history during 1956–1964; cf. *RH* 234 (1965), 129–158. The last report on Greek history, by Eduard Will, appeared in *RH* 238 (1967), 377–452.

Full bibliographies, giving titles of all books and journal articles, were published annually by the *Bibliotheca Philologica Classica* (1874–1938); its precision earned the admiration of scholars. For the years since 1938 one must depend on *Klassieke Bibliographie* (Utrecht 1929 ff.) and on France's *L'Année philologique*, ed. J. Marouzeau (Paris 1928 ff.), which covers the years from 1924 on, and is supplemented by J. Marouzeau, *Dix années de bibliographique classique, 1914–1924* (2 vols., Paris 1927–1928).

Another important tool is the bibliographic supplement (*Bibliographie*) published with the *Jahrbuch des Deutschen Archäologischen Instituts* (1923/24 ff.); it is concerned primarily with the monuments and their interpretation.

Finally there are important specialized bibliographies. An example is *Die Palästinaliteratur*, ed. P. Thomsen (6 vols.; vol. 6, covering 1935–1939, was published in Leipzig, 1953–1956), which covers all studies on all aspects of Palestine published during the years 1895–1939; a supplement covering the years 1878–1894 is in preparation; the first fascicle appeared 1957 in Berlin. Also noteworthy are the bibliography of the *Archiv für Orientforschung*, ed. E. F. Weidner, and of the *Indogermanisches Jahrbuch*.

BIBLIOGRAPHY

ENCYCLOPEDIAS: The *Real-Encyclopädie der classischen Altertumswissenschaft*, eds. Pauly and Wissowa (abbreviated *RE*) includes (as of 1968) vols. 1–24.1 in the first series, and in the second (letters R–Z) volumes 1A–9A, plus 11 supplementary volumes. A new edition in abbreviated form is now appearing, *Der Kleine Pauly: Lexikon der Antike*, eds. K. Ziegler and V. W. Sontheimer; so far 3 volumes (Stuttgart 1963–1968) have appeared, up to the article "Lyseis."

Also an important tool is the *Dictionnaire des antiquités grecques et romaines*, eds. C. Daremberg and E. Saglio (10 vols., Paris 1877–1918); it is a valuable guide to the material culture of Antiquity. For ancient art: *Enciclopedia dell' arte antica, classica ed orientale* (Rome 1956 ff.).

Useful brief manuals include: Fr. Lübker's *Reallexikon des klassischen Altertums*, eds. J. Geffcken and E. Ziebarth (Leipzig 1914), which has gaps; *The Oxford Classical Dictionary* (ed. 2, 1970); and *Lexikon der Alten Welt* (Zürich and Stuttgart 1965), unfortunately printed in a single, bulky volume.

For Roman history and constitutional law see *Dizionario epigrafico di antichitá romane*, ed. E. De Ruggiero (Rome 1895 ff.), not yet completed. Also still in course of publication is *Reallexikon für Antike und Christentum* (Leipzig 1941 ff.). Excellent articles on Antiquity by the best Italian scholars are in the *Enciclopedia Italiana* (35 vols., Milan and Rome 1929–1937).

For the prehistory and early history of the Mediterranean see, though it is partly out of date, the *Reallexikon der Vorgeschichte*, ed. Max Ebert (15 vols., Berlin 1924–1932).—Mythology is covered by the *Ausführliches Lexikon der griechischen und römischen Mythologie*, ed. W. H. Roscher (6 vols., Leipzig 1884–1937). For Indo-European studies see the *Reallexikon der Indogermanischen Altertumskunde*, eds. O. Schrader and A. Nehring (2 vols., ed. 2, 1917–1929). Not yet completed is the *Reallexikon der Assyriologie und der vorderasiatischen Altertumskunde*, eds. E. Ebeling, B. Meissner, and E. Weidner (Berlin 1932–1967); it has reached the article "Girsu."

PROSOPOGRAPHIES: Although nobody today questions the important results gained by the prosopographic method, which indeed has been adopted by other disciplines, it is important to realize its limitations. No matter how many careers and lives we know about, still the thoughts and values of the individuals concerned generally remain hidden—and these are essential for an understanding of the spirit of an age. On this topic see A. Momigliano, *Relazioni del X Congresso Intern. di Scienze storiche* VI (Rome 1955), 25–26.

Important prosopographies include: F. Justi, *Iranisches Namenbuch* (Marburg 1895), which now requires additions; J. Kirchner, *Prosopographia Attica* (2 vols., Berlin 1901–1903), "the Athenian address book"; supplements to it have been published by J. Sundwall, *Oeversigt af Finska Vetenskaps Societetens Foerhandlingar* 52 (1909–1910), vol. 1; a new edition with concordance was issued in 1966 by S. Lauffer. Also important for Greek prosopography are: the index volume to the journal *Hesperia* (1946); P. Poralla, *Prosopographie der Lakedämonier bis auf die Zeit Alexanders des Grossen* (Diss. Breslau 1913); H. Berve, *Das Alexanderreich auf prosopographischer Grundlage*, vol. 2 (Munich 1926), vol. 1 being an account of the administration and military system of Alexander's empire, a superb example of the historical use of prosopographic material.

For the Hellenistic period see P. Schoch, *Prosopographie der militärischen und politischen Funktionäre im hellenistischen Makedonien (323–168 v. Chr.)*, in typescript (Diss. Basel 1919); F. Heichelheim, *Die auswärtige Bevölkerung im Ptolemäerreich (Klio, Beiheft 18, 1925)*, with supplements in *Archiv für Papyrusforschung* 9, pp. 47 ff.; 12, pp. 54 ff.; H. Henne, *Liste des stratèges de nomes égyptiens à l'époque greco-romaine* (Cairo 1935). Further material in Hondius, *Saxa loquuntur* (1938), 187. Presently appearing is *Prosopographia Ptolemaica* by W. Peremans and E. van't Dack (5 vols. so far, Louvain 1950 ff.).

For Roman studies see *Prosopographia Imperii Romani saeculi I, II, III*, eds. E. Klebs, H. Dessau, P. v. Rohden (3 vols., 1897–1898: abbreviated *PIR*). A new edition by E. Groag, Leiva Petersen, and A. Stein has been in publication since 1933; vol. 3 appeared in 1958, vol. 4 (up to Zates) in 1966.—Roman prosopography also includes a number of studies devoted to the imperial officials of particular provinces, among them: A. Stein, *Römische Reichsbeamte der Provinz Thracia* (Sarajevo 1920), and *Die Legaten von Moesien* (*Diss. Pannonicae* 1.11, Budapest 1940), and *Die Reichsbeamten von Dazien* (*Diss. Pannonicae* 1.12, Budapest 1944), and *Die Präfekten von Ägypten in der röm. Kaiserzeit* (*Diss. Bern.* 1.1, Bern 1950); E. Groag, *Die römischen Reichsbeamten von Achaia bis auf Diokletian* (*Schriften d. Balkan-Komm. der Adad. d. Wiss. Wien, Antiqu. Abt.* 9, Vienna and Leipzig 1939), and *Die Reichsbeamten von Achaia im spätromischer Zeit* (*Diss. Pann.* 1.14, Budapest 1946); W. Kunkel, *Herkunft u. soziale Stellung der röm. Juristen* (ed. 2, 1967).

MANUALS: Ivan v. Müller founded the *Handbuch der Alter-tumswissenschaft*; he was succeeded as editor by W. Otto (who died in 1941), and in 1953 by Hermann Bengtson. The *Hand-buch* is planned to cover 12 divisions, as follows: (1) introductory and auxiliary disciplines; (2) language; (3) history and geography; (4) politics and law; (5) philosophy, science, and religion; (6) ar-cheology; (7) Greek literature; (8) Roman literature; (9) Latin literature of the Middle Ages; (10) legal history of Antiquity; (11) Germanic antiquities; (12) Byzantine studies.

The other major *Handbuch* is that edited by A. Gercke and E. Norden, the *Einleitung in die Altertumswissenschaft*. It was pub-lished in three volumes, which were issued in third editions and parts in a fourth. The first volume includes literary histories, language, and metrics; volume two includes private life, numismatics, art, re-ligion, the exact sciences, and philosophy; volume three includes history, constitutional law, and chronology.

JOURNALS: In the following list some journals are marked with an asterisk; this indicates that besides the regular issues the journal also publishes a separate series (variously called *Beihefte*, *Sonderschriften*, *Supplemente*, etc.). Journals mainly devoted to criticism are marked with two asterisks, and those which have not begun publishing since World War II are marked with a dagger.

AUSTRIA: (1) *Wiener Studien* (Vienna 1879 ff.).—(2) *Anzei-ger für die Altertumswissenschaft*** (Innsbruck 1948 ff.).

BELGIUM: (1) *L'Antiquité classique* (Louvain 1932 ff.).—(2) *Le Musée belge* (Liège 1897–1932).—(3) *Revue belge de Phil-ologie et d'Histoire* (Brussels 1922 ff.).—(4) *Les études classiques* (Namur 1932 ff.)—(5) *Latomus: Revue d'études latines* (Brussels 1937 ff.).

BRITAIN: (1) *Journal of Hellenic Studies* (London 1880 ff.). —(2) *Journal of Roman Studies* (London 1911 ff.).—(3) *Classical Quarterly* (London 1907 ff.).—(4) *Classical Review*** (London 1887 ff.).

FRANCE: (1) *Revue des études anciennes* (Bordeaux 1899 ff.)—(2) *Revue des études grecques* (Paris 1888 ff.).—(3) *Revue des études latines* (Paris 1923 ff.).—(4) *Revue historique* (Paris 1876 ff.).—(5) *Revue de philologie, de littérature, et d'histoire an-ciennes* (Paris 1845–1847, 1877 ff.).

GERMANY: (1) *Das Altertum* (Berlin 1955 ff.).—(2) *Die Antike*† (Berlin 1925 ff.).—(3) *Archiv für Religionswissenschaft**† (Leipzig 1898 ff.).—(4) *Gnomon*** (Berlin, then Munich, 1925 ff.).—(5) *Göttingische Gelehrte Anzeigen* (Göttingen and Berlin 1739 ff.).—(6) *Hermes: Zeitschrift für klassische Philologie** (Leipzig, now Wiesbaden, 1866 ff.)—(7) *Neue Jahrbücher für Wissenschaft und Jugendbildung*, then from 1938: *Neue Jahrbücher für Antike und deutsche Bildung*† (Leipzig 1898 ff.).—(8) *Klio: Beiträge zur Alten Geschichte** (Leipzig 1902 ff.; 1959 ff.).—(9) *Deutsche Literaturzeitung*** (Berlin 1880 ff.).—(10) *Rheinisches Museum für Philologie* (Bonn 1827 ff.).—(11) *Philologus** (Leipzig, now Wiesbaden, 1846 ff.).—(12) *Die Welt als Geschichte* (Stuttgart 1935–1962).—(13) *[Berliner] Philologische Wochenschrift*† (Berlin and Leipzig 1881 ff.).—(14) *Historia: Zeitschrift für alte Geschichte** (Baden-Baden, then Wiesbaden, 1950, 1953 ff.).—(15) *Historische Zeitschrift** (Munich 1846 ff.).

ITALY: (1) *Athenaeum: Studi periodici di letteratura e storia dell' antichità* (nuova serie, Pavia 1923 ff.).—(2) *Rivista di filologia e d'istruzione classica* (Rome, then Turin, 1873 ff.).—(3) *Studi italiani di filologia classica* (Florence and Rome 1893 ff.).—(4) *Paideia* (Milan 1946 ff.).—(5) *Parola del Passato* (Naples 1946 ff.).—(6) *Kokalos* (Palermo 1955 ff.).

NETHERLANDS: *Mnemosyne** (Leiden 1852 ff.).

NORWAY: *Symbolae Osloenses* (originally *Symbolae Arctoae*: Oslo 1922 ff.).

SWEDEN: *Eranos* (Uppsala 1896 ff.).

SWITZERLAND: *Museum Helveticum* (Basel 1944 ff.).

UNITED STATES: (1) *American Journal of Philology* (Baltimore 1880 ff.).—(2) *Classical Philology* (1906 ff.).—(3) *Classical World* (originally *Classical Weekly*: New York 1917 ff.).

──── IX ────

Select Bibliography

─────

Useful surveys and reference works are listed in Part One. Part Two follows the organization of the *Cambridge Ancient History* (12 vols., Cambridge 1924–1939), and is therefore arranged in twelve sections corresponding to the volumes of that work. A thirteenth section adds a few important works on late Antiquity.

PART ONE: GENERAL WORKS

I. REFERENCE AND BIBLIOGRAPHY

A. Breccia, *Avviamento e guida allo studio della storia e delle antichità classiche* (Pisa 1950).

M. Cary, *et al.*, eds., *Oxford Classical Dictionary* (Oxford 1949).

E. Manni, *Introduzione allo studio della storia greca e romana* (ed. 2, Palermo 1958).

P. Petit, *Guide de l'étudiant en histoire ancienne* (Paris 1959).

H. Scullard and A. v. d. Heyden, *Shorter Atlas of the Classical World* (New York 1967).

O. Seyffert, *Dictionary of Classical Antiquities*, rev. Nettleship and Sandys (1891; repr. Cleveland 1966).

W. Smith, *Smaller Classical Dictionary*, rev. Blakeney and Warrington (New York 1960).

C. Wachsmuth, *Einleitung in das Studium der Alten Geschichte* (Leipzig 1895).

II. SURVEYS

A. *General*

A. Bozeman, *Politics and Culture in International History* (Princeton 1960).

N. Fustel de Coulanges, *The Ancient City*, tr. W. Small (1864; repr. New York 1955).

F. Heichelheim, *An Ancient Economic History* (2 vols., Leiden 1958).

W. Heitland, *Agricola: A Study in Agriculture and Rustic Life in the Greco-Roman World* (Cambridge 1921).

M. Finley, ed., *Slavery in Classical Antiquity: Views and Controversies* (Cambridge 1960).

H. Marrou, *A History of Education in Antiquity*, tr. George Lamb (New York 1956).

O. Neugebauer, *The Exact Sciences in Antiquity* (ed. 2, Providence 1957).

R. Taton, ed., *Ancient and Medieval Science* (New York 1963).

L. Thorndike, *A History of Magic and Experimental Science* (vols. 1 and 2: the first 13 centuries A.D.; New York 1923, repr. 1958).

W. Westermann, *The Slave Systems of Greek and Roman Antiquity* (Philadelphia 1955).

B. *The Ancient Near East*

W. Albright, *From the Stone Age to Christianity* (ed. 2, Baltimore 1946).

H. Frankfort, *The Birth of Civilization in the Near East* (London 1951, repr. New York 1968). Also, *Kingship and the Gods: A Study of Ancient Near Eastern Religion as the Integration of Society and Nature* (Chicago 1948).

H. Hall, *The Ancient History of the Near East from the Earliest Times to the Battle of Salamis* (ed. 11, London 1952).

G. Maspero, *The Dawn of Civilization* (New York 1968).

C. *Greece*

C. Bowra, *The Greek Experience* (Cleveland 1958).

J. Bury, *A History of the Greek World to the Death of Alexander the Great* (ed. 3 by R. Meiggs, London 1951).

M. Cary, *A History of the Greek World from 323 to 146 B.C.* (New York 1963).

E. Dodds, *The Greeks and the Irrational* (Berkeley 1951).

W. Guthrie, *The Greeks and their Gods* (Boston 1950).

V. Ehrenberg, *The Greek State* (Oxford 1960).

M. Finley, *A History of Sicily* (vol. 1: Ancient Sicily to the Arab Conquest; London 1968).

M. Hammond, *City State and World State in Greek and Roman Political Theory until Augustus* (Cambridge, Mass. 1951).

N. Hammond, *A History of Greece to 322 B.C.* (ed. 2, Oxford 1967).

W. Jaeger, *Paideia. The Ideals of Greek Culture* (3 vols., tr. G. Highet, Oxford 1944–1945).

M. Laistner, *A History of the Greek World from 479 to 323 B.C.* (ed. 3, New York 1962).

M. Rostovtzeff, *Social and Economic History of the Hellenistic World* (3 vols., Oxford 1941).

B. Snell, *The Discovery of the Mind: The Greek Origins of European Thought* (Oxford 1953).

D. *Rome*

M. Cary, *A History of Rome down to the Reign of Constantine* (ed. 2, London 1962).

M. Charlesworth, *The Roman Empire* (Oxford 1954).

C. Cochrane, *Christianity and Classical Culture: A Study of Thought and Action from Augustus to Augustine* (ed. 2, Oxford 1944; repr. 1957).

G. Gianelli and S. Mazzarino, *Trattato di storia romana* (vol. 1, ed. 3, Rome 1965; vol. 2, ed. 2, Rome 1962).

W. Heitland, *The Roman Republic* (ed. 2, 3 vols., Cambridge 1923).

W. Kunkel, *An Introduction to Roman Legal and Constitutional History*, tr. J. Kelly (Oxford 1966).

N. Lewis and M. Reinhold, *Roman Civilization* (2 vols., New York 1951; repr. 1966): sources and bibliography.

A. Piganiol, *Histoire de Rome* (ed. 3, Paris 1949): outline and bibliography.

H. Parker, *History of the Roman World AD 138–337* (ed. 2, London 1958; repr. 1963).

M. Rostovtzeff, *The Social and Economic History of the Roman Empire* (2 vols., ed. 2 by P. Fraser, Oxford 1957): to A.D. 324.

E. Salmon, *History of the Roman World 31 B.C.–A.D. 138* (ed. 6, London 1968).

H. Scullard, *From the Gracchi to Nero* (ed. 2, London 1964).

———, *History of the Roman World 753–146 B.C.* (ed. 3, London 1961; repr. 1968).

PART TWO: STUDIES

I. and II. EGYPT AND BABYLONIA TO 1580 B.C., and THE EGYPTIAN AND HITTITE EMPIRES TO C. 1000 B.C.

A. *Egypt*

C. Bleeker, *Egyptian Festivals: Enactments of Religious Renewal* (Leiden 1967).

J. Breasted, *A History of Egypt from the Earliest Times to the Persian Conquest* (ed. 2, New York 1937).

F. Bratton, *A History of Egyptian Archaeology* (New York 1968).

J. Černý, *Ancient Egyptian Religion* (London 1952, repr. 1957).

W. Emery, *Archaic Egypt* (Baltimore 1961).

A. Erman, *The Literature of the Ancient Egyptians*, tr. A. Blackman (London 1927).

H. Frankfort, *Ancient Egyptian Religion; an Interpretation* (New York 1948, repr. 1961).

A. Gardiner, *Egypt of the Pharaohs, an Introduction* (Oxford 1961).

S. Glanville, ed., *The Legacy of Egypt* (Oxford 1942, repr. 1957).

W. Hayes, *The Scepter of Egypt* (2 vols., New York 1953–1959).

I. Edwards, *The Pyramids of Egypt* (West Drayton 1947).

A. Lucas, *Ancient Egyptian Materials and Industries* (ed. 4, London 1962).

P. Elgood, *Later Dynasties of Egypt* (Oxford 1951).

F. Petrie, *The Arts and Crafts of Ancient Egypt* (London 1923).

B. Rothenberg, *et al.*, *God's Wilderness, Discoveries in the Sinai* (London 1961).

J. Seters, *The Hyksos* (New Haven and London 1966).

J. Smith, *Tombs, Temples and Ancient Art* (Norman 1956).

W. Smith, *The Art and Architecture of Ancient Egypt* (Baltimore 1958).

———, *A History of Egyptian Sculpture and Painting in the Old Kingdom* (ed. 2, Oxford 1949).

G. Steindorff and K. Seele, *When Egypt Ruled the East* (Chicago 1957).

J. Wilson, *The Burden of Egypt; an Interpretation of Ancient Egyptian Culture* (Chicago 1951; repr. 1963 as *The Culture of Ancient Egypt*).

H. Winlock, *The Rise and Fall of the Middle Kingdom in Thebes* (New York 1947).

B. *The Near East*

S. Ahmed, *Southern Mesopotamia in the Time of Ashurbanipal* (Paris 1968).

G. Cameron, *History of Early Iran* (Chicago 1936).

S. Fiore, *Voices from the Clay: the Development of Assyro-Babylonian Literature* (Norman, Okla. 1965).

J. Finegan, *Light from the Ancient Past* (Princeton 1959).

H. Frankfort, *The Art and Architecture of the Ancient Orient* (Harmondsworth 1954).

H. Frankfort, *et al.*, *The Intellectual Adventure of Ancient Man* (Chicago 1946; repr. 1951 as *Before Philosophy*).

C. Gadd, *Ideas of Divine Rule in the Ancient East* (London 1948).

I. Gelb, *Hurrians and Subarians* (Chicago 1944).

O. Gurney, *The Hittites* (Harmondsworth 1954).

S. Hooke, *Babylonian and Assyrian Religion* (London 1953).

E. James, *Myth and Ritual in the Ancient Near East* (London 1958).

S. Kramer, *The Sumerians: Their History, Culture, and Character* (Chicago 1963).

W. Leemans, *Foreign Trade in the Old Babylonian Period* (Leiden 1960).

S. Lloyd, *The Art of the Ancient Near East* (London 1961).

I. Mendelsohn, *Slavery in the Ancient Near East* (New York 1948).

S. Moscati, *Ancient Semitic Civilizations* (New York 1960).

——, *The World of the Phoenicians* (London 1968).

D. Oates, *Studies in the Ancient History of Northern Iraq* (London 1968).

A. Oppenheim, *Ancient Mesopotamia* (Chicago 1964).

A. Parrot, *Sumer: The Dawn of Art* (New York and London 1960).

K. Polanyi, C. Arensberg, and H. Pearson, eds., *Trade and Market in the Early Empires* (Glencoe 1957).

G. Roux, *Ancient Iraq* (1964; repr. Harmondsworth 1966).

H. Saggs, *The Greatness That was Babylon* (London and New York 1962).

S. Smith, *The Early History of Assyria to 1000 B.C.* (London 1928).

J. Wilson, *et al.*, *Authority and Law in the Ancient Orient* (Baltimore 1954).

C. Woolley, *The Art of the Middle East including Persia, Mesopotamia and Palestine* (New York 1961).

C. *Bronze Age Greece*

C. Blegen, *Troy and the Trojans* (New York 1963).

J. Chadwick, *The Decipherment of Linear B* (Cambridge 1958).

V. Desborough, *The Last Mycenaeans and their Successors* (Oxford 1964).

G. Glotz, *The Aegean Civilization* (1925, repr. New York 1968).

J. Graham, *The Palaces of Crete* (Princeton 1962).

S. Hood, *The Home of the Heroes: the Aegean before the Greeks* (New York 1967).

R. Hutchinson, *Prehistoric Crete* (Harmondsworth and Boston 1962).

G. Huxley, *Achaeans and Hittites* (Oxford 1960).

F. Matz, *The Art of Crete and Early Greece* (New York 1962).

G. Mylonas, *Mycenae and the Mycenaean Age* (Princeton 1966).

M. Nilsson, *The Minoan-Mycenaean Religion and its Survival in Greek Religion* (ed. 2, Lund 1950).

D. Page, *History and the Homeric Iliad* (Berkeley 1959).

L. Palmer, *Mycenaeans and Minoans: Aegean Prehistory in the Light of the Linear B. Tablets* (ed. 2, New York 1965).

J. Pendlebury, *The Archaeology of Crete* (London 1939).

G. Thomson, *The Prehistoric Aegean* (ed. 3, London 1961).

E. Vermeule, *Greece in the Bronze Age* (Chicago 1964).

R. Willetts, *Everyday Life in Ancient Crete* (New York 1969).

III. THE ASSYRIAN EMPIRE C. 1000–C. 600 B.C.

  A. *Assyria*

    G. Contenau, *Everyday Life in Babylon and Assyria* (London 1959).

    J. Laesse, *People of Ancient Assyria* (London 1963).

    A. Olmstead, *A History of Assyria* (New York 1951; repr. Chicago 1960).

  B. *Palestine*

    W. Albright, *The Archaeology of Palestine* (Harmondsworth 1949).

    E. Anati, *Palestine before the Hebrews* (New York 1963).

    A. Burn, *Minoans, Philistines, and Greeks, B.C. 1400–900* (London 1968).

    J. Gray, *The Legacy of Canaan* (Leiden 1957).

    T. Meek, *Hebrew Origins* (New York 1960).

    W. Oesterley and T. Robinson, *A History of Israel* (2 vols., Oxford 1932).

    A. Olmstead, *A History of Palestine and Syria* (New York 1931).

H. Rowley, *The Old Testament and Modern Study* (Oxford 1961).

G. Wright, ed., *The Bible and the Ancient Near East* (Garden City 1961).

Y. Yadkin, *The Art of Warfare in Biblical Lands in the Light of Archaeological Study* (New York 1963).

C. *Greece*

L. Brea, *Sicily before the Greeks* (London 1957).

A. Burn, *The Lyric Age of Greece* (New York 1960).

———, *The World of Hesiod; a Study of the Greek Middle Ages c. 900–700 B.C.* (ed. 2, New York 1966).

R. Carpenter, *Folk Tale, Fiction, and Saga in the Homeric Epics* (Berkeley 1946).

T. Dunbabin, *The Western Greeks: The History of Sicily and South Italy from the Foundation of the Greek Colonies to 480 B.C.* (Oxford 1948).

M. Finley, *The World of Odysseus* (London 1956).

G. Kirk, *The Songs of Homer* (Cambridge 1962).

H. Lorimer, *Homer and the Monuments* (London 1950).

J. Morrison and R. Williams, *Greek Oared Ships, 900–322 B.C.* (London 1968).

J. Myres, *Homer and His Critics* (London 1958).

H. Parke, *Greek Oracles* (London 1967).

G. Richter, *Archaic Greek Art against its Historical Background* (New York 1949).

C. Starr, *The Origins of Greek Civilization 1100–650 B.C.* (New York 1961).

B. Warmington, *Carthage* (Harmondsworth 1964).

T. Webster, *From Mycenae to Homer* (London 1958).

IV. THE PERSIAN EMPIRE AND THE WEST C. 600–478 B.C.

A. *Persia*

H. Bengtson, *et al.*, *The Greeks and the Persians from the Sixth to the Fourth Centuries* (London 1969).

A. Burn, *Persia and the Greeks: the Defence of the West, c. 546–478 B.C.* (London 1962).

R. Ghirshman, *Iran* (Harmondsworth 1954).

G. Grundy, *The Great Persian War and its Preliminaries* (London 1901).

W. Henning, *Zoroaster, Politician or Witch-doctor?* (Oxford 1951).

E. Herzfeld, *Zoroaster and His World* (2 vols., Princeton 1947).

C. Hignett, *Xerxes' Invasion of Greece* (Oxford 1963).

A. Olmstead, *A History of the Persian Empire* (Chicago 1948; repr. 1959).

B. *Greece*

A. Andrewes, *The Greek Tyrants* (ed. 2, London 1958).

G. Beardsley, *The Negro in Greek and Roman Civilization: A Study of the Ethiopian Type* (1929; repr. New York 1967).

W. den Boer, *Laconian Studies* (Amsterdam 1954).

V. Ehrenberg, *From Solon to Socrates: Greek History and Civilization During the Sixth and Fifth Centuries* (London 1968).

W. Forrest, *The Emergence of Greek Democracy* (London 1966).

C. Hignett, *A History of the Athenian Constitution to the End of the Fifth Century B.C.* (Oxford 1958).

G. Huxley, *Early Sparta* (London 1962).

J. Larsen, *Greek Federal States: Their Institutions and History* (Oxford 1968).

H. Michell, *Sparta* (Cambridge 1952; repr. 1964).

M. Pohlenz, *Freedom in Greek Life and Thought: The History of an Ideal* (New York 1966).

M. Rostovtzeff, *Iranians and Greeks in South Russia* (Oxford 1922).

C. Seltman, *Athens: Its History and its Coinage before the Persian Invasion* (Cambridge 1924).

C. Starr, *The Awakening of the Greek Historical Spirit* (New York 1968).

W. Woodhouse, *Solon the Liberator* (Oxford 1938).

C. *The Western Mediterranean*

J. Boardman, *The Greeks Overseas* (Baltimore 1964).

H. Hencken, *Tarquinia and Etruscan Origins* (London 1968).

———, *Tarquinia, Villanovans, and Early Etruscans* (Cambridge, Mass. 1968).

J. Heurgon, *The Daily Life of the Etruscans* (London 1964).

Z. Mayani, *The Etruscans Begin to Speak* (New York 1962).

M. Pallottino, *The Etruscans* (Harmondsworth 1955).

E. Richardson, *The Etruscans: Their Art and Civilization* (Chicago 1964).

H. Scullard, *The Etruscan Cities and Rome* (Ithaca 1967).

V. ATHENS 478–401 B.C.

F. Adcock, *The Greek and Macedonian Art of War* (Berkeley 1957).

A. Andréadès, *A History of Greek Public Finances* (Cambridge, Mass. 1933).

E. Barker, *Greek Political Theory: Plato and His Predecessors* (ed. 4, London 1951).

H. Bolkestein, *Economic Life in Greece's Golden Age* (Leiden 1958).

A. Bonnard, *Greek Civilization* (Glasgow 1961).

C. Cochrane, *Thucydides and the Science of History* (London 1929).

W. Connor, *Theopompus and Fifth-Century Athens* (Cambridge 1968).

V. Ehrenberg, *The People of Aristophanes: A Sociology of Old Attic Comedy* (ed. 2, Oxford 1951).

―――, *Sophocles and Pericles* (Oxford 1954).

J. Finley, *Three Essays on Thucydides* (Cambridge, Mass. 1967).

―――, *Thucydides* (Cambridge, Mass. 1942).

M. Finley, *Studies in Land and Credit in Ancient Athens* (New Brunswick 1951).

R. Flacelière, *Daily Life in Greece at the Time of Pericles* (New York 1965).

A. French, *The Growth of the Athenian Economy* (London 1964).

A. Gomme, *Historical Commentary on Thucydides* (3 vols., Oxford 1945–1953).

―――, *Population of Athens in the Fifth and Fourth Centuries B.C.* (Oxford 1933).

G. Grundy, *Thucydides and the History of His Age* (2 vols., Oxford 1911–1948).

J. Hasebroek, *Trade and Politics in Ancient Greece* (London 1933).

K. Johansen, *The Attic Grave Reliefs of the Classical Period: An Essay in Interpretation* (Copenhagen 1951).

A. H. M. Jones, *Athenian Democracy* (Oxford 1957).

J. W. Jones, *The Law and Legal Theory of the Greeks: An Introduction* (Oxford 1956).

B. Knox, *Oedipus at Thebes* (New Haven 1957).

M. Lang and C. Eliot, *The Athenian Agora* (Athens 1954).

A. Lawrence, *Greek Architecture* (Harmondsworth 1957).

H. Michell, *The Economics of Ancient Greece* (ed. 2, Cambridge 1956).

J. Milne, *Greek and Roman Coins and the Study of History* (London 1939).

J. Myres, *Herodotus, Father of History* (Oxford 1953).

M. Nilsson, *Cults, Myths, Oracles and Politics in Ancient Greece* (Lund 1951).

G. Sarton, *A History of Science through the Golden Age of Greece* (London 1953).

R. Sealey, *Essays in Greek Politics* (New York 1965).

T. Sinclair, *A History of Greek Political Thought* (London 1952).

T. Webster, *Everyday Life in Classical Athens* (New York 1969).

W. Woodhouse, *King Agis of Sparta and his Campaign in Arkadia in 418 B.C.* (Oxford 1933).

A. Zimmern, *The Greek Commonwealth* (ed. 5, Oxford 1961).

G. Zuntz, *The Political Plays of Euripides* (Manchester 1955).

VI. MACEDON 401–301 B.C.

J. F. Dobson, *The Greek Orators* (London 1919).

W. Ferguson, *Greek Imperialism* (New York 1913; repr. 1963).

———, *Hellenistic Athens* (London 1911).

G. Griffith, *The Mercenaries of the Hellenistic World* (1935; repr. Groningen 1968).

F. Jacoby, *Atthis: The Local Chronicles of Ancient Athens* (Oxford 1949).

W. Jaeger, *Demosthenes: The Origin and Growth of His Policy* (1938; repr. New York 1963).

A. H. M. Jones, *The Greek City from Alexander to Justinian* (Oxford 1940).

P. Jouguet, *Macedonian Imperialism and the Hellenization of the East* (New York 1928).

J. Larsen, *Representative Government in Greek and Roman History* (Berkeley and Los Angeles 1955).

H. Parke, *Greek Mercenary Soldiers from the Earliest Times to the Battle of Ipsos* (Oxford 1933).

C. Robinson, Jr., *The History of Alexander the Great* (2 vols., Providence 1953–1963).

W. Tarn, *Alexander the Great* (2 vols., Cambridge 1948).

———, *Hellenistic Military and Naval Developments* (1930; repr. New York 1966).

T. Webster, *Art and Literature in Fourth Century Athens* (Bristol 1956).

M. Wheeler, *Flames over Persepolis: Turningpoint in History* (London 1968).

U. Wilcken, *Alexander the Great* (New York 1932).

VII. THE HELLENISTIC MONARCHIES AND THE RISE OF ROME
  A. *Celts and Gauls*
    N. Chadwick, *Celtic Britain* (New York 1964).
    H. Hubert, *The Rise of the Celts* (1934, repr. New York 1966).
    ———, *Les Celts depuis l'époque de La Tène et la civilization celtique* (ed. 2, Paris 1950).
    T. Kendrick, *The Druids* (London 1927).
    R. Pernoud, *Les Gaulois* (Paris 1957).
    T. Powell, *The Celts* (New York 1958).
    A. Ross, *Pagan Celtic Britain* (London 1967).
  B. *Hellenistic States*
    F. Adcock, *The Greek and Macedonian Art of War* (Berkeley 1957).
    ———, "Greek and Macedonian Kingship," *PBA* 39 (1953), 163–180.
    H. Bell, *Egypt from Alexander the Great to the Arab Conquest* (Oxford 1956).
    E. Budge, *A History of Egypt from the End of the Neolithic Period to the Death of Cleopatra VII* (8 vols., 1902; repr. Oosterhout 1968).
    G. Downey, *A History of Antioch in Syria* (Princeton 1961): ch. 1–6.
    S. Eddy, *The King is Dead: Studies in the Near Eastern Resistance to Hellenism 334–31 B.C.* (Lincoln, Nebraska 1961).
    P. Hitti, *History of Syria, including Lebanon and Palestine* (London 1951): ch. 17–20.
    ———, *Lebanon in History* (ed. 3, London 1967): ch. 11–12.
    A. Jirku, *The World of the Bible*, tr. A. Keep (New York 1967).
    W. Tarn, *The Greeks in Bactria and India* (ed. 2, Cambridge 1951).
    W. Tarn, *Antigonos Gonatas* (Oxford 1913).
    F. Walbank, *Aratos of Sicyon* (Cambridge 1933).
  C. *Hellenistic Civilization*
    E. Barber, *et al., The Hellenistic Age* (Cambridge 1923).
    B. Farrington, *Science and Politics in the Ancient World* (London 1946).
    B. Farrington, *Greek Science: Its Meaning for Us* (ed. 2, Baltimore 1961).
    M. Hadas, *Hellenistic Culture* (New York 1959).
    T. Heath, *Aristarchus of Samos, the Ancient Copernicus: A*

History of Greek Astonomy to Aristarchus (Oxford 1913; repr. 1959).

T. Heath, *A History of Greek Mathematics* (2 vols., Oxford 1921; repr. 1960).

A. Körte, *Hellenistic Poetry*, tr. J. Hammer and M. Hadas (New York 1929).

C. Kraeling, *Anthropos and Son of Man: A Study in the Religious Syncretism of the Hellenistic Orient* (New York 1927).

W. Tarn and G. Griffith, *Hellenistic Civilization* (ed. 3, London 1959).

F. Wright, *A History of Later Greek Literature* (London 1932).

D. *Early Rome: Politics and Society*

F. Adcock, *Roman Political Ideas and Practice* (Ann Arbor 1959, repr. 1964).

R. Bloch, *The Origins of Rome* (New York 1960).

G. Botsford, *The Roman Assemblies from their Origin to the End of the Republic* (New York 1909, repr. 1968).

T. Frank, *Roman Imperialism* (New York 1914).

E. Gjerstad, *Early Rome* (*Acta Inst. Romani Regni Sueciae*, ser. 4, vol. 17.1; Lund 1953).

L. Holland, *Janus and the Bridge* (*Papers ... Am. Ac. Rome* 21, Rome 1961).

L. Homo, *Roman Political Institutions*, tr. M. Dobie (New York 1962).

A. McDonald, *Republican Rome* (New York 1966).

H. Rose, *Primitive Culture in Italy* (London 1926).

J. Thiel, *A History of Roman Sea-Power before the Second Punic War* (Amsterdam 1954).

C. Westrup, *Introduction to Early Roman Law: Comparative Sociological Studies* (5 vols., Copenhagen 1934–1954).

E. *Early Rome: Expansion*

A. Alföldi, *Early Rome and the Latins* (Ann Arbor 1963).

L. Homo, *Primitive Italy and the Beginnings of Roman Imperialism*, tr. V. G. Childe (New York 1926).

A. Piganiol, *La Conquête romaine* (ed. 5, Paris 1967).

J. Thiel, *A History of Roman Sea-Power before the Second Punic War* (Amsterdam 1954).

VIII. ROME AND THE MEDITERRANEAN 218–133 B.C.

A. *Polybius*

K. v. Fritz, *The Theory of the Mixed Constitution in An-*

tiquity: A Critical Analysis of Polybius' Political Ideas (New York 1954).

Polybius, *The Histories*, tr. E. Shuckburgh (1889; repr., 2 vols., Bloomington 1962); also *LCL*, tr. W. Paton (6 vols., London 1922–1927).

F. Walbank, *A Historical Commentary on Polybius* (2 vols., Oxford 1957–1967).

B. *Roman Expansion*

H. Scullard, *Scipio Africanus in the Second Punic War* (Cambridge 1930).

R. Smith, *Rome and Carthage: The Punic Wars* (New York 1923).

F. Walbank, *Philip V of Macedon* (1940; repr. Hamden, Conn. 1967).

B. Warmington, *Carthage* (New York 1960).

A. Wilson, *Emigration from Italy in the Republican Age of Rome* (Manchester 1966).

C. *Roman Politics and Society*

A. Allcroft, *Rome under the Oligarchs: A History of Rome 202–133 B.C.* (London 1892).

R. Haywood, *Studies on Scipio Africanus* (Baltimore 1933).

H. Scullard, *Roman Politics 220–150 B.C.* (Oxford 1951).

D. *Latin Literature*

L. Bieler, *History of Roman Literature*, tr. J. Wilson (London 1966).

J. Duff, *A Literary History of Rome: From the Origins to the Close of the Golden Age* (ed. 3, London 1960).

F. Leo, *Geschichte d. römischen Literatur* I: *Die Archäische Literatur* (1913, repr. Berlin 1958).

E. Segal, *Roman Laughter: The Comedy of Plautus* (Cambridge, Mass. 1968).

E. *Roman Religion*

F. Altheim, *A History of Roman Religion*, tr. H. Mattingly (New York 1938).

E. Burriss, *Taboo, Magic Spirits: A Study of Primitive Elements in Roman Religion* (New York 1931).

J. Carter, *The Religion of Numa* (New York 1906).

W. Fowler, *The Roman Festivals of the Period of the Republic* (London 1899).

F. Grant, *Ancient Roman Religion* (New York 1957).

F. *Seleucids and Jews*

R. Charles, *A Critical and Exegetical Commentary on the Book of Daniel* (London 1929).

S. Dubnov, *History of the Jews* I: *From the Beginnings to Early Christianity*, tr. M. Spiegel (South Brunswick, 1967, based on 1938 Russian edition).

W. Farmer, *Maccabees, Zealots, and Josephus* (New York 1956).

W. Oesterley, *A History of Israel* II: *From the Fall of Jerusalem, 586 B.C. to the Bar-Kokhba Revolt, A.D. 135* (Oxford 1932; repr. 1957).

H. Rowley, *Darius the Mede and the Four World Empires in the Book of Daniel* (Cardiff 1935).

D. Russell, *The Jews from Alexander to Herod* (Oxford 1967).

A. Tcherikovev, *Hellenistic Civilization and the Jews*, tr. S. Appelbaum (Philadelphia 1959).

IX. THE ROMAN REPUBLIC 133–44 B.C.
  A. *The Gracchi, Marius, Sulla*
    A. Astin, *Scipio Aemilianus* (Oxford 1967).
    J. Balsdon, "Sulla Felix," *JRS* 41 (1951), 1 ff.
    T. Carney, *A Biography of C. Marius* (*PACA*, supp. no. 1; 1961).
    D. Earl, *Tiberius Gracchus: A Study in Politics* (Brussells 1963).
    P. Kildahl, *Caius Marius* (New York 1968).
    C. Oman, *Seven Roman Statesmen of the Later Republic: The Gracchi, Sulla, Crassus, Cato, Pompey, Caesar* (1902, repr. London 1957).
  B. *Cicero, Pompey, Caesar*
    J. Carcopino, *Cicero: The Secrets of His Correspondence*, tr. E. Lorimer (2 vols., London 1951).
    Cicero, *Letters to Atticus*, ed. D. Shackleton-Bailey, with translation and commentary (6 vols., Cambridge 1965–1968).
    F. Cowell, *Cicero and the Roman Republic* (London 1948).
    H. Frisch, *Cicero's Fight for the Republic: The Historical Background of Cicero's Philippics* (Copenhagen 1946).
    M. Gelzer, *Caesar: Politician and Statesman*, tr. P. Needham (Cambridge, Mass. 1968).
    H. Haskell, *This was Cicero: Modern Politics in a Roman Toga* (New York 1942).
    E. Meyer, *Caesars Monarchie und das Principat des Pompejus* (ed. 3, Stuttgart 1922; repr. 1963).
    P. Jal, *La guerre civil à Rome: Étude litteraire et moral* (Paris 1963).

J. Strachan-Davidson, *Cicero and the Fall of the Roman Republic* (New York 1894).

C. *Politics and Society*

D. Earl, *The Political Thought of Sallust* (Cambridge 1961).

T. Frank, ed., *An Economic Survey of Ancient Rome* I: *Rome and Italy, the Republic* (Baltimore 1933).

E. Gruen, *Roman Politics and the Criminal Courts 149–78 B.C.* (Cambridge, Mass. 1968).

J. Heaton, *Mob Violence in the Late Roman Republic 133–49 B.C.* (1939, repr. Ann Arbor 1968).

L. Homo, *Roman Political Institutions*, tr. M. Dobie (New York 1962).

L. Taylor, *Party Politics in the Age of Caesar* (Berkeley 1949; repr. 1961).

———, *Roman Voting Assemblies from the Hannibalic War to the Dictatorship of Caesar* (Ann Arbor 1966).

A. Toynbee, *Hannibal's Legacy: The Hannibalic War's Effects on Roman Life* (2 vols., Oxford 1965).

C. Wirszubski, *Libertas as a Political Idea at Rome during the Late Republic and Early Principate* (Cambridge 1950).

D. *Army and Provinces*

E. Badian, *Foreign Clientelae 264–70 B.C.* (Oxford 1958).

A. Boak, "The Extraordinary Commands from 80 to 48 B.C.: A Study in the Origins of the Principate," *AHR* 24 (1918–19), 1–25.

P. Brunt, "The Army and the Land in the Roman Revolution," *JRS* 52 (1962), 69–86.

J. Cobban, *Senate and Provinces 78–49 B.C.* (Cambridge 1935).

E. Jonkers, *Social and Economic Commentary on Cicero's De imperio Cn. Pompei* (Leiden 1959).

R. Smith, *Service in the Post-Marian Roman Army* (Manchester 1958).

G. Stevenson, *Roman Provincial Administration till the Age of the Antonines* (Oxford 1939).

E. *Wars and Conquests*

E. Badian, *Roman Imperialism in the Late Republic* (ed. 2, Ithaca 1968).

S. Brady, *Caesar's Gallic Campaigns* (Harrisburg 1947).

G. Anderson, "Pompey's Campaign against Mithridates," *JHS* 12 (1922), 99 ff.

T. Holmes, *Caesar's Conquest of Gaul* (Oxford 1907).

M. Rostovtzeff, *Iranians and Greeks* (Oxford 1927).

P. Sands, *The Client Princes of the Roman Empire under the Republic* (Cambridge 1908; repr. Ann Arbor 1968).

F. *Roman Civilization*

F. Brown, *Roman Architecture* (New York 1961): ch. 1–3.

D. Daube, *Roman Law* (Edingburgh 1969).

W. Fowler, *Roman Ideas of Deity in the Last Century before the Christian Era* (London 1914).

T. Frank, *Life and Literature in the Roman Republic* (Berkeley 1930).

A. Jitta, *Ancestral Portraiture in Rome and the Art of the Last Century of the Republic* (Amsterdam 1932).

H. Jolowicz, *Historical Introduction to Roman Law* (ed. 2, Oxford 1952).

J. Kelly, *Roman Litigation* (Oxford 1966).

K. Quinn, *The Catullan Revolution* (Melbourne 1959).

F. Schulz, *Classical Roman Law* (Oxford 1954).

R. Syme, *Sallust* (Berkeley 1964).

X. THE AUGUSTAN EMPIRE: 44 B.C.–A.D. 70

A. *The Augustan Settlement*

Augustus, *Res gestae*, eds. P. Brunt and J. Moore (Oxford 1967).

G. Bowersock, *Augustus and the Greek World* (Oxford 1965).

T. Holmes, *The Architect of the Roman Empire* (2 vols., Oxford 1928–1931).

F. Marsh, *The Founding of the Roman Empire* (ed. 2, 1927; repr. Cambridge 1959).

K. Scott, "The Political Propaganda of 44–30 BC," *MAAR* 11 (1933), 7–49.

R. Syme, *The Roman Revolution* (Oxford 1939; repr. 1960).

B. *The Julio-Claudians*

J. Balsdon, *The Emperor Gaius (Caligula)* (Oxford 1934).

M. Charlesworth, "The Tradition about Caligula," *Cambridge Hist. Journal* 4 (1933), 105 ff.

M. Hammond, *The Augustan Principate in Theory and Practice during the Julio-Claudian Period* (ed. 2, New York 1968).

M. Levi, *Nerone e i suoi tempi* (Milan 1949).

F. Marsh, *The Reign of Tiberius* (London 1931).

A. Momigliano, *Claudius: The Emperor and His Achievement*, tr. W. Hogarth (Oxford 1934; repr. with new bib., 1961).

R. Rosborough, *An Epigraphic Commentary on Suetonius' Life of Gaius Caligula* (Philadelphia 1920).

C. *Bureaucracy, Army, Provinces*

F. Abbott and A. Johnson, *Municipal Administration in the Roman Empire* (Princeton 1926): with texts.

W. Arnold, *Studies of Roman Imperialism* (Manchester 1906).

P. Baillie Reynolds, "The Troops Quartered in the Castra Peregrinorum," *JRS* 13 (1923), 168–189.

F. Bourne, *The Public Works of the Julio-Claudians and Flavians* (Princeton 1946).

M. Charlesworth, "The Virtues of a Roman Emperor: Propaganda and the Creation of Belief," *PBA* 23 (1937), 105 ff.

G. Cheesman, *The Auxilia of the Roman Imperial Army* (Oxford 1914).

A. Jones, *Studies in Roman Government and Law* (Oxford 1960).

M. Lewis, *The Official Priests of Rome under the Julio-Claudians (Papers and Monographs of Am. Academy* 16, Rome 1955).

H. Mattingly, *The Imperial Civil Service of Rome* (Cambridge 1910).

W. Oldfather and H. Canter, *The Defeat of Varus and the German Frontier Policy of Augustus (Univ. Illinois Studies in Social Sciences* 4.2, Urbana 1915).

D. *Roman Civilization*

J. Carcopino, *Daily Life in Ancient Rome*, ed. H. Rowell and tr. E. Lorimer (New Haven 1940).

E. Fraenkel, *Horace* (Oxford 1951).

L. Friedlander, *Roman Life and Manners under the Early Empire* (ed. 7, tr. L. Magnus *et al.*; 4 vols., New York 1908–1913).

O. Kiefer, *Sexual Life in Ancient Rome*, tr. G. and H. Highet (London 1938; repr. 1956).

B. Otis, *Ovid as an Epic Poet* (Cambridge 1966).

W. J. Knight, *Vergil: Epic and Anthropology*, ed. J. Christie (London 1967).

B. Otis, *Virgil: A Study in Civilized Poetry* (Oxford 1964).

H. Rowell, *Rome in the Augustan Age* (Norman 1962).

E. *Politics and Civil War*

B. Henderson, *Civil War and Rebellion in the Roman Empire A.D. 69–70* (London 1908).

R. MacMullen, *Enemies of the Roman Order* (Cambridge, Mass. 1966).

C. Starr, *Civilization and the Caesars: The Intellectual Revolution in the Roman Empire* (Ithaca 1954).

J. Toynbee, "Dictators and Philosophers in the First Century A.D.," *G&R* 13 (1944), 43–58.

XI. THE IMPERIAL PEACE: A.D. 70–192
  A. *The Flavians*
    R. Gephart, *Suetonius' Life of Domitian, with Notes and Parallel Passages* (Philadelphia 1922).
    S. Gsell, *Essai sur le regne de l'empereur Domitien* (Paris 1893).
    B. Henderson, *Five Roman Emperors: Vespasian, Titus, Domitian, Nerva, Trajan, A.D. 69–117* (Cambridge 1927).
    C. Sutherland, "The State of the Imperial Treasury at the Death of Domitian," *JRS* 25 (1935), 150 ff.
    R. Syme, "The Imperial Finances under Domitian, Nerva and Trajan," *JRS* 20 (1930), 55 ff.
  B. *The Antonines*
    A. Birley, *Marcus Aurelius* (London 1966).
    E. Bryant, *The Reign of Antoninus Pius* (Cambridge 1895).
    F. Gregorovius, *The Emperor Hadrian: A Picture of the Graeco-Roman World in His Time*, tr. M. Robinson (London and New York 1898).
    B. Henderson, *The Life and Principate of the Emperor Hadrian A.D. 76–138* (London 1923).
    T. Lepper, *Trajan's Parthian War* (Oxford 1948).
  C. *Bureaucracy and Army*
    W. Arnold, *The Roman System of Provincial Administration to the Accession of Constantine the Great* (ed. 3, Oxford 1914).
    E. Birley, *Roman Britain and the Roman Army* (Kendal 1953).
    P. Brunt, "Pay and Superannuation in the Roman Army," *PBSR* 18 (1950), 50–71.
    J. Crook, *Consilium Principis* (Cambridge 1955).
    M. Hammond, *The Antonine Monarchy (Papers and Monographs of the American Academy in Rome* 19, Rome 1959).
    ———, "Pliny the Younger's Views on Government," *HSCP* 49 (1938), 115 ff.
    M. Nilsson, *Imperial Rome* (New York 1962); part 2, "The Empire and Its Inhabitants."

J. Oliver, *The Ruling Power: A Study of the Roman Empire in the Second Century after Christ through the Roman Oration of Aelius Aristides* (Philadelphia 1953).

H. Pflaum, *Les procurateurs equestres sous le Haut-Empire romain* (Paris 1950).

A. Sherwin-White, *The Letters of Pliny: A Historical and Social Commentary* (Oxford 1966); cf. rev. F. Millar, *JRS* 58 (1968), 218–224.

A. Sherwin-White, *The Roman Citizenship* (Oxford 1939).

W. Sinnigen, "The Origins of the Frumentarii," *MAAR* 27 (1962), 213 ff.

C. Starr, *The Roman Imperial Navy, 31 B.C.–A.D. 324* (Ithaca 1941).

Tacitus, *De vita Agricolae*, eds. R. Ogilvie and I. Richmond (Oxford 1967).

S. Wallace, *Taxation in Egypt from Augustus to Diocletian* (Princeton 1938).

W. Wannemacher, *The Development of Imperial Civil Officia during the Principate* (Diss. Univ. Mich., 1940).

G. Webster, *The Roman Imperial Army of the First and Second Centuries A.D.* (London 1969).

D. *Provinces and Economy*

J. Wacher, ed., *The Civitas Capitals of Roman Britain* (Leicester 1966).

W. Ramsay, *The Social Basis of Roman Power in Asia Minor* (Aberdeen 1941).

J. Broughton, *The Romanization of Africa Proconsularis* (Baltimore 1929).

T. Mommsen, *The Provinces of the Roman Empire from Caesar to Diocletian*, tr. W. Dickson (2 vols., New York 1887 and London 1909).

D. Magie, *Roman Rule in Asia Minor* (Princeton 1950).

A. Rivet, *Town and Country in Roman Britain* (London 1958).

P. Louis, *Ancient Rome at Work: An Economic History of Rome from the Origins to the Empire*, tr. E. Wareing (New York 1927; repr. 1965).

T. Frank, ed., *An Economic Survey of Ancient Rome*; vols. 2–5 (Baltimore 1936–1940) cover the Empire; vol. 6 is a general index.

M. Charlesworth, *Trade-routes and Commerce of the Roman Empire* (Cambridge 1924; repr. Hildesheim 1961).

B. Levick, *Roman Colonies in Southern Asia Minor* (Oxford 1967).

C. Starr, *The Roman Imperial Navy 31 B.C.–A.D. 324* (ed. 2, Cambridge 1960).

G. Boissier, *Roman Africa: Archaeological Walks in Algeria and Tunis*, tr. A. Ward (New York and London 1899).

C. Thomas, ed., *Rural Settlement in Roman Britain* (London 1966).

E. Warmington, *The Commerce between the Roman Empire and India* (Cambridge 1928).

E. *Roman Civilization*

F. Altheim, *A History of Roman Religion*, tr. H. Mattingly (New York 1938).

T. Dorey, ed., *Latin Historians* (London 1966).

T. Glover, *The Conflict of Religions in the Early Roman Empire* (ed. 9, London 1920).

A. Grenier, *The Roman Spirit in Religion, Thought, and Art*, tr. M. Dobie (New York 1926).

P. Hamberg, *Studies in Roman Imperial Art: with Special Reference to the State Reliefs of the Second Century* (Uppsala 1945).

G. Highet, *Juvenal the Satirist* (Oxford 1954; repr. 1961).

H. Rose, *The Roman Questions of Plutarch: A New Translation with Introductory Essays and a Running Commentary* (Oxford 1924).

I. Ryberg, *Panel Reliefs of Marcus Aurelius* (*Monographs on Archaeology and Fine Arts, Archaeological Institute of America* 14, New York 1967).

R. Syme, *Tacitus* (2 vols., Oxford 1958).

F. *Early Christianity*

S. Brandon, *The Fall of Jerusalem and the Christian Church* (ed. 2, London 1957).

S. Brandon, *Jesus and the Zealots* (New York 1969).

P. Carrington, *The Early Christian Church* (2 vols., Cambridge 1957).

G. Dix, *Jew and Greek: A Study in the Primitive Church* (Westminster 1953).

M. Goguel, *The Birth of Christianity*, tr. C. Snape (London 1953).

A. Harnack, *The Mission and Expansion of Christianity in the First Three Centuries*, tr. J. Moffatt (London and New York 1908; repr. 1961).

H. Lietzmann, *A History of the Early Church*, tr. B. Woolf
(4 vols., London 1960): vols. 1–2.

C. Richardson, *The Christianity of Ignatius of Antioch*
(New York 1935).

A. Sherwin-White, *Roman Society and Roman Law in the
New Testament* (Oxford 1963).

XII. THE IMPERIAL CRISIS AND RECOVERY: A.D. 193–324

A. *The Severi*

M. Hammond, "Septimius Severus, Roman Bureaucrat,"
HSCP 51 (1940), 137 ff.

M. Platnauer, *The Life and Reign of the Emperor Lucius
Septimius Severus* (London 1928).

W. Westerman and A. Schulter, *Apokrimata: Decision of
S. Severus on Legal Matters* (New York 1954).

B. *Imperial Crisis (A.D. 249–270)*

A. Alföldi, "La grande crise du monde romain au IIIᵉ siècle,"
AC 7 (1938), 5–18.

A. Boak, *Manpower Shortage and the Fall of the Roman
Empire in the West* (Ann Arbor 1955).

S. Bolin, *State and Currency in the Roman Empire to 300
A.D.* (Stockholm 1958); cf. rev. T. Pekary, *Historia* 9
(1960), 380 ff.

P. Oliva, *Pannonia and the Onset of Crisis in the Roman Empire*, tr. I. Urevin (Prague 1962).

C. Oman, "The Decline and Fall of the Denarius in the Third
Century," *NC* (1916), 37 ff.

S. Oost, "The Death of the Emperor Gordian III," *CP* 53
(1958), 106 ff.

M. Rostovtzeff, *Social and Economic History of the Roman
Empire* (ed. 2, Oxford 1957): ch. 9–12.

C. *Frontier Peoples*

N. Debevoise, *A Political History of Parthia* (Chicago 1938).

F. Millar, ed., *The Roman Empire and its Neighbors* (London 1967): ch. 14–17.

D. Saddington, "Roman Attitudes to the 'Externae Gentes'
of the North," *AC* 4 (1961), 90 ff.

E. Thompson, *The Early Germans* (Oxford 1965).

J. Ward-Perkins, "The Roman West and the Parthian East,"
PBA 51 (1967), 175–199.

D. *Bureaucracy, Army, Provinces*

A. Alföldi, "A Teutonic Contingent in the Service of Constantine the Great," *DOP* 13 (1959), 169 ff.

H. Bell, *et al.*, *The Abinneus Archive* (Oxford 1962).

A. Boak and H. Youtie, "Flight and Oppression in IVth Century Egypt," *Studi ... Calderini* (Milan 1957), 325 ff.

P. Brunn, "Roman Imperial Administration as Mirrored in the Early Fourth Century Coinage," *Actes XI Cong. Int. Sc. Hist.* (Uppsala 1960), 87 ff.

G. Downey, *A Study of the Comites Orientis and the Consulares Syriae* (Princeton 1939).

C. Keyes, *The Rise of the Equites in the Third Century of the Roman Empire* (Princeton 1915).

R. MacMullen, *Soldier and Civilian in the Later Roman Empire* (Cambridge, Mass. 1963).

W. Sinnigen, *The Officium of the Urban Prefecture during the Later Roman Empire* (*Papers and Monographs of the Am. Academy in Rome* 17, Rome 1957).

L. West and A. Johnson, *Currency in Roman and Byzantine Egypt* (Princeton 1944).

E. *Imperial Recovery*

A. Alföldi, *The Conversion of Constantine and Pagan Rome*, tr. H. Mattingly (Oxford 1948).

N. Baynes, *Constantine the Great and the Christian Church* (London 1929).

J. Burckhardt, *The Age of Constantine the Great*, tr. M. Hadas (New York 1949, 1956; from 1853 edition).

L. Homo, *Essai sur le regne de l'empereur Aurelien (270–275)* (Paris 1904).

A. Jones, "Capitatio and Jugatio." *JRS* 47 (1957), 88 ff.

W. Seston, *Dioclétien et la Tetrarchie* (Paris 1946).

C. Sutherland, "Diocletian's Reform of the Coinage," *JRS* 51 (1961), 94 ff.

F. *Paganism and Christianity*

T. Barnes, "Legislation against the Christians," *JRS* 58 (1968), 32–50.

P. Brown, "Aspects of the Christianization of the Roman Aristocracy," *JRS* 51 (1961), 1 ff.

V. Corwin, *St. Ignatius and Christianity in Antioch* (New Haven 1960).

F. Cumont, *After Life in Roman Paganism* (New Haven 1923).

———, *The Mysteries of Mithra*, tr. T. McCormack (Chicago 1903).

———, *The Oriental Religions in Roman Paganism* (New York 1911; repr. 1956).

L. Duchesne, *Early History of the Christian Church*, tr. C. Jenkins (3 vols., New York 1912–1924).

W. Frend, *Martyrdom and Persecution in the Early Church* (Oxford 1965, New York 1967).

A. Momigliano, ed., *Paganism and Christianity in the Fourth Century* (London 1962).

J. Fest, *Plotinus: The Road to Reality* (Cambridge 1967).

E. Swift, *Roman Sources of Christian Art* (New York 1951).

XIII. LATE ANTIQUITY

A. Alföldi, *A Conflict of Ideas in the Late Roman Empire*, tr. H. Mattingly (Oxford 1952).

A. Jones, *The Decline of the Ancient World* (London and New York 1966): a summary of the following work.

——, *The Later Roman Empire, 284–602: A Social, Economic, and Administrative Survey* (3 vols., Oxford 1963).

F. Lot, *The End of the Ancient World and the Beginning of the Middle Ages*, tr. P. Leon (London 1931; repr. 1953).

A. Piganiol, *L'empire Chrétien (325–395)* (Paris 1947).

E. Thompson, *The Historical Work of Ammianus Marcellinus* (Cambridge 1947).

J. Vogt, *The Decline of Rome*, tr. J. Sondheimer (New York 1967).

Abbreviations

The following list is in two parts. First are abbreviations of books and collections of books; some of these are used only in the present work, but most are in general use. Second are standard abbreviations of periodicals likely to be cited in studies of ancient history.

PART I: BOOKS

BT   *Biblioteca Scriptorum Graecorum et Romanorum Teubneriana*

CAH   *Cambridge Ancient History*

CB   *Collection Budé*

CIG   *Corpus Inscriptionum Graecarum*

CIL   *Corpus Inscriptionum Latinarum*

CIS   *Corpus Inscriptionum Semiticarum*

CSEL   *Corpus Scriptorum Ecclesisticorum Latinorum*

CVA   *Corpus Vasorum Antiquorum*

FGrH   Jacoby, *Die Fragmente der griechischen Historiker*

FHG   Müller, *Fragmenta Historicorum Graecorum*

Gercke-Norden   A. Gercke and E. Norden, *Einleitung in die Altertumswissenschaft* (ed. 3, Berlin 1927)

IG   *Inscriptiones Graecae*

ILS   Dessau, *Inscriptiones Latinae Selectae*

LCL   *Loeb Classical Library*

MGH   *Monumenta Germaniae Historica*

Müller   I. v. Müller, *et al.*, eds., *Handbuch der Altertumswissenschaft*

OCD   *Oxford Classical Dictionary*

OCT   *Oxford Classical Texts* = *Scriptorum Classicorum Bibliotheca Oxoniensis*

PIR   *Prosopographia Imperii Romani*

PW   See *RE*

RE A. Pauly and G. Wissowa, eds., *Real-Encyclopädie der classischen Altertumswissenschaft*

Rosenberg A. Rosenberg, *Einleitung und Quellenkunde zur römischen Geschichte* (Berlin 1921)

SB *Sitzungsberichte*

Schanz-Hosius M. Schanz, *Geschichte der römischen Literatur*, revised by C. Hosius (4 vols.: vol. 1, ed. 4, 1927; vol. 2, ed. 4, 1935; vol. 3, ed. 3, 1922; vol. 4, 2 parts, 1914 and 1920): part of *Müller*

Schmid-Stählin W. Schmid and O. Stählin, *Geschichte der griechischen Literatur* (2 vols. in 4 parts: vol. 1.1, 1929; 1.2, 1934; 2.1, ed. 6, 1920; 2.2, ed. 6, 1924): part of *Müller*

SEG *Supplementum Epigraphicum Graecum*

SIG Dittenberger, *Sylloge Inscriptionum Graecarum*

PART II: PERIODICALS

AA *Archäologischer Anzeiger* (Supplement to *JDAI*)

ABAW *Abhandlungen der Bayerischen Akademie der Wissenschaften, Philos.-Hist. Klasse*

ABSA *Annual of the British School at Athens*

ABull *The Art Bulletin*

AC *L'Antiquité Classique*

ADAW *Abhundlungen der Deutschen Akademie der Wissenschaften zu Berlin, Klasse für Sprachen, Literatur und Kunst*

AHAW *Abhandlungen der Heidelberger Akademie der Wissenschaften, Philos.-Hist. Klasse*

AHR *American Historical Review*

AJ *The Archaeological Journal*

AJA *American Journal of Archaeology*

AJPh *American Journal of Phililogy*

AK *Antike Kunst*

AKG *Archiv für Kulturgeschichte*

AO *Der Alte Orient*

AOF *Archiv für Orientforschung*

APF *Archiv für Papyrusforschung und verwandte Gebiete*

APh *L'Année Philologique*

ARW *Archiv für Religionswissenschaft*

ÄZ *Zeitschrift für ägyptische Sprache*

Altertum *Das Altertum*

Antiquity *Antiquity*

ArchClass *Archeologia Classica*

Archaeology *Archaeology*

Arion *Arion*

Athenaeum   *Athenaeum*
A&R   *Atene e Roma*
BASO   *Bulletin of the American Schools of Oriental Research in Jerusalem and Baghdad*
BCH   *Bulletin de Correspondance Hellénique*
BO   *Bibliotheca Orientalis*
Berytus   *Berytus*
ByzZ   *Byzantinische Zeitscrift*
Byzantion   *Byzantion*
CJ   *The Classical Journal*
CPh   *Classical Philology*
CQ   *Classical Quarterly*
CR   *Classical Review*
CT   *Les Cahiers de Tunisie*
CW   *The Classical World*
DLZ   *Deutsche Literaturzeitung*
EHR   *English Historical Review*
Eranos   *Eranos*
F&F   *Forschungen und Fortschritte*
GGA   *Göttingische Gelehrte Anzeigen*
GJ   *The Geographical Journal*
GRBS   *Greek, Roman and Byzantine Studies*
Glotta   *Glotta*
Gnomon   *Gnomon*
Gymnasium   *Gymnasium*
G&R   *Greece and Rome*
HSPh   *Harvard Studies in Classical Philology*
HT   *History To-day*
HThR   *Harvard Theological Review*
HZ   *Historische Zeitschrift*
Hermathena   *Hermathena*
Hermes   *Hermes*
Hesperia   *Hesperia*
Historia   *Historia*
History   *History*
IF   *Indogermanische Forschungen*
Iraq   *Iraq*
Isis   *Isis*
JA   *Journal Asiatique*
JAOS   *Journal of the American Oriental Society*
JAS   *Journal of the Asiatic Society of Great Britain and Ireland*
JAW   *Bursian's Jahresbericht*

JCUN Journal of Cuneiform Studies
JDAI Jahrbuch des Deutschen Archäologischen Instituts
JEA Journal of Egyptian Archaeology
JEH Journal of Ecclesistical History
JHI Journal of the History of Ideas
JHS Journal of Hellenic Studies
JNES Journal of Near Eastern Studies
JNG Jahrbuch für Numismatik und Geldgeschichte
JRH Journal of Religious History
JRS Journal of Roman Studies
JWI Journal of the Warburg and Courtauld Institute
JbAC Jahrbuch für Antike und Christentum
Klio Klio
LEC Les Études Classiques
Latomus Latomus
MAAR Memoirs of the American Academy in Rome
MAL Memorie della Classe di Scienze morali e storiche dell-'Accademia dei Lincei
MDOG Mitteilungen der Deutschen Orient-Gesellschaft
MH Museum Helveticum
Mnemosyne Mnemosyne
NC Numismatic Chronicle and Journal of the Numismatic Society
NClio La Nouvelle Clio
NJA Neue Jahrbücher
NSA Notizie degli Scavi di Antichità
NT Novum Testamentum
NTS New Testament Studies
NZ Numismatische Zeitschrift
OLZ Orientalistische Literaturzeitung
PAPhS Proceedings of the American Philosophical Society
PBA Proceedings of the British Academy
PBSR Papers of the British School at Rome
PCA Proceedings of the Classical Association
PCPhS Proceedings of the Cambridge Philological Society
PP La Parola del Passato
Paideia Paideia
Philologus Philologus
Phoenix Phoenix
Phronesis Phronesis
P&P Past and Present
RA Revue Archéologique

RAL　*Rendiconti della Classe di Scienze morali, storiche e filologiche dell'Accademia dei Lincei*

REA　*Revue des Études Anciennes*

REByz　*Revue des Études Byzantines*

REG　*Revue des Études Grecques*

REL　*Revue des Études Latines*

RH　*Revue Historique*

RLAC　*Reallexikon für Antike und Christentum*

RN　*Revue Numismatique*

RSI　*Rivista Storica Italiana*

RhM　*Rheinisches Museum*

SAWW　*Sitzungsberichte der Akademie der Wissenschaften in Wien*

SBAW　*Sitzungsberichte der Bayerischen Akademie der Wissenschaften, Philos.-Hist. Klasse*

SDAW　*Sitzungsberichte der Deutschen Akademie der Wissenschaften zu Berlin, Klasse für Philosophie, Geschichte, Staats—, Rechts— und Wirtschaftswissenschaften*

SE　*Studi Etruschi*

SHAW　*Sitzungsberichte der Heidelberger Akademie der Wissenschaften, Philos.-Hist. Klasse*

SO　*Symbolae Osloenses*

Saeculum　*Saeculum*

SPAW　*Sitzungesberichte der Preussischen Akademie der Wissenschaften*

StudRom　*Studi Romani*

Syria　*Syria*

TAPhA　*Transactions and Proceedings of the American Philological Association*

VChr　*Vigiliae Christianae*

VT　*Vetus Testamentum*

WG　*Die Welt als Geschichte*

YClS　*Yale Classical Studies*

ZA　*Zeitschrift für Assyriologie*

ZATW　*Zeitschrift für die Alttestamentliche Wissenschaft*

ZDMG　*Zeitschrift der Deutschen Morgenländischen Gesellschaft*

ZII　*Zeitschrift für Indologie und Iranistik*

ZNTW　*Zeitschrift für die Neutestamentliche Wissenschaft und die Kunde der älteren Kirche*

ZRG　*Zeitschrift der Savigny-Stiftung für Rechtsgeschichte (Romanistische Abteilung)*

Index of Names

Index of Topics

Academies, 169 f.
Anthropology, 164
Archeology, 15 f., 22, 127–129
Art, historical: 126–127

Biography, 98–100, 170 f.

Calendars, 26–28
City-plans, 128
Climate, 40, 44 f.
Commerce, 41
Coins: study of, 144–146, 156 f.; Greek, 147, 158; Roman, 146 f., 158

Dictionaries, 168
Disease, 64
Documents, 65 ff.

Encyclopedias, 168, 172

Fasti, 30 f.
Frontiers, 127–129

Geography, 2 ff.

Historian, 2
Historiography: of Rome, 8 f., 11; of Greece, 9 f., 14 f., 18 f.; of Hellenistic Age, 15, 19; of ancient Near East, 19; of religion, 19; ancient, 87 ff.; local, 90; universal, 93

Individual, 59–60, 62
Inscriptions: Latin, 11, 12, 13, 137 ff., 151 ff.; Greek, 26, 137, 148 ff.; importance of, 136–141; restoration of, 137; distribution of, 137–138.

Journals, scholarly: 169, 174–175

Language, 53–54, 57
Law, 164, 167; Roman, 11, 12, 13, 70, 71, 72, 153; Greek, 69–70; Egyptian, 71
Letters, 74–75, 85–87
Linguistics, 164, 166–167

Manuals, 169, 174
Maps, 40–42
Masses, 62–63
Memoirs, 72–73, 81–83
Military Diplomas, 153

Nation, 54–56; Greek, 62
National Consciousness, 55
Neohumanism, 14–15, 19–20

Orators, 73–74, 83–85

Pamphlets, 75–76
Panegyric, 87
Papyri: study of, 141–142; literary, 142; documentary, 143–144
Periodization, 4, 6, 162
Philology, 162–163
Popular Tradition, 120–121
Population, 17, 63–64
Propaganda, 63, 160
Prosopography, 141, 168–169, 172–173

Race, 49–50; in Attica, 50–51; and language, 60

Script, 67
Series, 170
Synchronism, 28–29

Treaties, 68–69, 78 f., 79 f.